IMAGES
of Modern America

West Brighton

On the Front Cover: Clockwise from top left: Boomerang Toys (courtesy of Boomerang Toys, see page 29), Beans & Leaves (courtesy of Beans & Leaves, see page 66), Book Nook (courtesy of Trifoglio family, see page 41), Scott Edwards (courtesy of Preservation League of Staten Island, see page 10), St. Benedicta's Church (courtesy of Joseph Yaccarino, see page 72).

On the Back Cover: Clockwise from left to right: Rustic Music (courtesy of Rustic Music, see page 28), Columbian Lyceum Red & Gold Room (courtesy of the Morand family, see page 18), Staten Island Zoo (courtesy of the Staten Island Zoological Society, see page 61).

IMAGES
of Modern America

West Brighton

Jim Harkins and Cecelia N. Brunner

ARCADIA
PUBLISHING

ISBN 978-1-4671-2194-1

Published by Arcadia Publishing
Charleston, South Carolina

Printed in the United States of America

Library of Congress Control Number: 2013954624

For all general information, please contact Arcadia Publishing:
Telephone 843-853-2070
Fax 843-853-0044
E-mail sales@arcadiapublishing.com
For customer service and orders:
Toll-Free 1-888-313-2665

Visit us on the Internet at www.arcadiapublishing.com

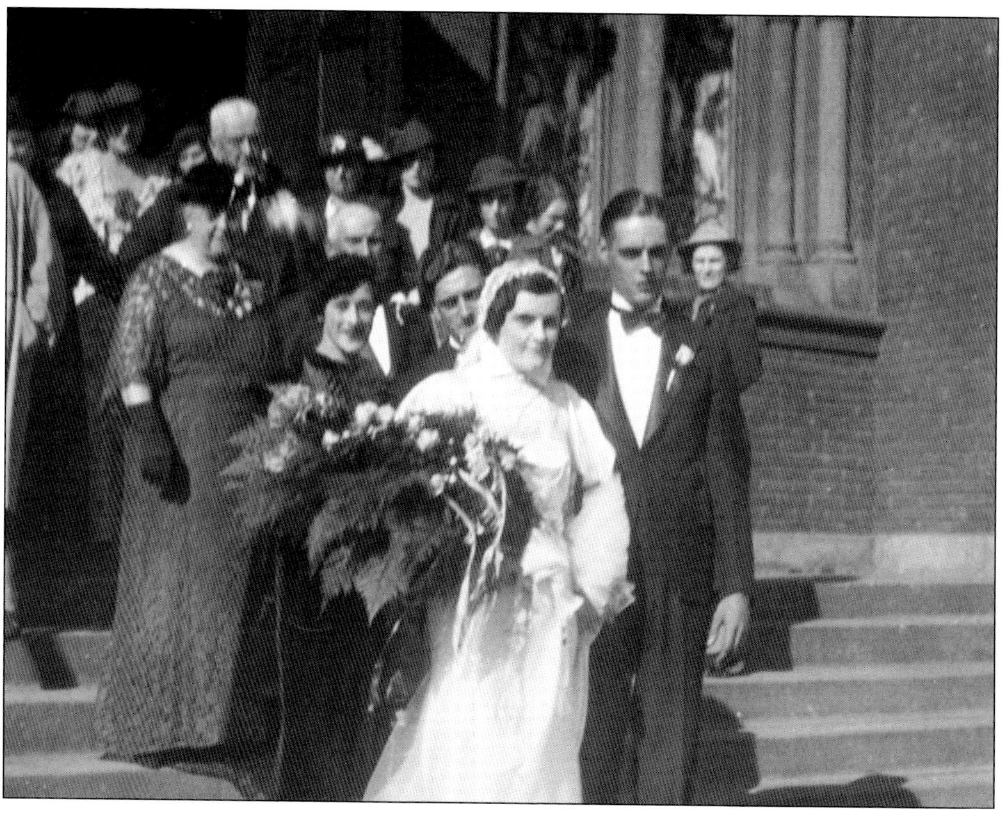

This book is dedicated to Gerard and Helen Brunner (pictured) and Dorothy Brunner Kelly, parents and grandparents, sister and aunt. We miss you. Love, Cecelia, Jim, and Debbie.

Contents

ACKNOWLEDGMENTS

The authors want to thank everyone who took part in creating this book. Of course, we have to start with the third member of our creative team, Debbie Harkins. This book would not have been possible without Debbie scanning all of the photographs. Next, we want to thank Sal Marino, of Wallich's Camera Shop and Photo Lab, not only for the photography work but also for getting us contact information for Pal Joey's. We are very lucky to have had the Staten Island Zoo in West Brighton for over 70 years. We want to thank Kenneth Mitchell, executive director of the Staten Island Zoological Society, and Brian Morris for their contributions to both West Brighton books. We also want to express our gratitude to Caroline Diamond Harrison, of the *Staten Island Advance*, the O'Connor family of West Brighton, and Gene DiGiacomo and Danny Ingellis of the Vietnam Veterans of America Thomas J. Tori Chapter 421.

We also want to acknowledge some folks for their assistance in locating some of the store owners who are no longer in business, including Awilda Campbell, Mary Beth Van Cott Delmar, and RoseMarie Krumrey. The life's blood of any church is its congregation, or worshipers, and West Brighton is blessed with many religious institutions. The authors would like to thank the following individuals for their contributions of photographs and detailed stories about the history of their churches: Msgr. Peter Finn of Blessed Sacrament, Rev. Eli D. Smith and Mr. Damon Tucker of Shiloh A.M.E. Zion Church, Pastor Larry Miraldi, Henry and Barbara Ann Kiedrowski of Salem Evangelical Free Church, and Mary Bruno Nolan for the photographs of St. Benedicta's Church and the family photographs as well.

Social media played a part in compiling this book. We are grateful for the support and encouragement of our friends on the West Brighton book and Growing Up in West Brighton Facebook pages. We always enjoy the nostalgic discussions about long-forgotten West Brighton characters and the lively debates about which pizzeria had the best pizza in the neighborhood, Happy Days or Pal Joey's.

INTRODUCTION

We always knew the Images of America: *West Brighton* book would be very popular, and that's not just self-confidence. We knew we were telling the story of a very supportive community. The population of Staten Island has grown considerably since the opening of the Verrazano Narrows Bridge in 1964, so there are very few Staten Island neighborhoods that can claim to be "old Staten Island," but West Brighton is one of them. It is a place where generations have grown up but remained rooted in the same close-knit town.

When we began our four-and-a-half month journey to complete the first book, West Brighton was very receptive to the idea. We compiled some photographs from the Staten Island Historical Society and Staten Island Sports Hall of Fame, but most of the photographs and information in the book came from West Brighton families. When reaching out to the descendants of longtime West Brighton residents, over and over again we were told how much they appreciated the fact that their families would be celebrated and remembered, and those descendants came through with an abundance of photographs and stories. During that spring, we must have talked to 500 people. Everyone gave us five more people to call. And even if they had nothing to contribute, they were excited to see West Brighton's story told. That level of enthusiasm kept us focused on doing the book correctly. Since Images of America: *West Brighton* debuted in January 2011, we have received so many kind words of congratulations on a job well done, and that made us proud.

We believed we wrote the comprehensive history of West Brighton, but unfortunately, some stories were left out of the first book. Most were due to various circumstances. We did not have enough information to find some folks. There were some photographs that could not be located then but since have been found. Some West Brighton descendants who moved away from Staten Island discovered the book online and offered us photographs if we decided to do a sequel. All of these factors helped us to include so many things that were not in the first book.

Some of our favorite interviews were with the spouses and descendants of Staten Island politicians who have passed away. We would like to thank Miriam Cusick, Ollie Gaeta, and Kathleen Murphy, who are proof of the old saying "Behind every man, there's a good woman." We also spent some time with Jane Stilwell, daughter of Justice Thomas Sullivan. All of these ladies gave us some wonderful stories about the successful men in their lives.

While working on the new book, certain themes emerged in different chapters. Since the book covers 1960 to the present, we were trying to find things that were nostalgic but also current or something old that looked new. We contacted the Preservation League of Staten Island and worked with historian Barnett Shepherd to find some West Brighton homes with interesting stories, and we were able to tour some of these beautiful houses that have been restored to their former glory.

Longevity did not just apply to structures. As we were compiling pictures for the "Generations" chapter, many of the photographs celebrated golden anniversaries of 50 years or more. And the happy couples are surrounded by multiple generations of family members, most of whom are also West Brighton residents.

Images of America: *West Brighton* drew upon a deep well of history from the last two centuries. For this new book, we are very fortunate to have many more stories from the past 50 years without having to repeat anything from the first book. We look forward to the challenge of bringing the West Brighton story into the 21st century.

We are confident that this new West Brighton book will be as popular as the first one, but at the same time, we believe it may exceed its success, because a modern book will appeal to current West Brighton residents who want to see their story told. That is a legacy they can pass on to their children, who will hopefully continue to live in one of the finest communities in New York City.

One

HISTORY

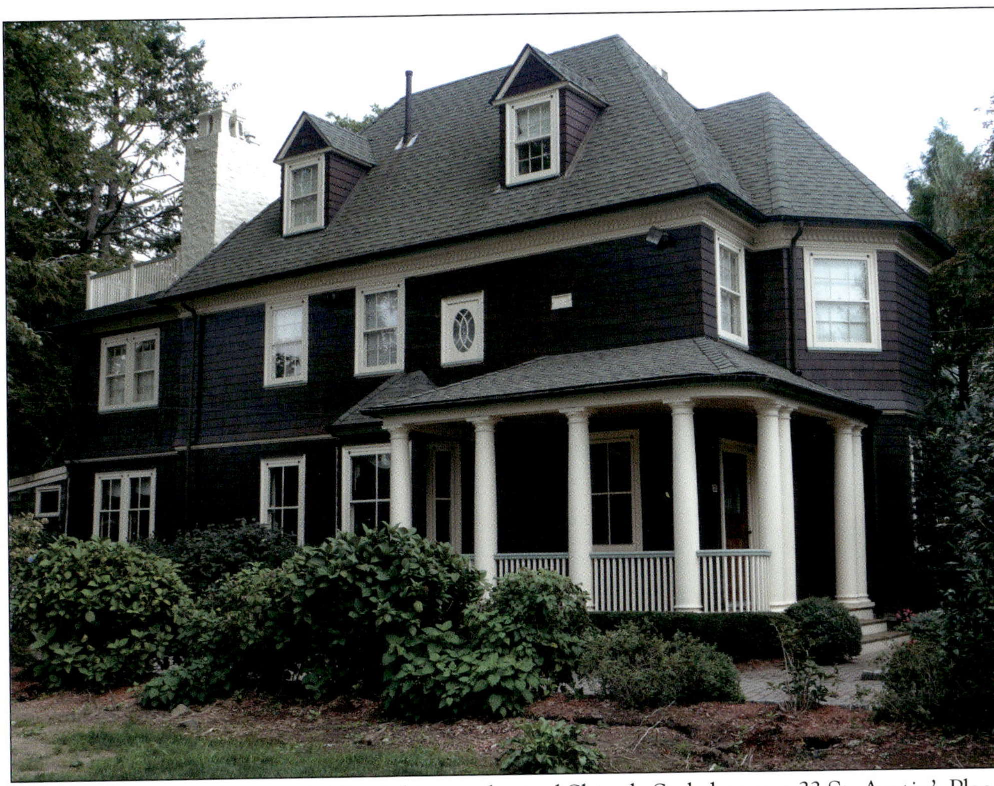

The completion in the early 1890s of this neoclassical Shingle Style home at 33 St. Austin's Place (and its mirror image at 34 St. Austin's Place) coincided with the opening of the St. Austin's School for Boys in the nearby Garner Mansion. The house was McKim, Mead & White's smallest commission, costing $5,500 to design during the recession of the early 1890s. A thorough interior and exterior restoration culminated in 2007. (Courtesy of John C. Gustafsson.)

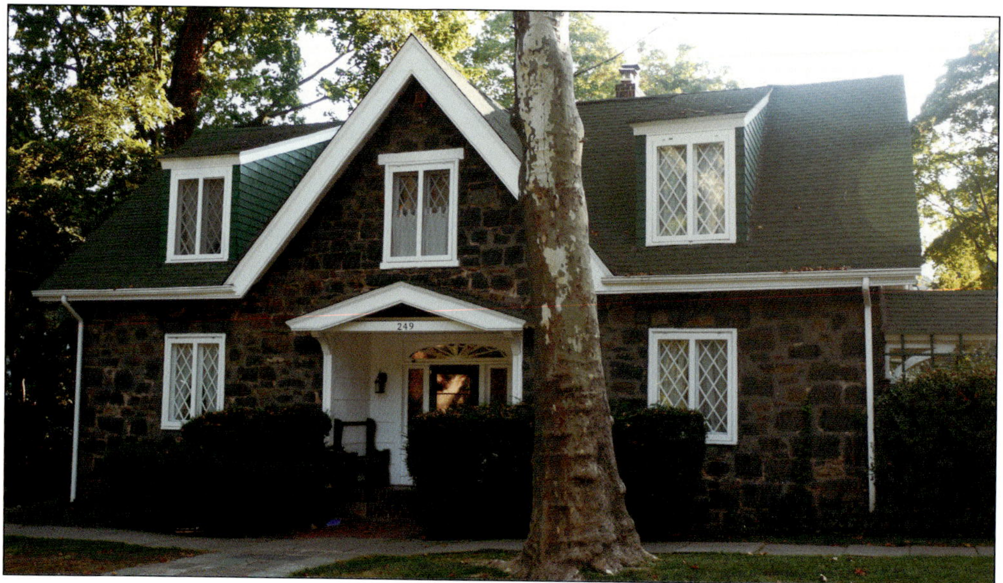

The mansion that was once known as the Willow Brook estate is long gone, but the gatehouse on the property, which was also built in 1830, still remains at 249 Bard Avenue and Rokeby Place. The Kissel family owned the land in the 1870s and 1880s. Elizabeth N. Outerbridge is listed as the owner of the Willow Brook estate in 1898, and R.T. Rokeby is listed as the owner in 1907. (Courtesy of Joyce Baldassarri.)

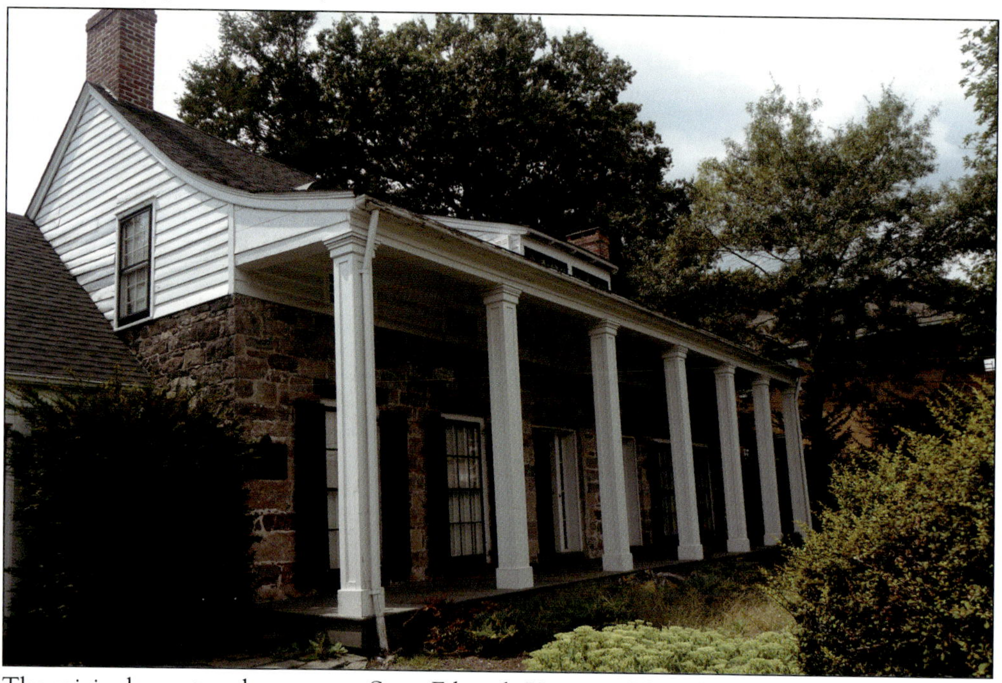

The original one-story brownstone Scott-Edwards House at 752 Delafield Avenue was probably erected in the first part of the 18th century. The second story was added later, and the Greek portico was most likely added to the building in the 1840s, perhaps by Judge Ogden Edwards, the first New York State Supreme Court justice from Staten Island, shortly after he purchased the house. (Courtesy of Preservation League of Staten Island.)

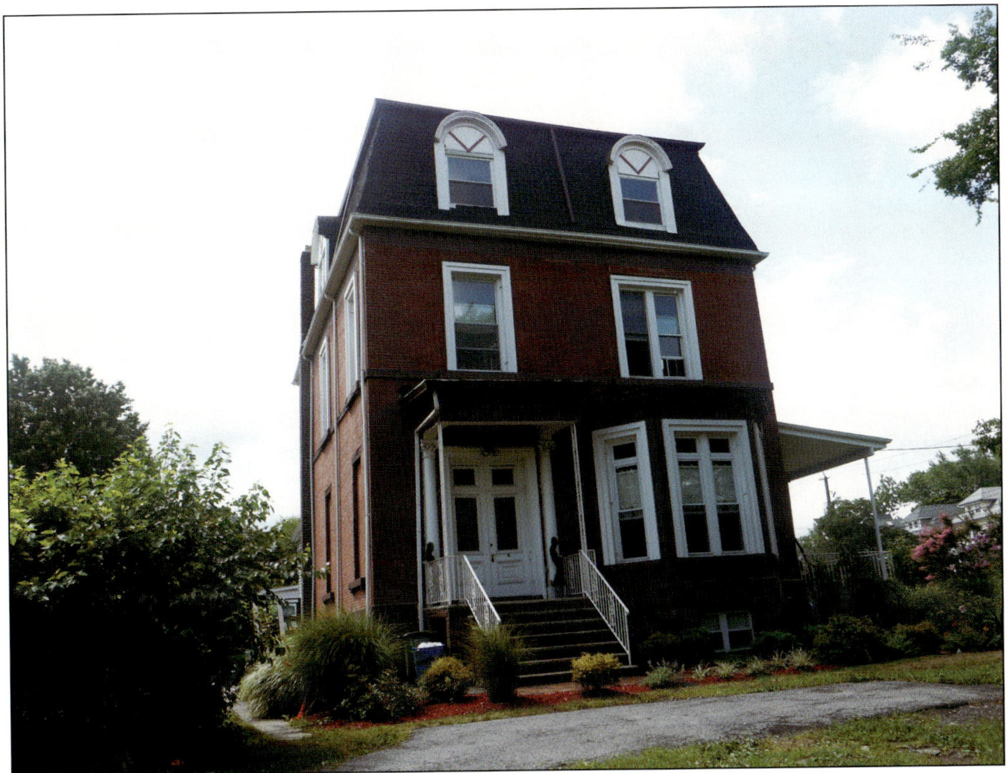

The home at 15 Bement Avenue, near Richmond Terrace, was once owned by Eberhard Faber, who is credited with building the first large-scale pencil factory in the United States. The home, built in 1870, also included a boathouse and dock across Richmond Terrace. It went on to become the headquarters of the Staten Island Athletic Club, but is now a private home. Faber Pool and Faber Street were named in honor of the Faber family. (Courtesy of the Johnson family.)

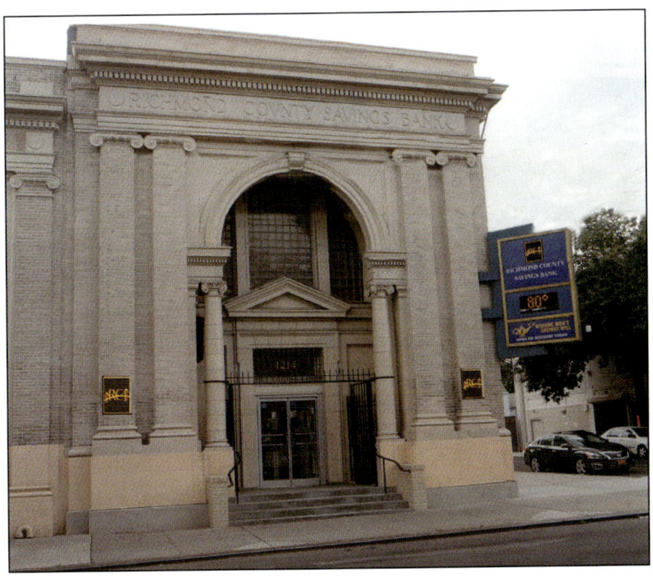

Richmond County Savings Bank was established on October 30, 1886. Its original site was in the Independent Order of Odd Fellows Building at the corner of Richmond Terrace and Broadway. As business continued to grow, the bank moved to 1619 Richmond Terrace and again in August 1921 to much larger space at 1214 Castleton Avenue (pictured) in West Brighton. This location is still used as the main office for Richmond County Savings Banks. (Courtesy of Richmond County Savings Bank.)

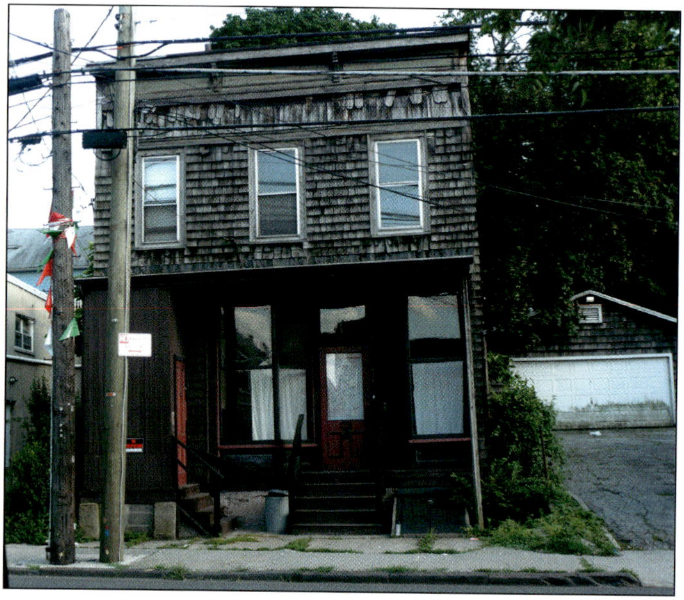

Around 1900, the Henderson Estate Company constructed this two-story commercial building at 848 Castleton Avenue. The original shop windows are a rare surviving example of 19th-century commercial architecture. For over 40 years, Andrea Phillips, a painter and collage artist, resided in the building, which also served as her studio and gallery. Her husband, Maurice, was a leader in Staten Island's African American artist community until his death in 1972. (Courtesy of the authors.)

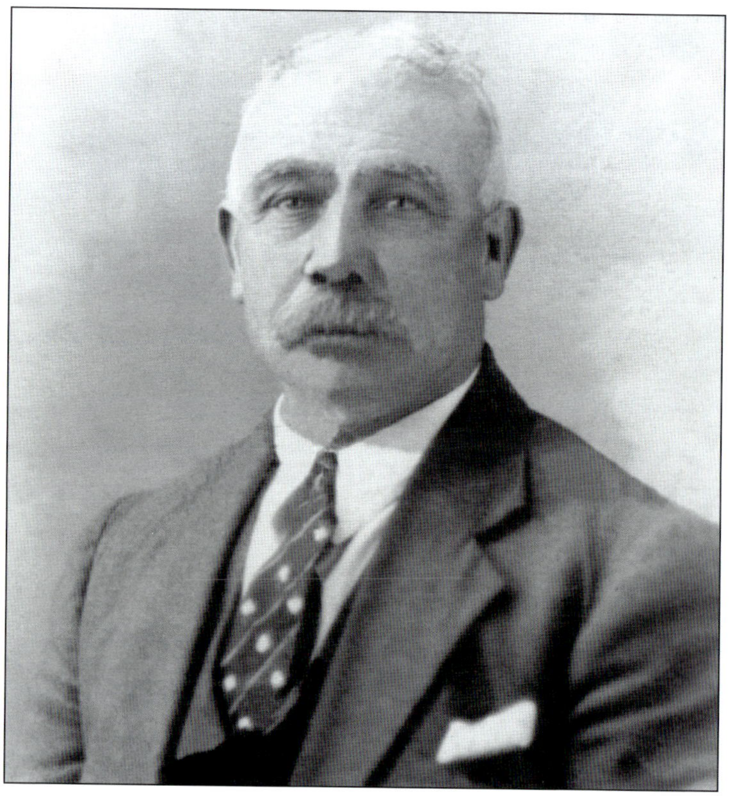

In 1908, John P. O'Connor and his wife, Alice, started the O'Connor Construction Company in West Brighton with a single team of horses and a cart. They eventually built a stable of 14 teams that operated across Staten Island. For years, they ran the business from their home on Birch Avenue. The O'Connors had nine children—six boys and three girls. All of the sons worked for the family business. (Courtesy of the O'Connor family.)

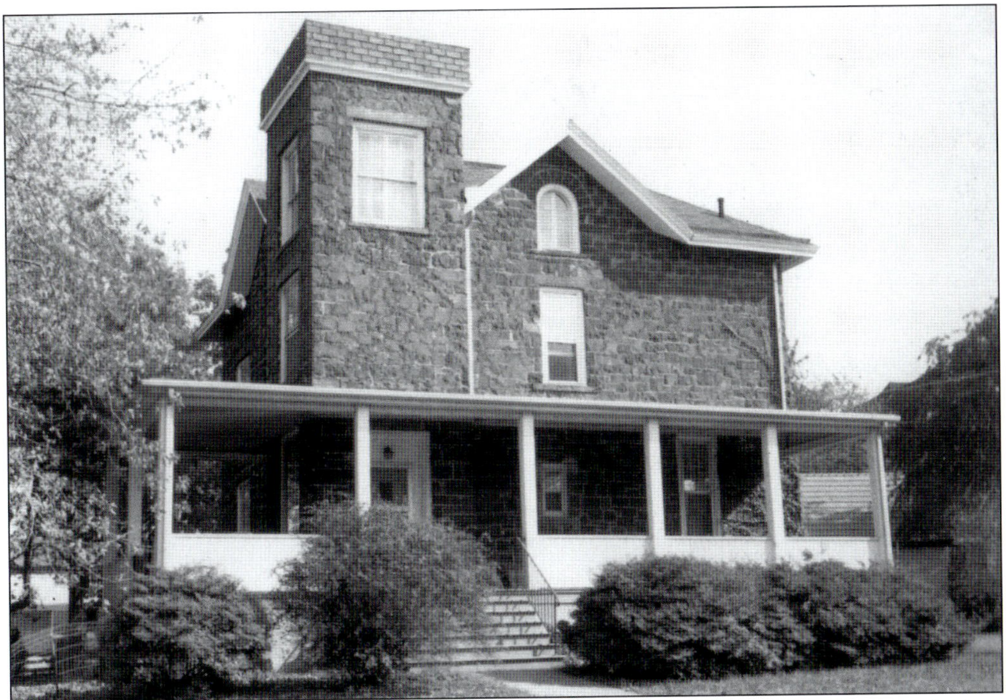

Oculist Dr. Samuel MacKenzie Elliot constructed the building at 557 Bard Avenue in the late 1850s. He erected several other stone buildings in the area, which was once known as "Elliotville." In October 1956, the congregation of Our Saviour Lutheran Church purchased the property and building; it is now used as the church parsonage. (Courtesy of Our Saviour Lutheran Church.)

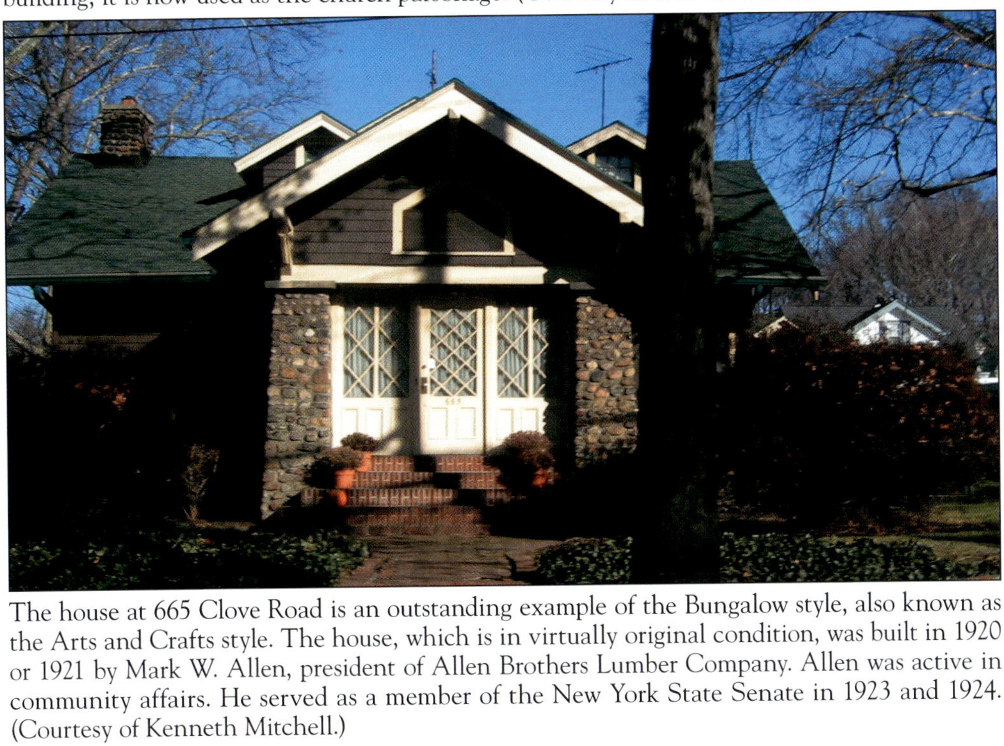

The house at 665 Clove Road is an outstanding example of the Bungalow style, also known as the Arts and Crafts style. The house, which is in virtually original condition, was built in 1920 or 1921 by Mark W. Allen, president of Allen Brothers Lumber Company. Allen was active in community affairs. He served as a member of the New York State Senate in 1923 and 1924. (Courtesy of Kenneth Mitchell.)

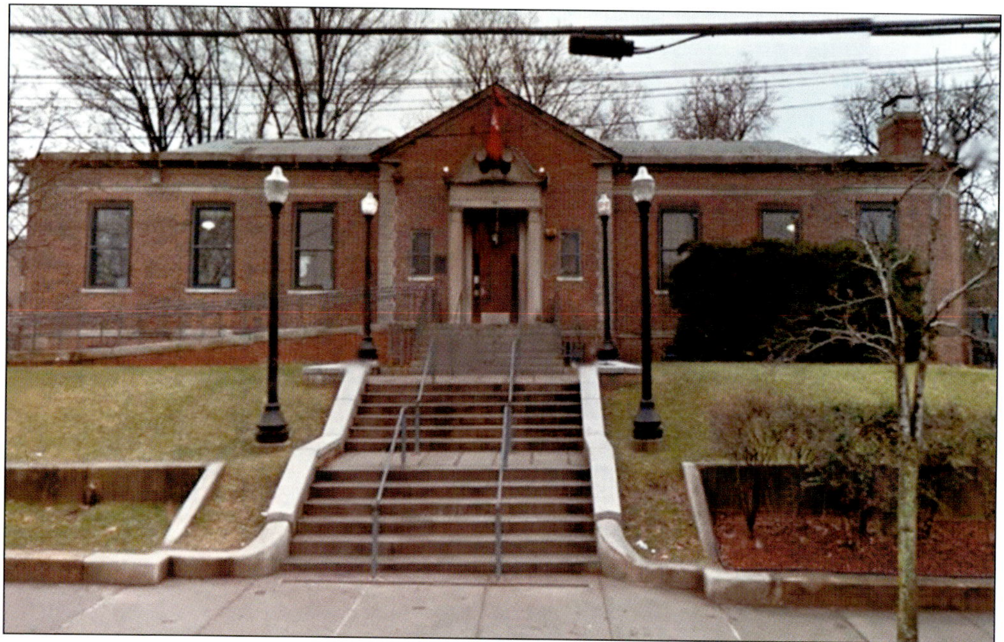

The West New Brighton branch of the New York Public Library (NYPL) was established in 1913 as a "home station" at a residence at 1006 Castleton Avenue. The following year, it relocated to a "community station" in a store at 996 Castleton Avenue. Then, the NYPL opened a sub-branch at 85 State Street. By 1928, strong demand from the reading public of West Brighton called for a branch library of the community's own. The construction of the building on the corner of North Burgher and Castleton Avenues commenced at the height of the Great Depression. Financial difficulties caused a delay in opening the branch that lasted for several months. Finally, on April 1, 1933, the West New Brighton Library opened its doors. Now, 80 years later, it remains a vital part of the community that offers programs for children and adults. (Both, courtesy of West New Brighton Library.)

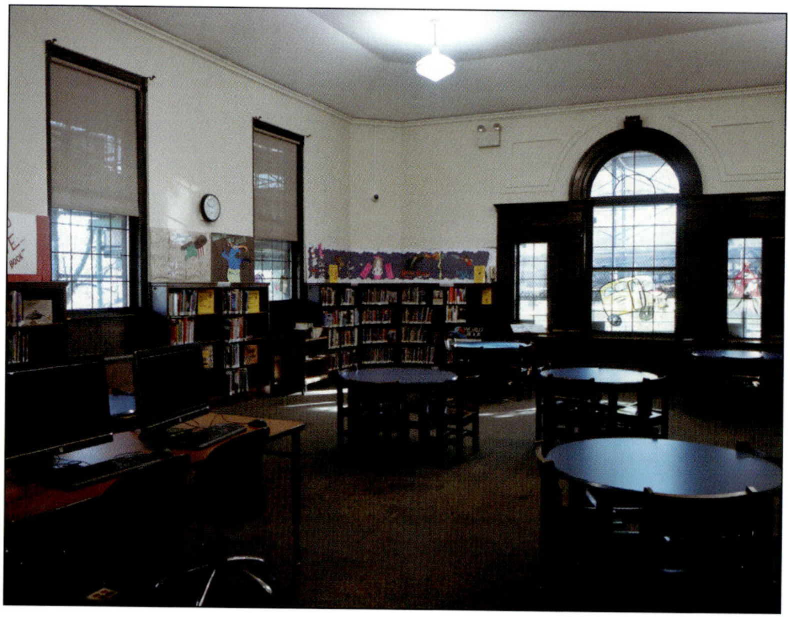

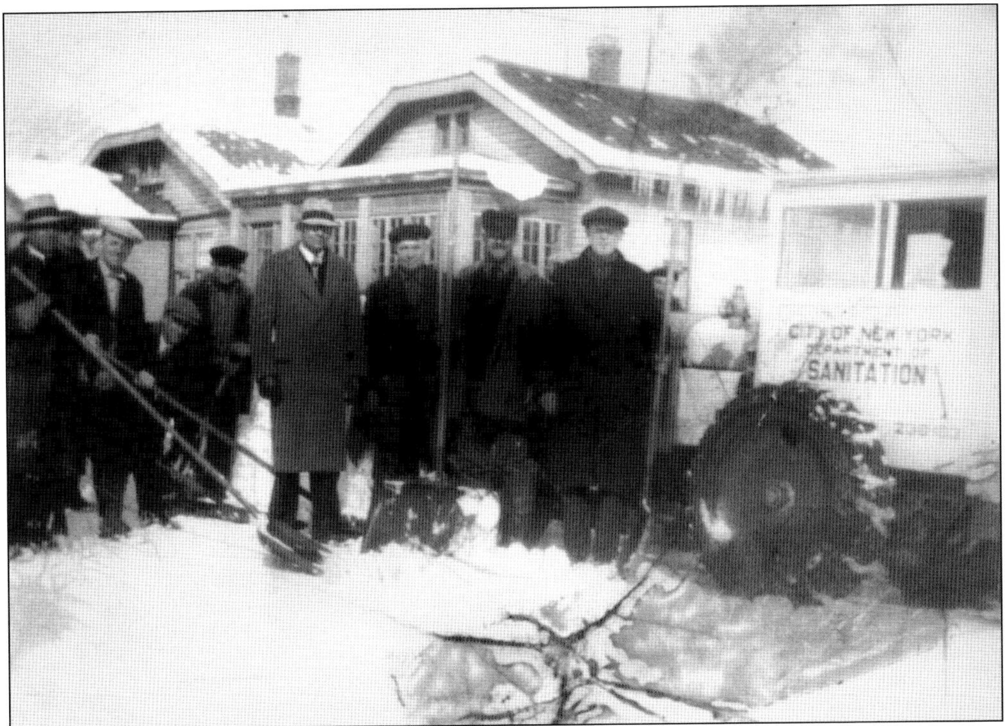

These two photographs represent the many seasons of West Brighton. In the image above, the men of the O'Connor Construction Company are shoveling snow. The photograph below shows bathing beauties on the South Beach boardwalk representing the Blue White Laundry. (Above, courtesy of the O'Connor family; below, courtesy of the DePaolo family.)

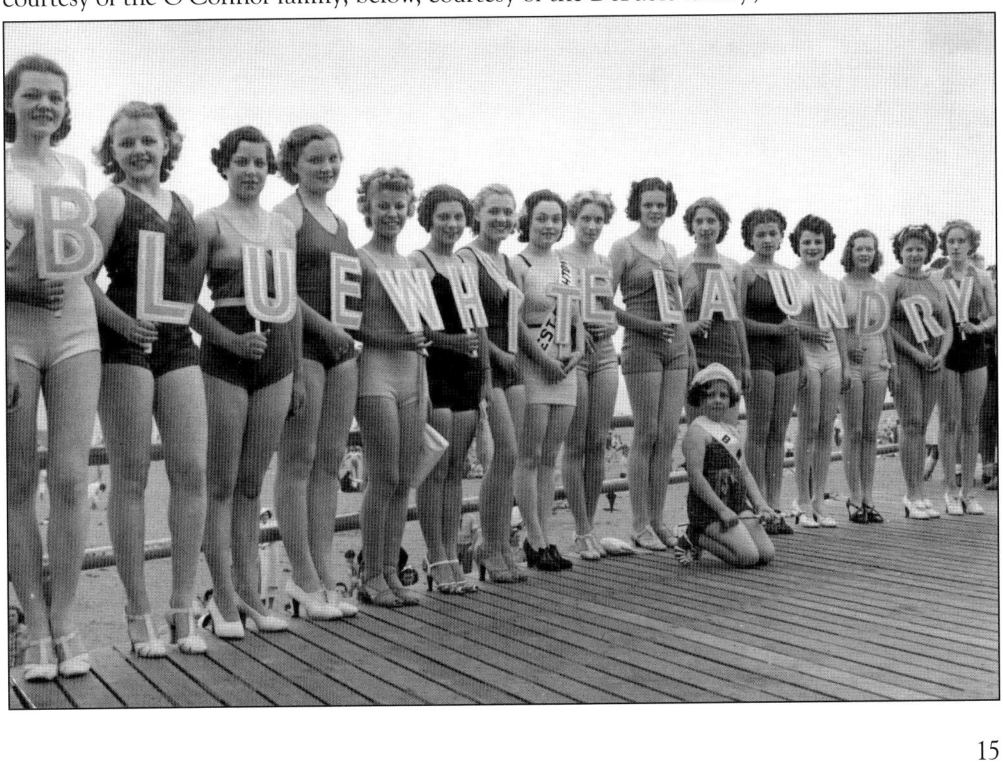

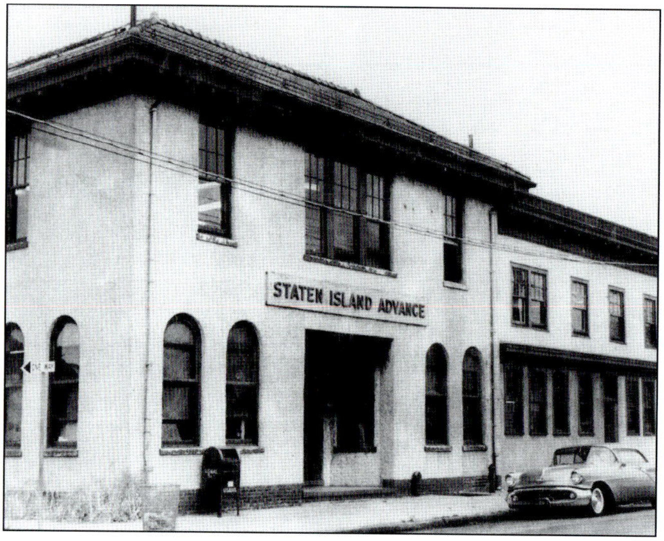

In 1886, John J. Crawford Jr. founded the *Richmond County Advance* as a weekly newspaper published on Saturdays. It began in a small building on Broadway in West Brighton. In 1913, a new building (pictured) was erected at 1267 Castleton Avenue. It became a daily newspaper in 1918 and changed its name to the *Staten Island Advance* in 1921. The paper's headquarters remained at the Castleton Avenue location until 1960. (Courtesy of the *Staten Island Advance*.)

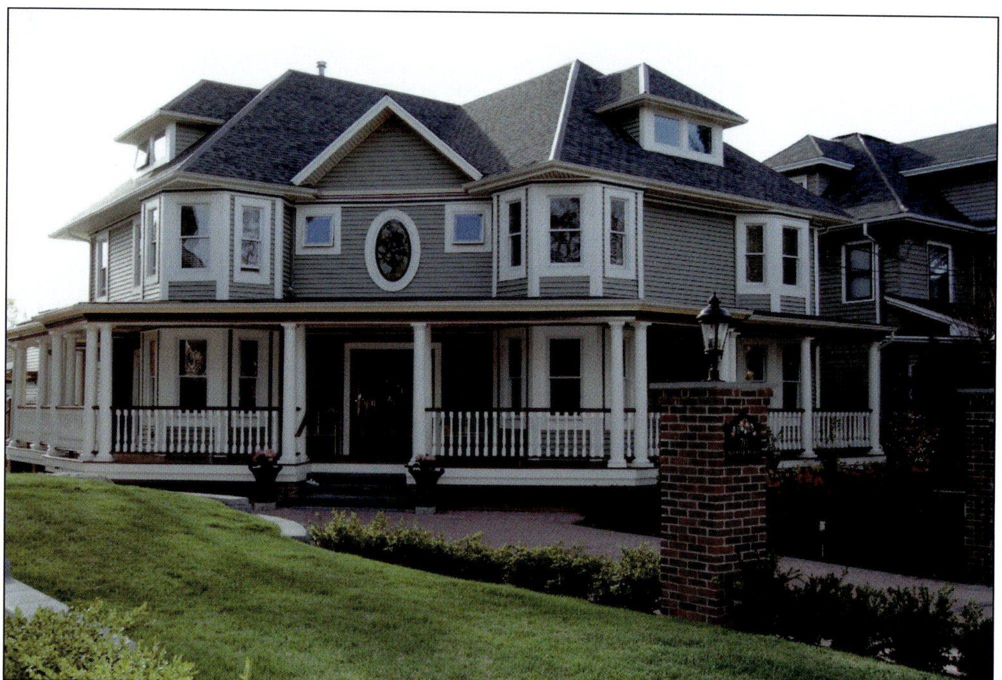

Richmond County Advance founder John J. Crawford Jr. built this home at 70 Manor Road around 1902. Crawford was among the first Staten Islanders to own an automobile, and he built a precursor to the shock absorber in his garage. In 2004, the home at 70 Manor Road was completely remodeled, but the current owners retained the outside structure of the old house in order to preserve the memories they had made in the residence. (Courtesy of the Spach family.)

Two

Recreation and Entertainment

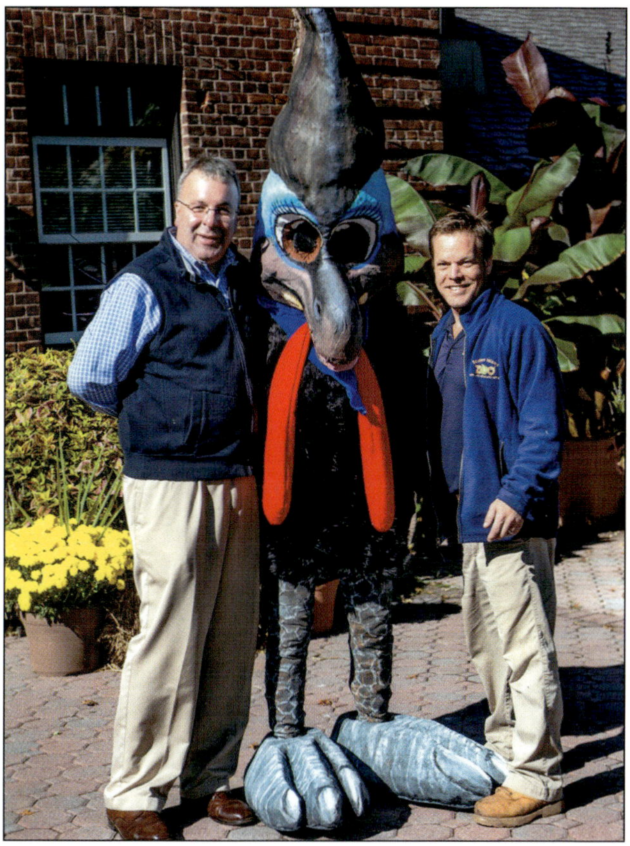

Kenneth C. Mitchell (left), executive director of the Staten Island Zoological Society, and Mark Lamberti, the Staten Island Zoo's facilities manager, pose with a replica of a cassowary, a flightless bird native to the forests of New Guinea, which the zoo is attempting to add to its collection. Both Mitchell and Lamberti are third-generation West Brighton residents. (Courtesy of the Staten Island Zoological Society.)

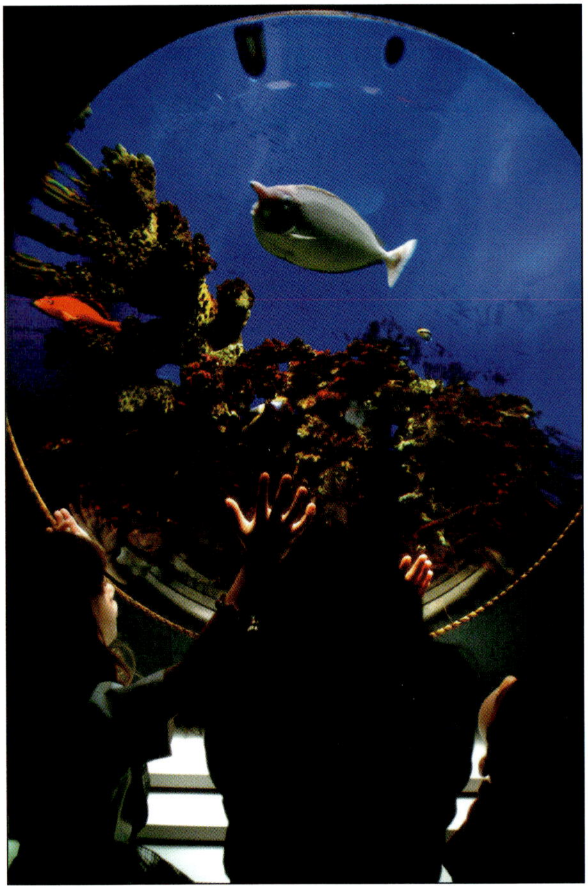

At first, the aquarium at the Staten Island Zoo had freshwater species. It was not until the 1950s that the zoo was successful in maintaining saltwater marine life—no easy task in a closed water system. The zoo had a puffin, clownfish, and an angelfish. Beginning in 1983, the aquarium underwent a complete renovation. The John J. Marchi Aquarium was dedicated on April 13, 1986, to honor the longtime state senator. The renovation took a bold approach to include larger exhibit tanks. The zoo now has 15 tanks, including four bubble tanks in the corners that contain reef exhibits from different parts of the world. The largest of the 15 are the three freestanding center tanks, which hold large reef predators including moray eels, groupers, and sharks. (Both, courtesy of the Staten Island Zoological Society.)

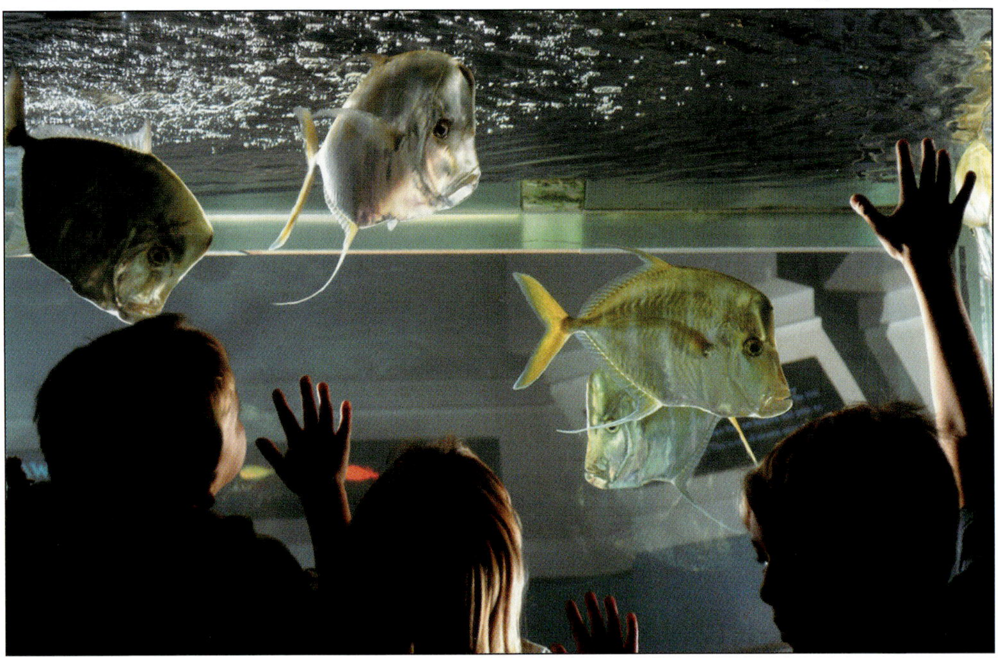

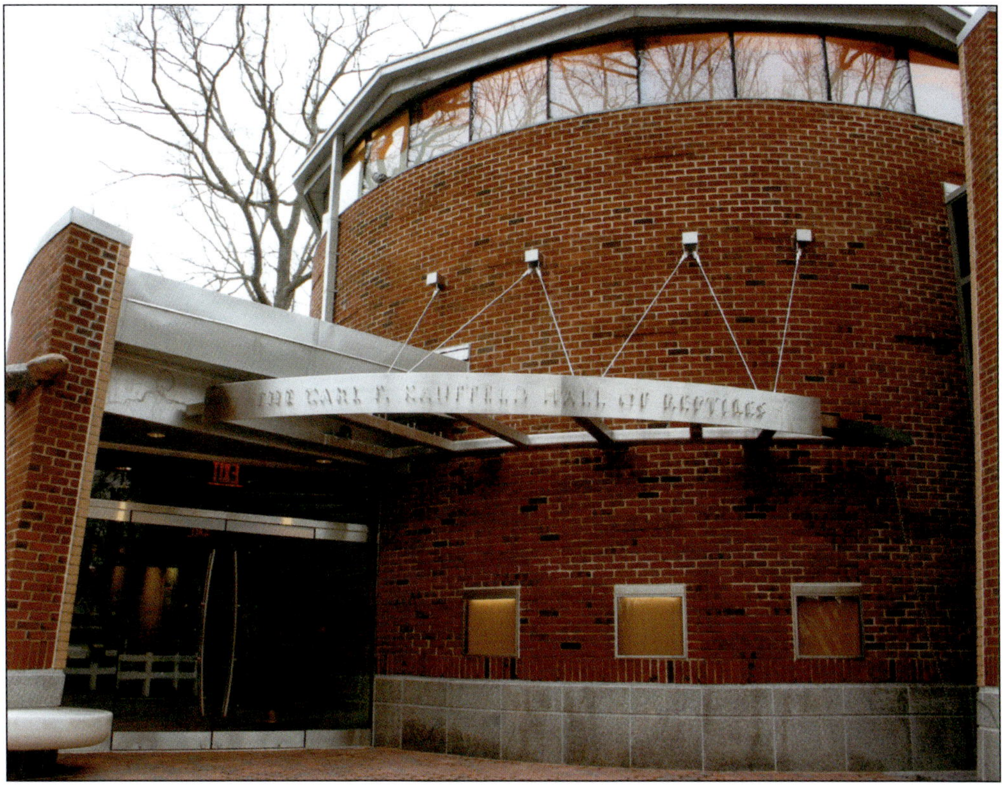

The reptile wing at the Staten Island Zoo—one of the original exhibits when the zoo opened in 1936—continued to grow over the years thanks largely to the curator of reptiles, Carl Kauffeld. Kauffeld worked at the zoo for 34 years and was zoo director from 1963 to 1973. Under Kauffeld's direction, the Staten Island Zoo realized that in order to compete with larger institutions like the Bronx Zoo, it would have to specialize in certain areas. With the reptile wing, it prided itself on presenting a collection the public could not see elsewhere. By 1968, the zoo's rattlesnake collection contained a new record of 39 forms (species and subspecies). Kauffeld resigned in 1973 due to health and died the following year. In 1977, the reptile wing was dedicated to the memory of Carl Kauffeld. The wing underwent an extensive renovation in 2007. (Both, courtesy of the Staten Island Zoological Society.)

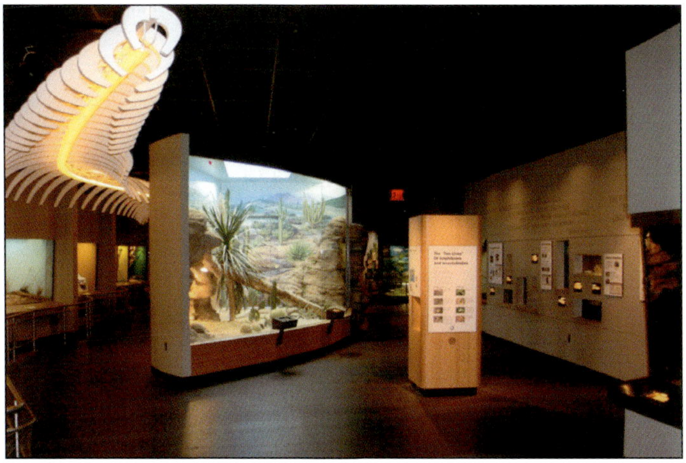

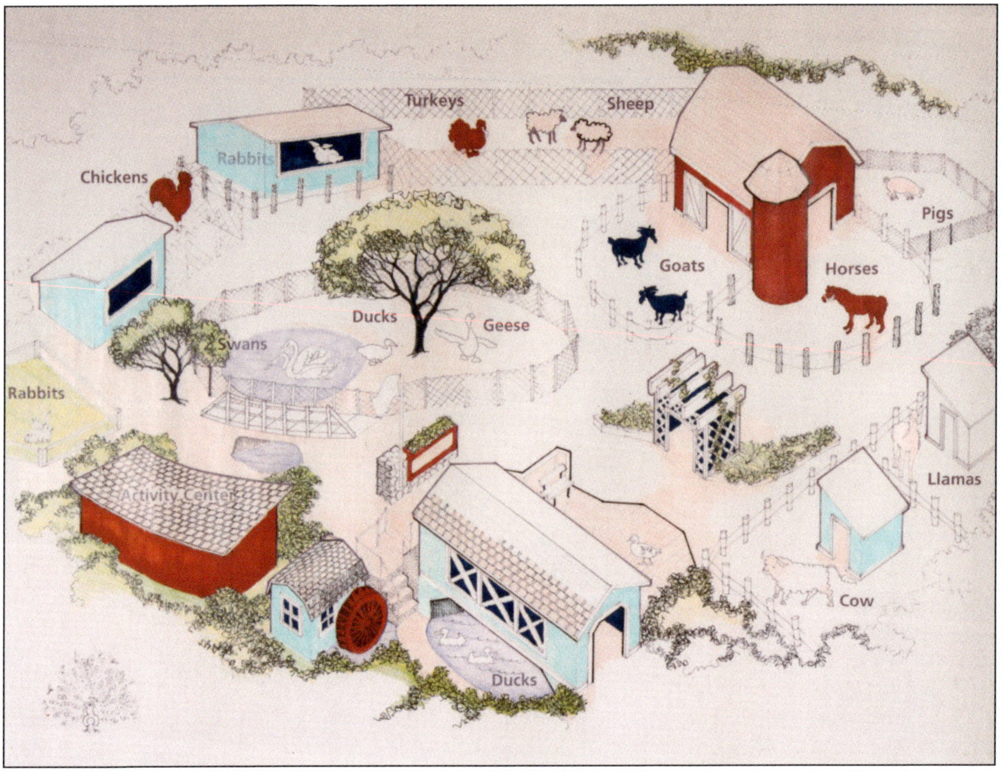

The Staten Island Zoo provided an artist's rendering (above) from the late 1960s that shows the proposal for its children's zoo. It opened May 4, 1970, at a cost of $140,754. The admission that day was 15¢ for children and 25¢ for adults. The new facility featured a barn, a covered bridge, and a waterwheel to create an atmosphere of farm life. Children were offered the chance to stroll through the corrals and pens in a leisurely manner. The first animals in the children's zoo included calves, goats, sheep, a Shetland pony, a donkey, four geese, and a dozen each of chickens, ducks, and rabbits. (Both, courtesy of the Staten Island Zoological Society.)

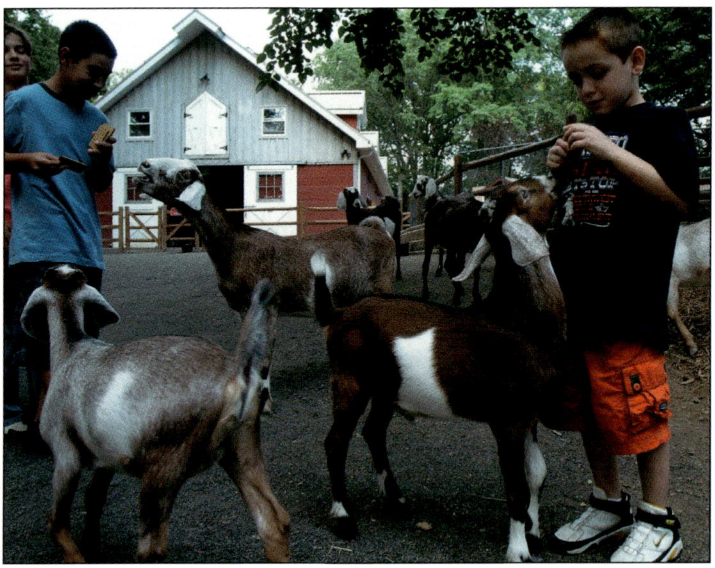

YMCA programs have been offered on Staten Island since before the Civil War. As early as 1857, an independent Staten Island association organized activities for young men. The image at right is of 1590 Richmond Terrace near Van Street. The 1871 building's facade looks much the same as it did in the 19th century (although it did undergo a restoration by current occupant Lennie Construction Corp.), when the YMCA operated in West Brighton from 1871 to 1886. This may be the oldest surviving YMCA building in the country. In 1952, the YMCA acquired land for a permanent YMCA branch on Broadway across from the Staten Island Zoo. The Robjohn Estate (below), a 100-year-old stone homestead on the property, was used as a temporary headquarters until a new facility was built. (Right, courtesy of Lennie Construction; below, courtesy of the Staten Island Historical Society.)

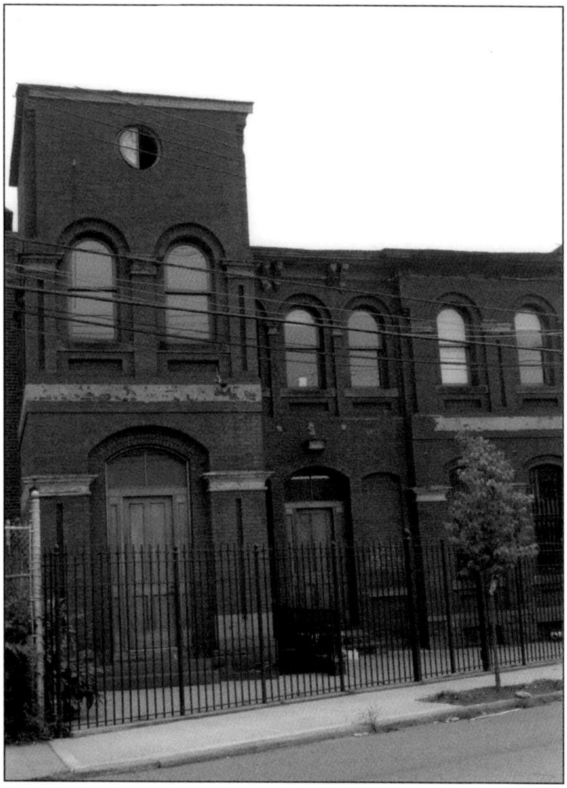

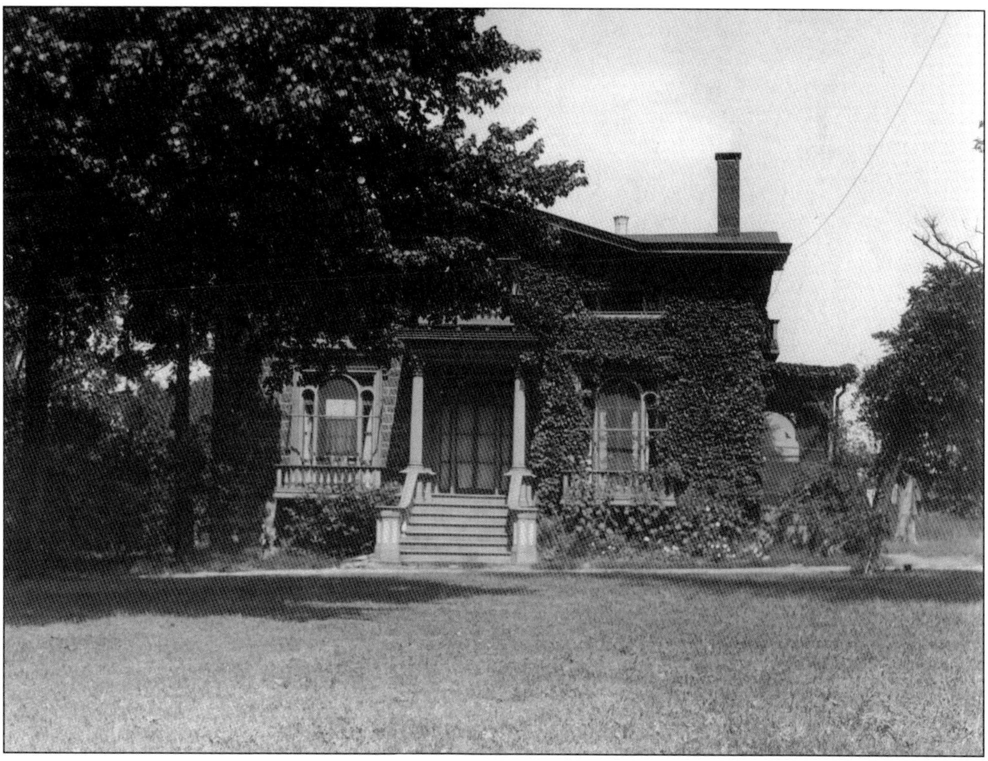

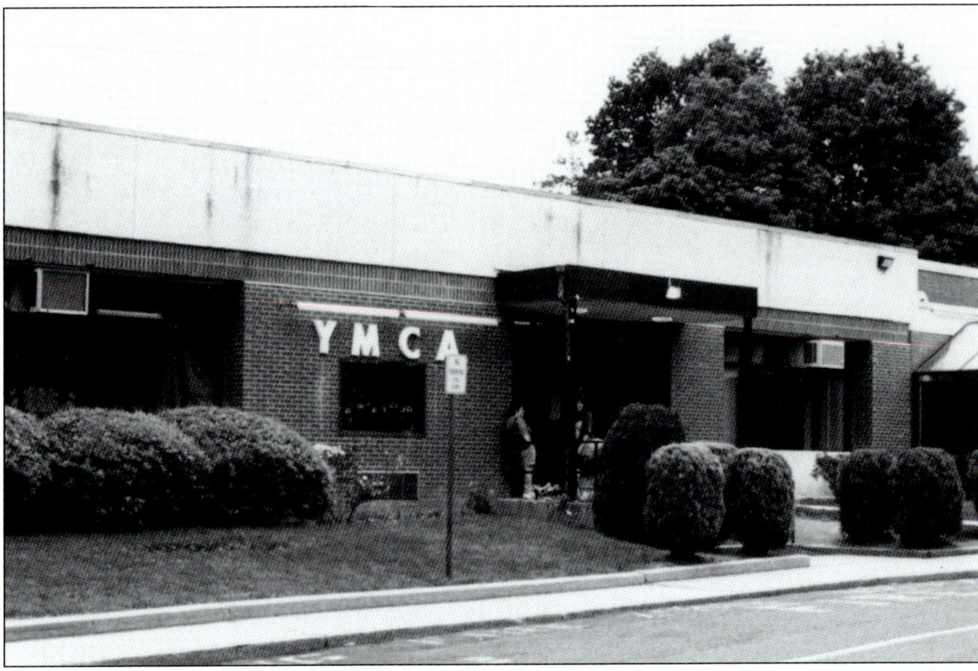

The YMCA on Broadway was dedicated on October 25, 1953. The building, pictured above, received a $1 million expansion and was renamed the Broadway branch in 1976 with a new gym, classrooms and tennis courts. Since then, the facility has been expanded several times. Pictured below are the 2013 directors of the Broadway branch of the YMCA. They are, from left to right, (first row) Joyce Strype, youth and family coordinator; Audrey Urcia, membership director; Allison Sicuranza, early childhood director; and Stella Bennardello, senior director of healthy lifestyles; (second row) Romulus Staton, aquatics director; Erik Bradley, building manager; Heather Scapp, executive assistant; and Joseph Verhey, executive director. (Both, courtesy of the YMCA.)

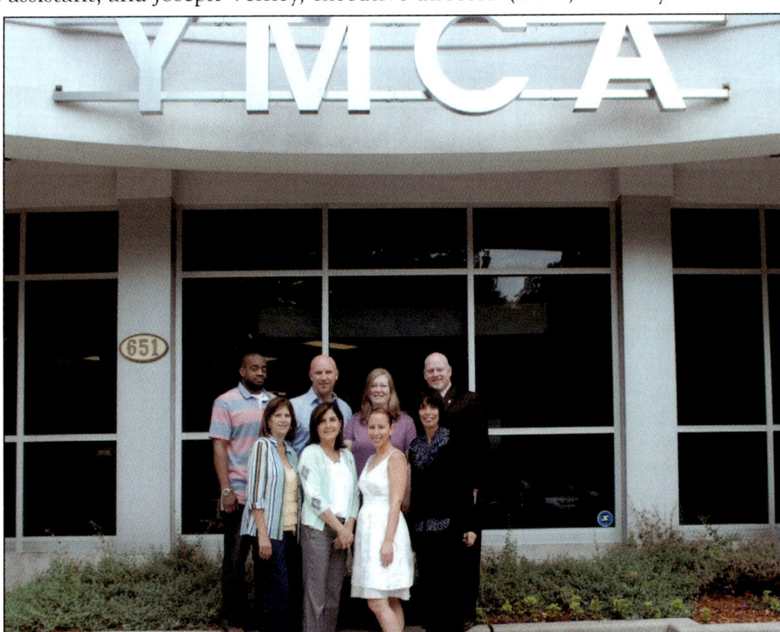

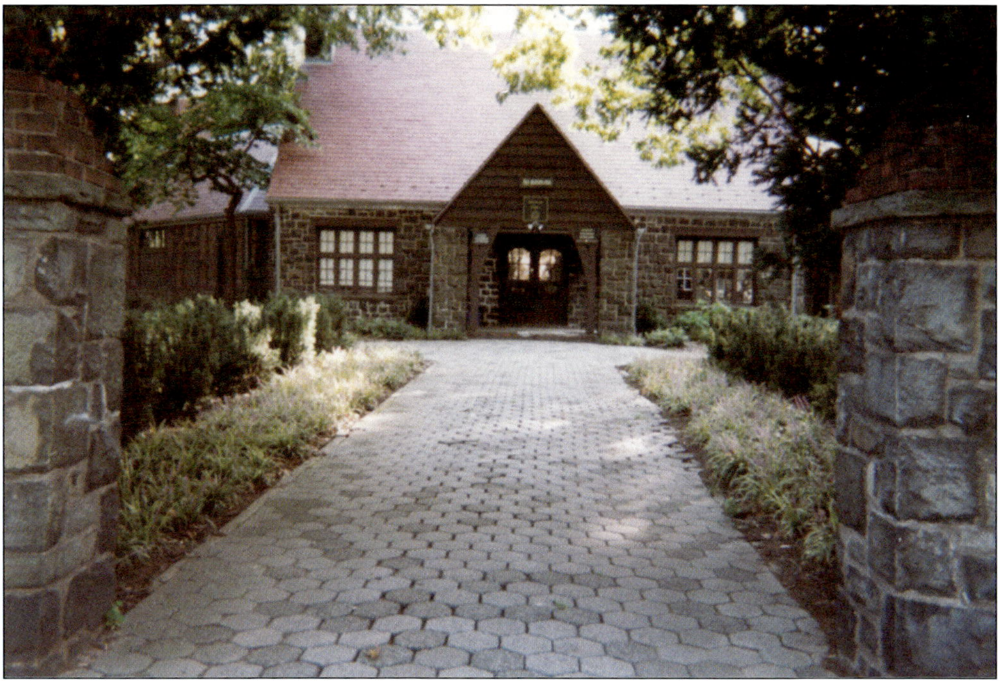

At one time, the five acres of Walker Park were the Henry P. Delafield estate. The Staten Island Cricket and Tennis Club purchased the estate in 1886, and Staten Island Academy owned it in 1923. The New York City Parks Department bought the estate in 1930 and dedicated it to the memory of World War I hero Randolph St. George Walker Jr. in 1934. The park grounds include a French Provincial clubhouse. (Courtesy of Nancy Vanderbilt.)

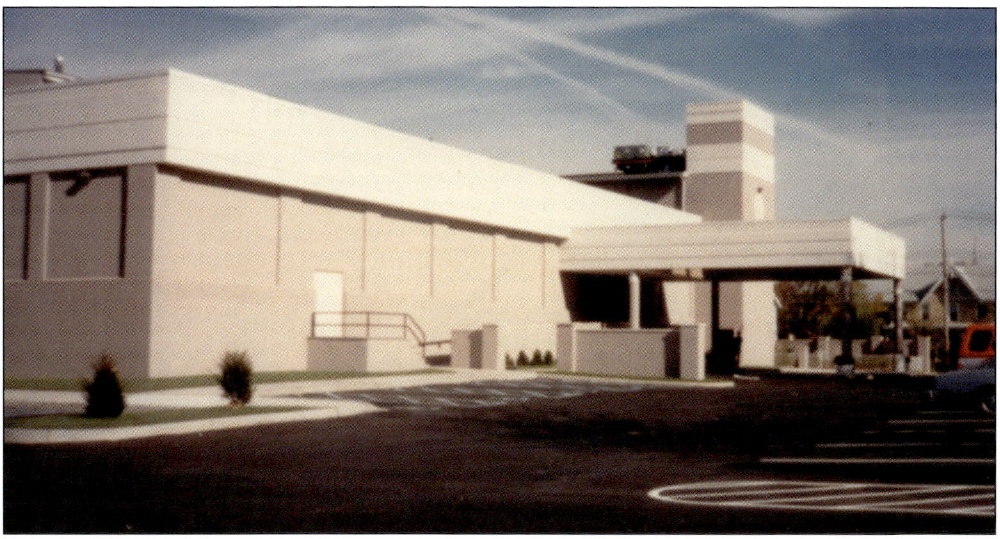

The Columbian Lyceum was originally on Richmond Terrace. In August 1959, it was moved to 386 Clove Road. The main hall on the second floor was called the Red and Gold Room. Some of the affairs held in this building through the years included weddings, charity balls, Christmas parties, and local sports dinners. The bowling alley in the structure had many leagues, such as the Knights of Columbus island-wide league and the Larry McSorley P.A.L. league for children. (Courtesy of Robert and Ann Marie Scott.)

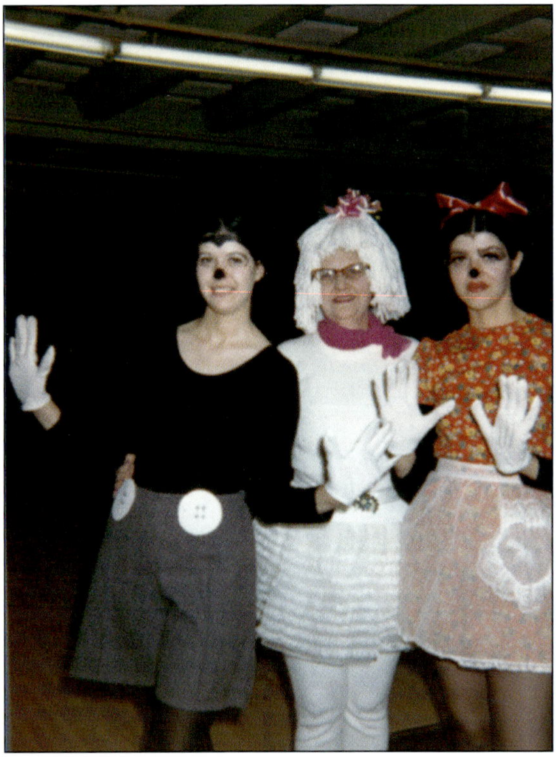

These photographs from the 1960s and 1970s capture some Halloween fun for the ladies of the Sacred Heart Thursday night bowling league at the Columbian Lanes on Clove Road. Pictured at left are Rosemary Morrison Tarnacki (left), Beatrice Morrison (center), and Jean Morrison Cronin. Pictured below are, from left to right, Margaret Smith, Dorothy Farley, Catherine Mulligan, and Ethel Dugan. (Both, courtesy of Jean Morrison Cronin.)

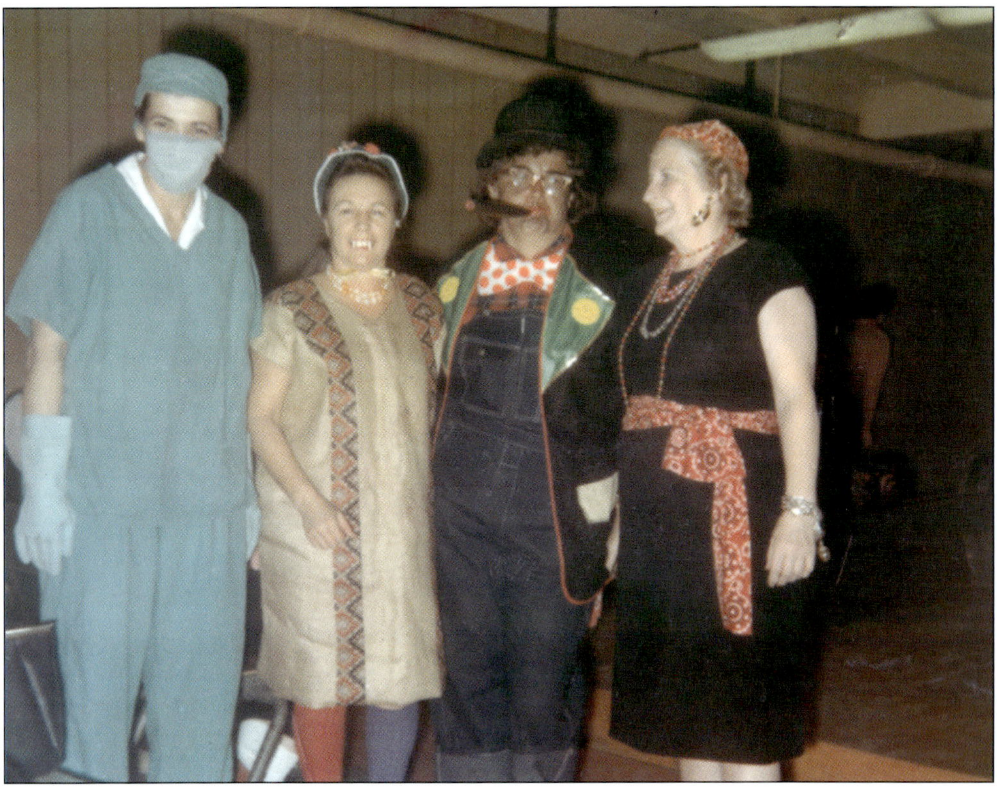

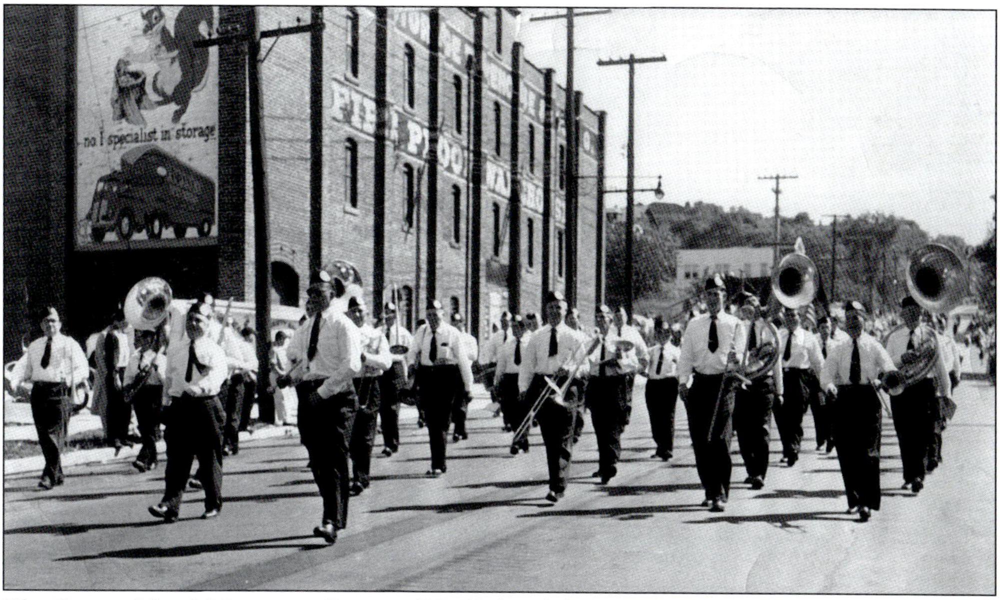

The Staten Island Musicians Society (SIMS) band (pictured above) was founded in 1955 by Maestro Al Cardone, Louis "Lou Russ" Russo, Patty "O'Day" Rufolo, Johnny DiMauro, Ceasar DiMauro, and Rocco Faciola. The band was very popular until 1990 (when the group disbanded) and contained many Staten Island players, such as Joe and Al Cardone Jr., Larry Laurenzano, Dan "Sy" Seymour, and the "Febb" brothers—Jimmy, Johnny, and Joe Fevelo. The SIMS band played free concerts at many Staten Island parks and took part in countless parades and festivities throughout the five boroughs. The musical tradition continues in the Cardone family, as shown in a recent photograph of The Silas Knight Project (below). Pictured are, from left to right, Troy Roberts, Bryson Barnes, Al Cardone Jr., Talia Cardone, Joe Weitekamp, Silas Knight, Steve Elias, Eric Tolnes, and Alex Lopez. (Both, courtesy of the Cardone family.)

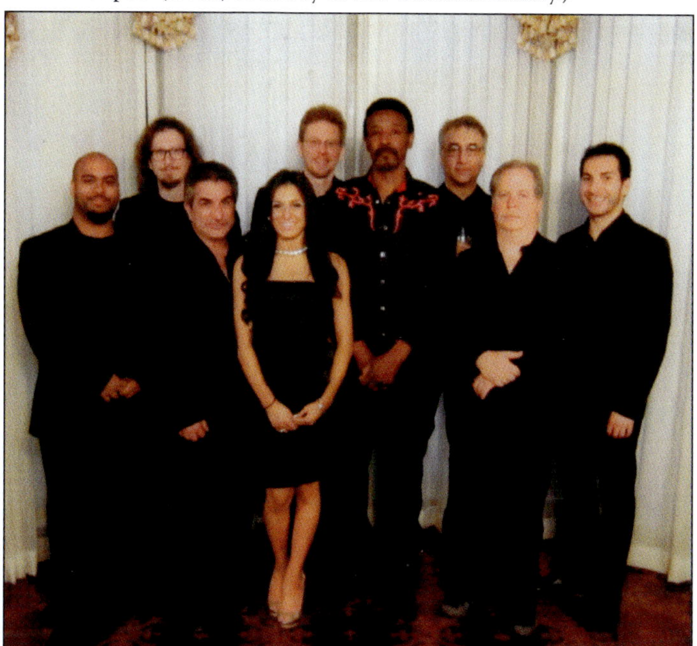

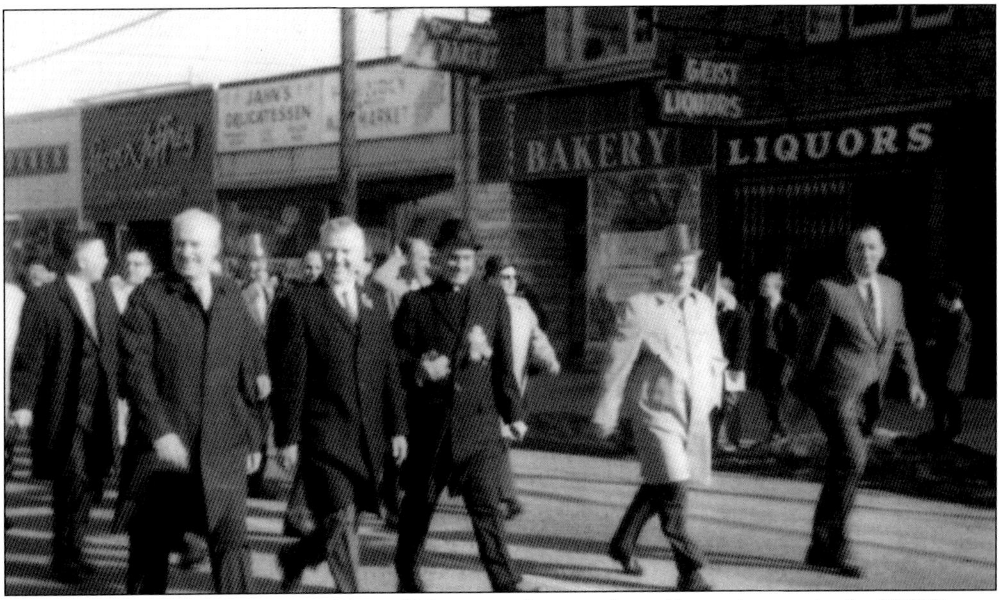

Fr. Vincent Clyne leads a group of Sacred Heart parishioners down Forest Avenue in the 1969 Staten Island St. Patrick's Day parade. Clyne passed away in June 2013 at age 95. Many West Brighton residents recalled that when he was a parish priest, he would walk the Catholic students from PS 45 down Bement Avenue to Sacred Heart School for CCD instruction. He also started the "First Friday" roller-skating trips for Sacred Heart students. (Courtesy of Dr. Craig Campbell.)

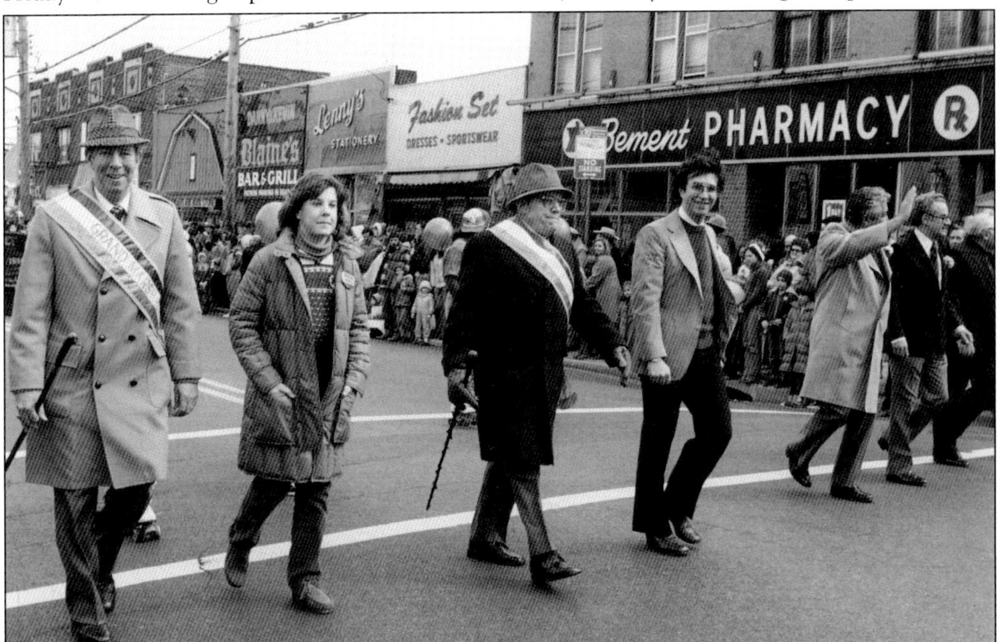

No book about West Brighton would be complete without a few photographs of the annual Staten Island St. Patrick's Day parade. This photograph from the early 1980s shows some Staten Island politicians proudly marching down Forest Avenue. From left to right are Judge Thomas Sullivan and his daughter Caroline, John Kearney, Robert Straniere, Anthony Gaeta, and Guy Molinari. (Courtesy of the Sullivan family.)

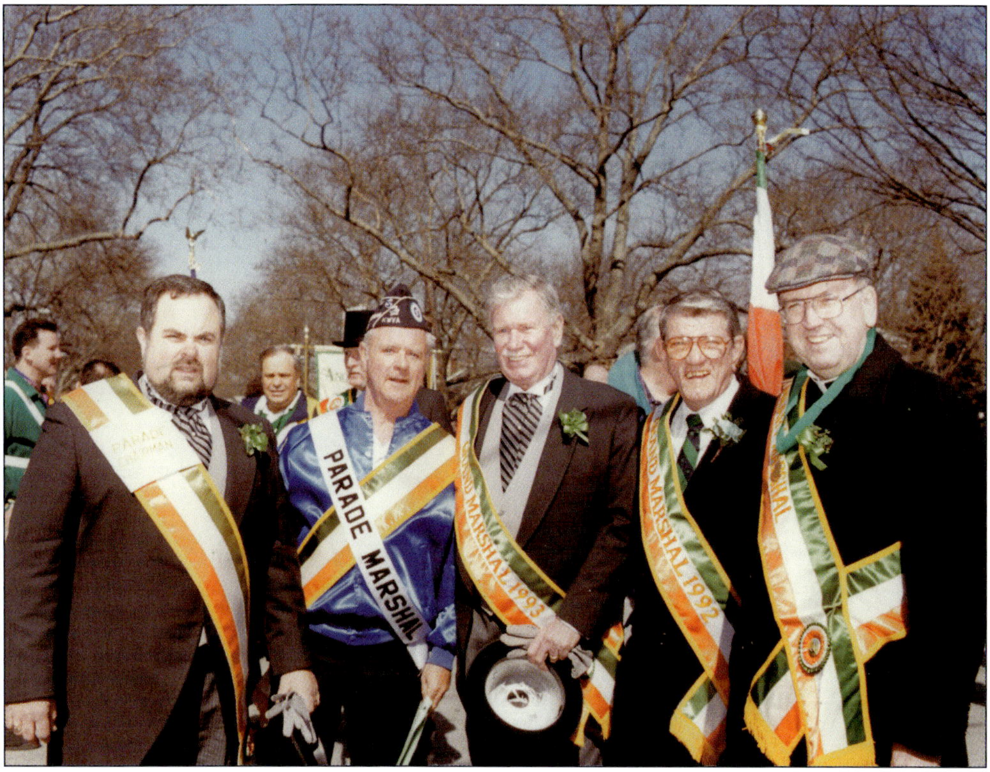

West Brighton is well represented in these two 1990s photographs from the Staten Island St. Patrick's Day parade. The above photograph includes, from left to right, parade organizer Charles "Chip" McLean; parade marshal Joe Ferris; Judge Peter Cusick; Raymond Taylor, owner of the Claddagh Gift Shop; and Msgr. Peter Finn. The below photograph shows, from left to right, Staten Island district attorney William Murphy, Robert Helbock, and Edgar Sweeney. (Above, courtesy of the Cusick family; below, courtesy of the Murphy family.)

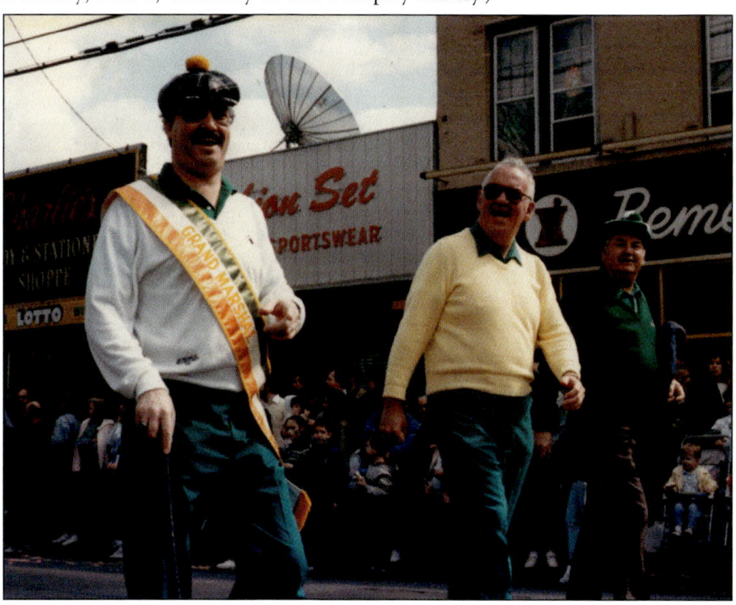

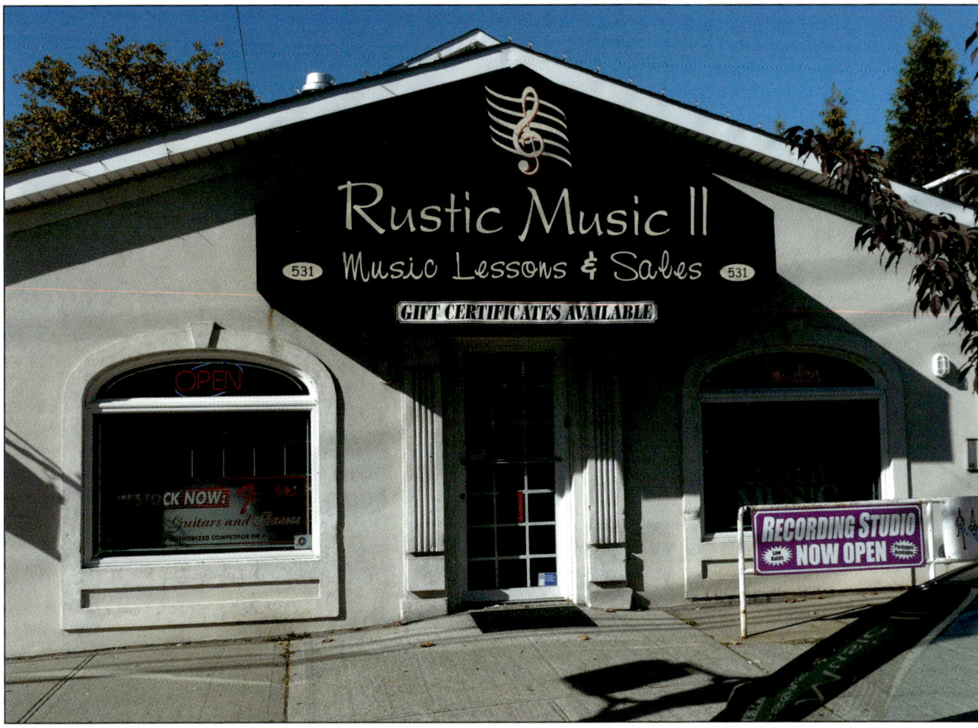

Rustic Music Center, founded in 1969, operated a small shop at the top of Forest Avenue until it closed in 1991. The second Rustic Music store, on Richmond Road, continues to operate. Between 1995 and 1996, Michael Caldarella, a teacher at Rustic, purchased Rustic Music Center and became partners with Christina Caldarella, another teacher at the store. In 1999, Rustic Music II was reborn at 531 Forest Avenue, where it resides today. In the past four years, the store has grown and continues to bring new and exciting inventory to customers. Rustic Music is a full-service music shop. Some things it offers include music lessons, instruments, sheet music, rentals, and stage lighting. Rustic Music Studios is available for recording and rehearsals. Rustic Music is the longest-operating music store on Staten Island. (Both, courtesy of Rustic Music Center.)

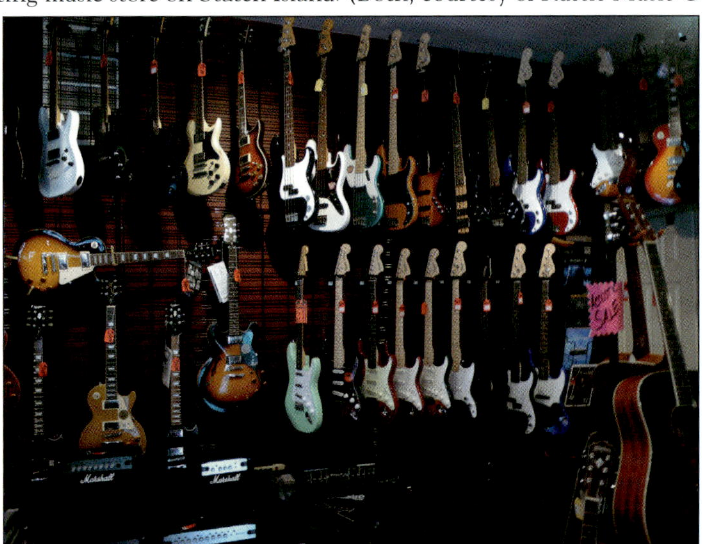

Three

Business

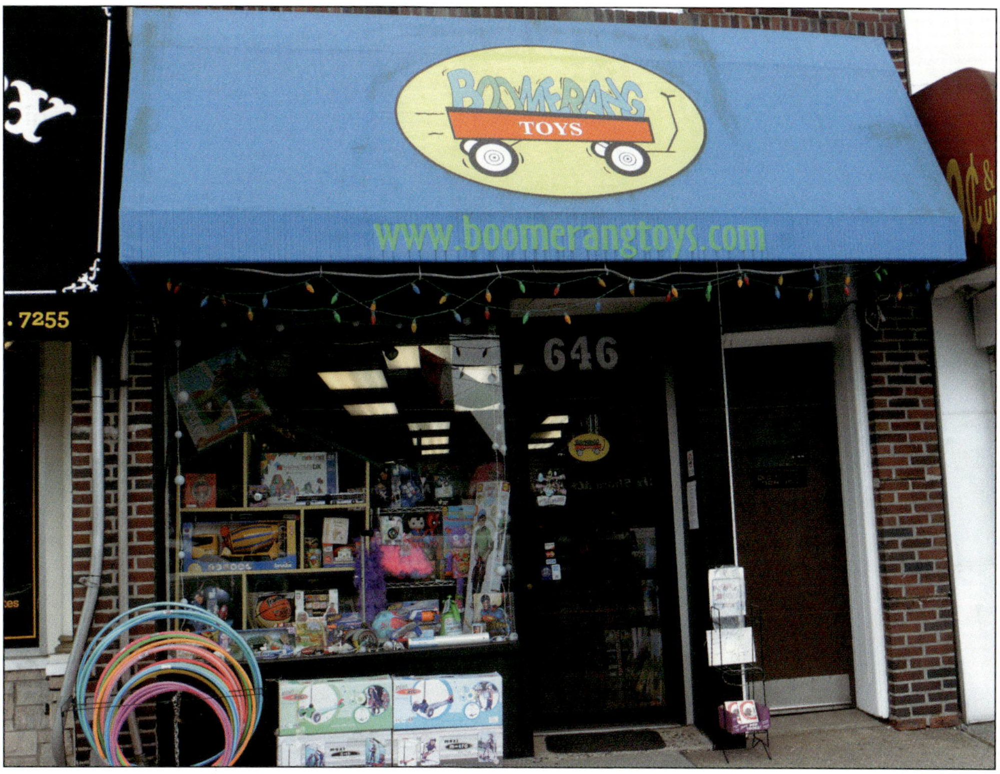

Karen Barwick opened Boomerang Toys in 2002 in Tribeca, Manhattan, after she was unable to find quality educational toys for young children in her neighborhood. She opened a second store in the World Financial Center. Originally from West Brighton, she chose her hometown for the third Boomerang Toys location. Her mother, RoseMarie Krumrey, manages the store. (Courtesy of Boomerang Toys.)

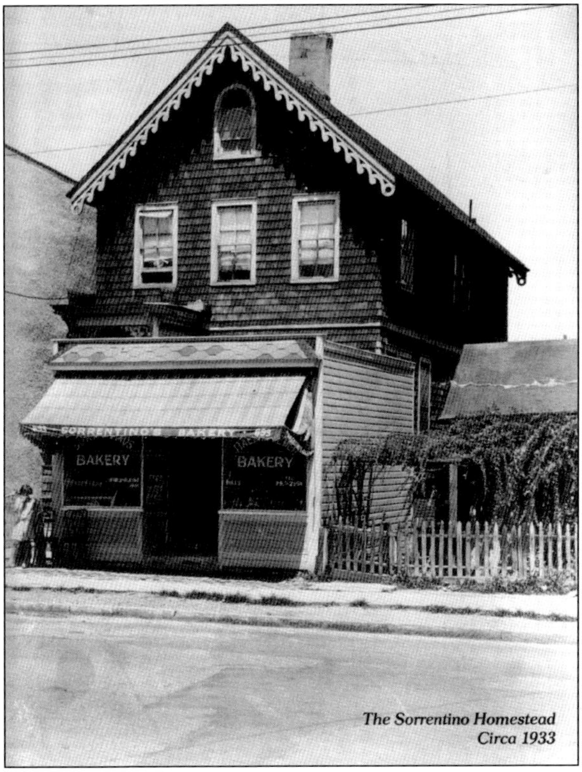

The Sorrentino Homestead
Circa 1933

For parts of six decades, a Sorrentino's Bakery (left) existed in West Brighton. Frank and Caroline Sorrentino (below) opened their first bakery at Henderson and Campbell Avenues in 1928. In 1931, they moved the bakery to 693 Henderson Avenue, where the business thrived until 1955. Their daughter Sylvia Sorrentino Prestia, who was born in the apartment above the bakery, recalled how her parents would bake all night, then her brothers would make deliveries across Staten Island while she worked in the bakery. She also remembered that in October 1946, she had to make 450 cream puffs for her own wedding. In the late 1950s, her brother Joseph bought Daylight Bakery on the corner of Castleton and Oakland Avenues. (Both, courtesy of the Sorrentino family.)

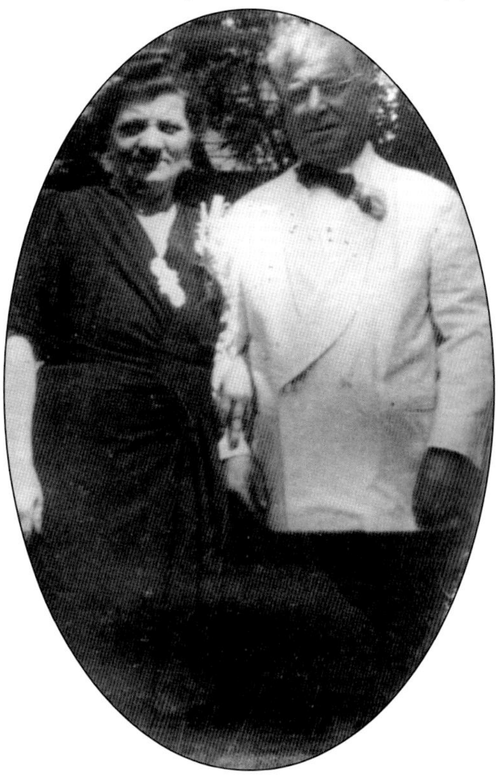

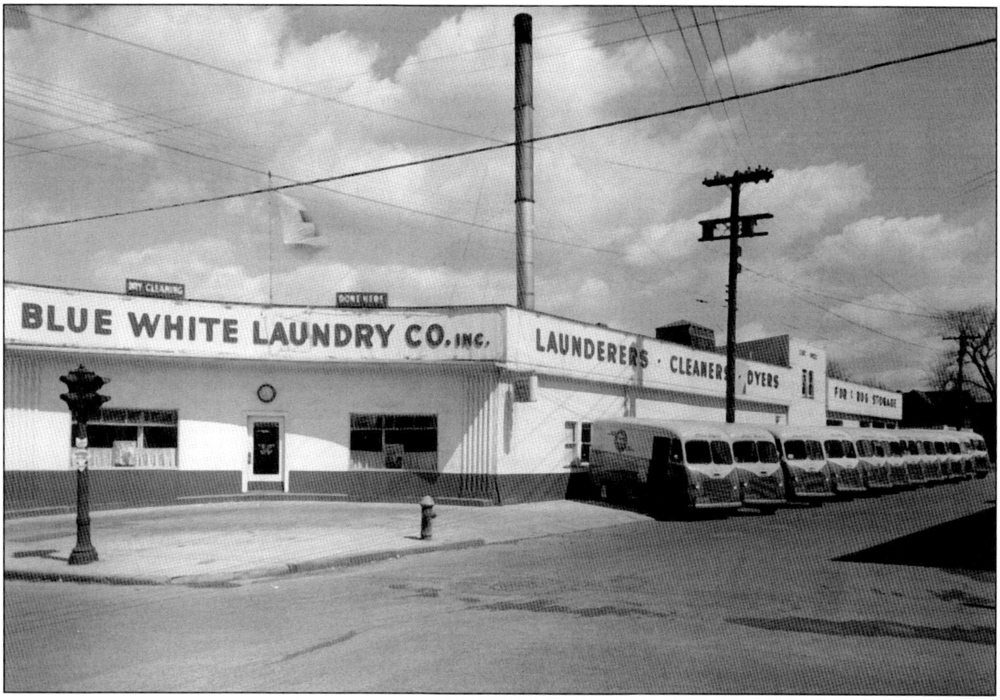

After arriving in the United States from Italy, Frank Giaco established the Blue White Laundry in 1923 at Cary Avenue and Clove Road. By 1947, the company had 150 employees and was Staten Island's largest and most successful laundry. That year, Giaco sold the Blue White Laundry and began building the Plaza Casino on Castleton Avenue with his son-in-law Leonard DePaolo. (Courtesy of the DePaolo family.)

Shoemaker Giovanni "John" Pillarella opened his shop on Broadway, just below Castleton Avenue, in 1939, and it remained open until his death in 1979. For 40 years, Pillarella repaired shoes for just about everyone in West Brighton. He and his wife, Mary, lived on Seneca Street with their eight children. When Mary was not making homemade pasta in her basement, she worked at Macrae and Rose, a dress factory located at 400 Broadway. (Courtesy of the Pillarella family.)

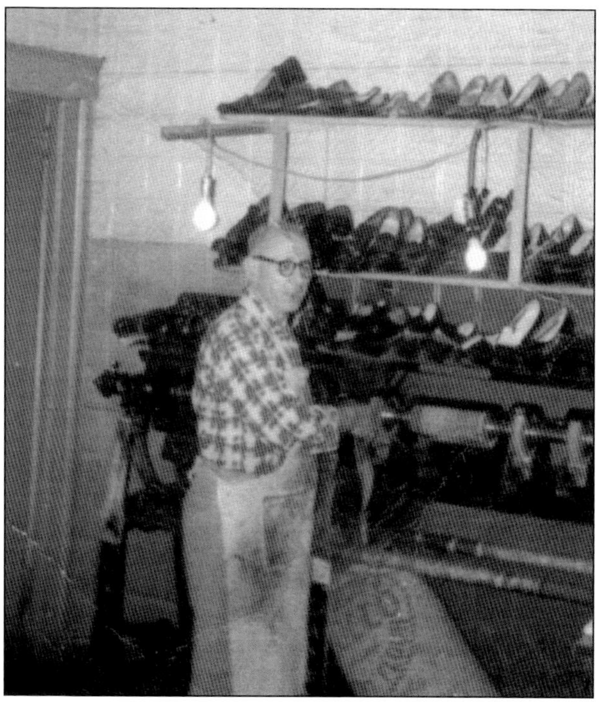

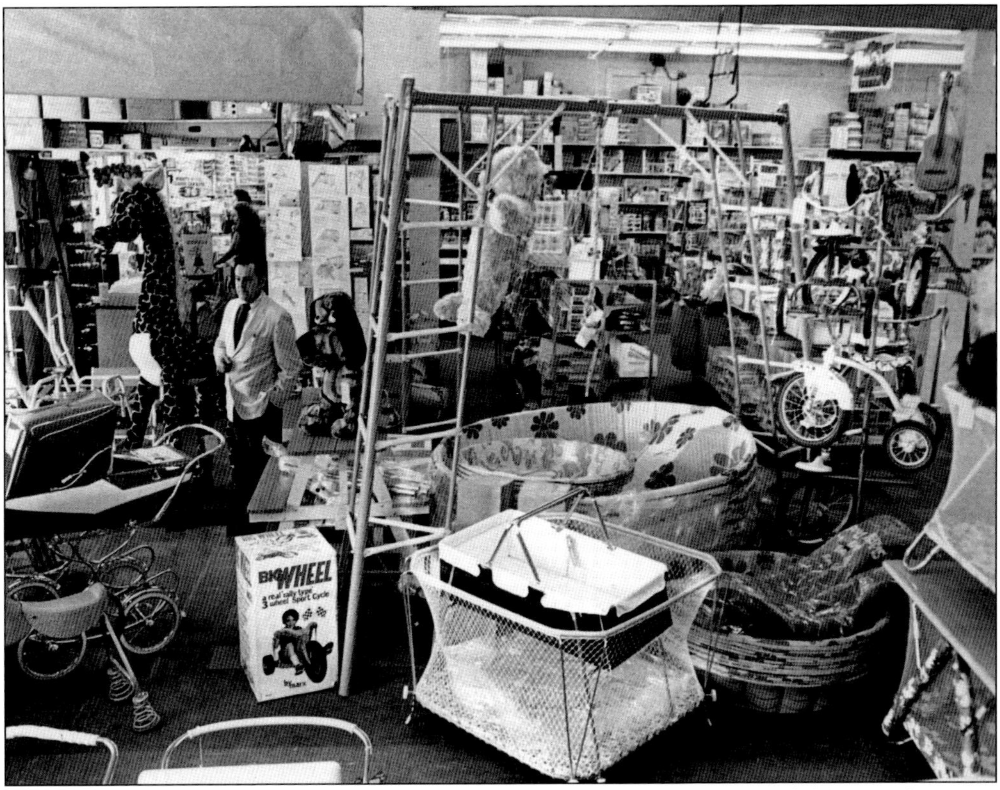

Martin Colby's store, Smiling Sunny's Toy Corner, was so popular among children and parents that Colby, known to everyone as Smiling Sunny, became a household name on Staten Island. Smiling Sunny's Toy Corner was first located in Tompkinsville before Colby and his wife, Florence, (pictured below at a toy fair) moved the business to Forest and Oakland Avenues in West Brighton. There, the successful toy store thrived through the 1950s, 1960s, and 1970s. Martin and Florence's son Russ recalled, "Everyone shopped at our store. And all the kids knew my parents very well." The Colbys sold Smiling Sunny's in the early 1980s. (Both, courtesy of Russ Colby.)

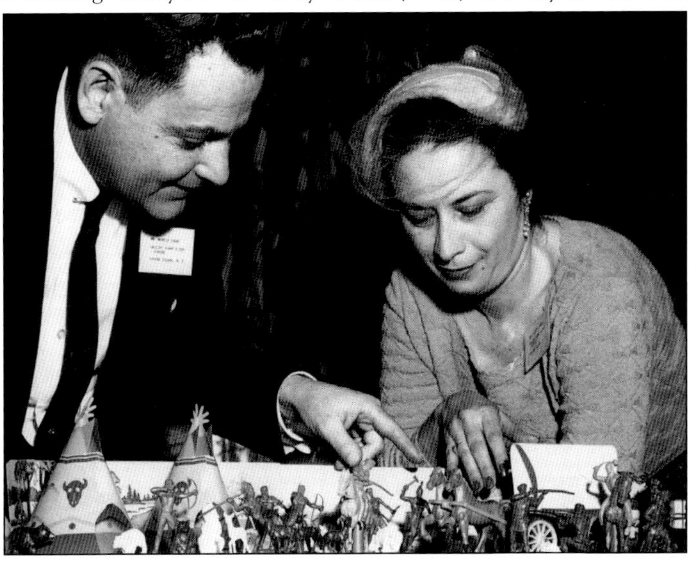

Charles Kennedy founded Kennedy's Men's Store and first operated it from the family home on Delafield Avenue before moving it to Forest Avenue. The store was a mainstay in West Brighton for 50 years until its closing in 1996. Charles (on the left in the image at right; pictured with employee Al Sankewich) eventually handed the store over to his son, Joseph (on the right in the image below; shown with an unidentified man). Kennedy's was well known for its fine men's clothing and its famous "suit club," for which members would contribute money each week and receive store credit in the future. Charles also had a column in the *Staten Island Advance* called Kennedy's Komments, in which he would talk about the Staten Island social scene. Joseph was assisted in running the store by his brother Charles, his sister Corinne Kennedy O'Brien, and many great employees over the years. (Both, courtesy of the Kennedy family.)

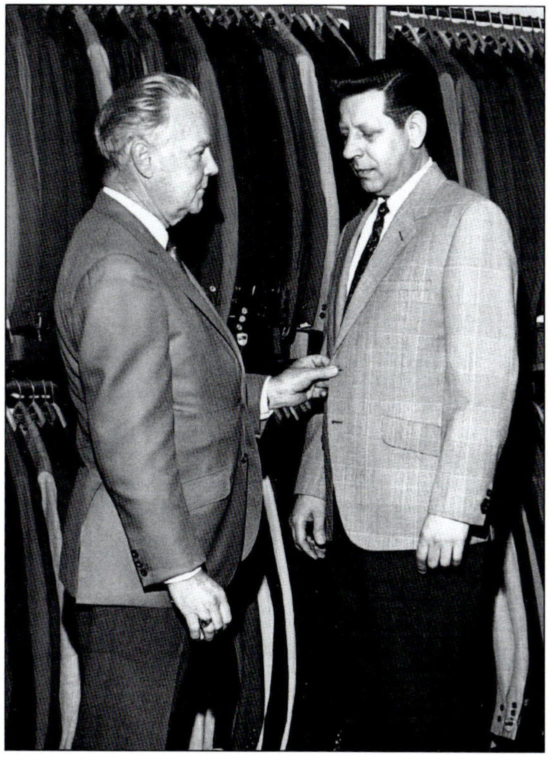

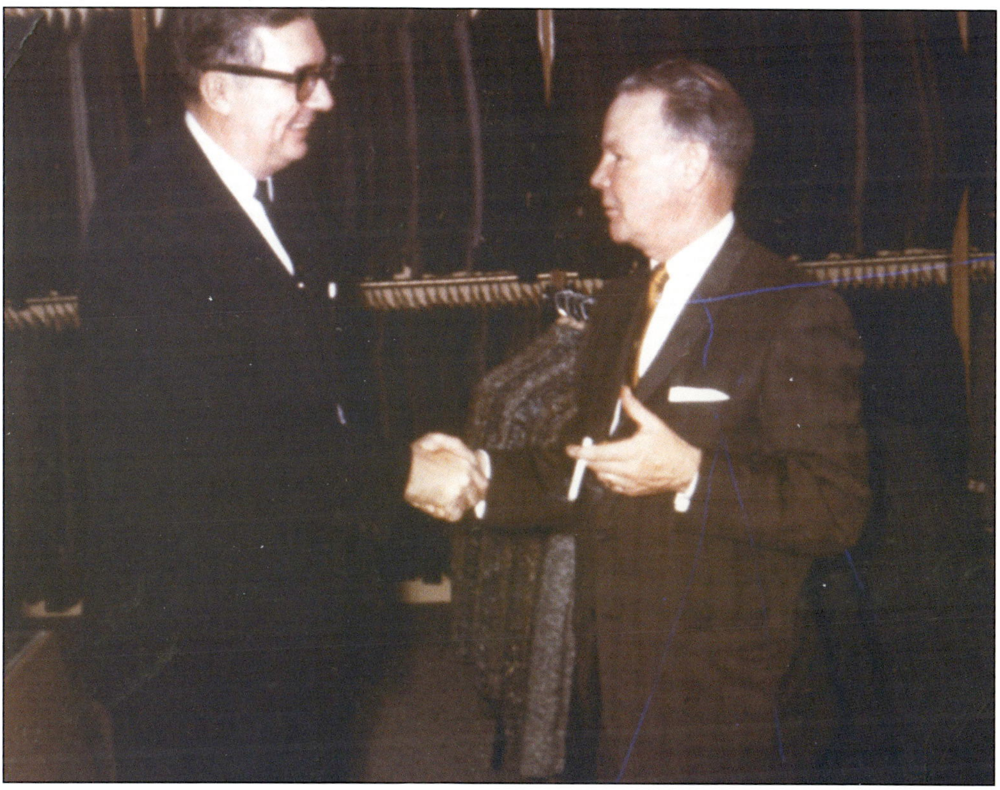

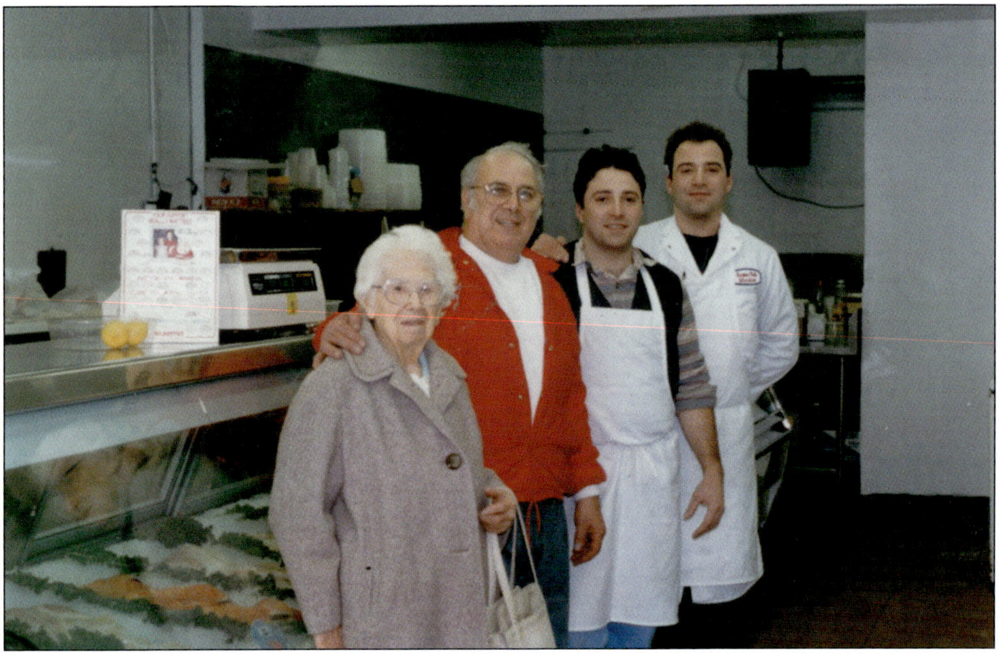

The above photograph represents three generations and 91 years of the Boston Fish Market. Fannie Cucuzza (far left in the above image) learned the fish market business from her father. She and her husband, Vito, opened Boston Fish Market in 1918. For a time, they had a store on Broadway before moving to 1065 Castleton Avenue, where they lived above the shop. After Vito passed away, Fannie continued to raise the family and run the business. Fannie was known in the community for her generosity. She worked extremely long hours. As her children grew, they worked alongside her. Her eldest son, Salvatore (aka Tutti) operated the store for a while before he was called into the service. The youngest son, Vito, (second from left in the above image) took an interest and learned the fish market business from his mother. Also shown are Vito Jr. and Salvatore Cucuzza. The below image includes, from left to right, Carlos Moran, Vito Cucuzza Jr., Marilyn Cucuzza Ciaburri, and George Moran. (Both, courtesy of the Cucuzza family.)

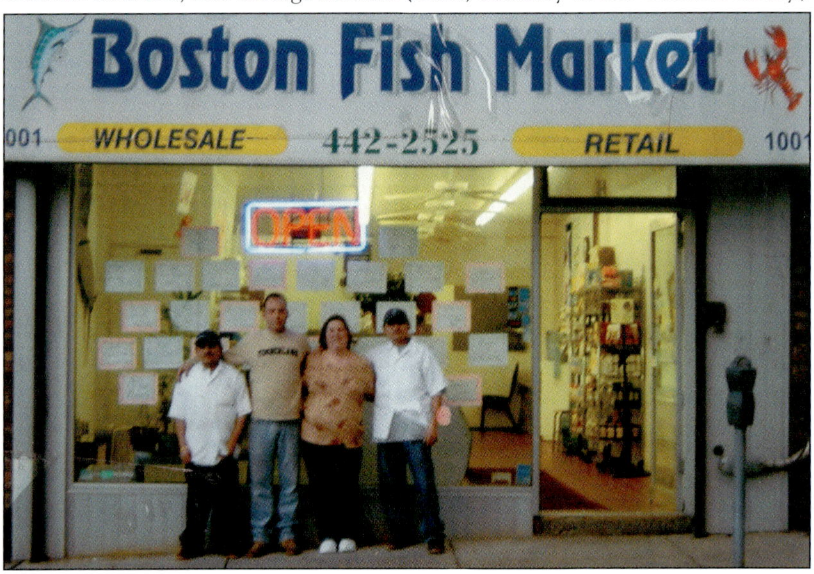

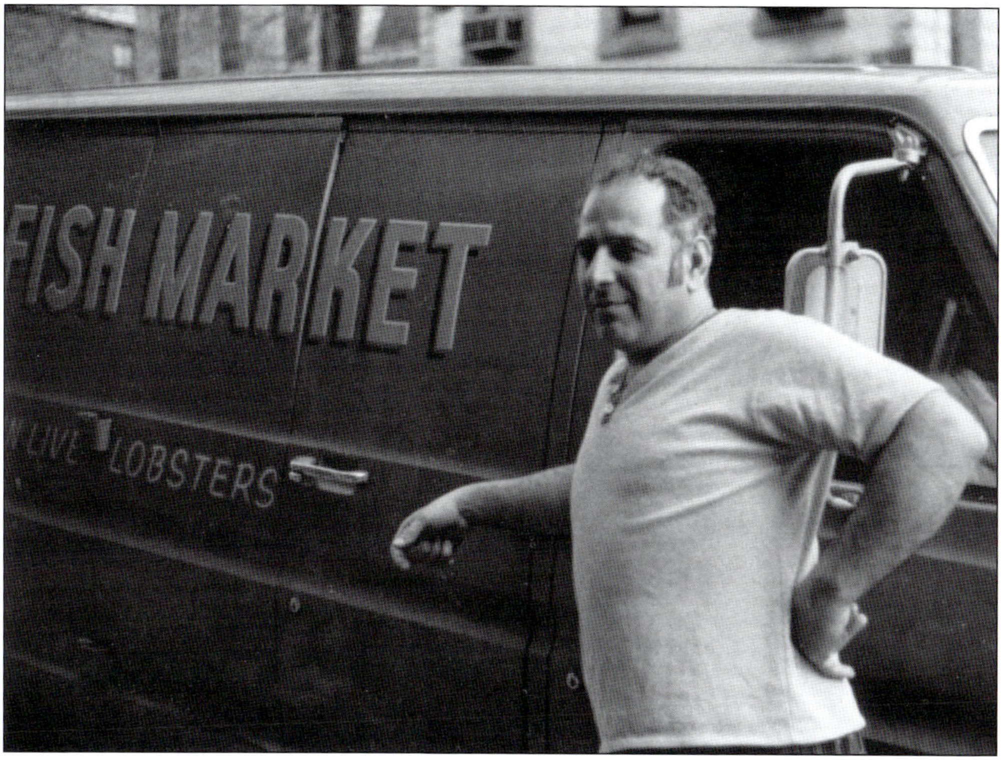

Vito Cucuzza Sr., pictured above, took over Boston Fish Market in 1959. Soon after, the store relocated to 1001 Castleton Avenue. Cucuzza was determined to bring customers the freshest seafood possible, and he was a perfectionist who worked seven days each week to maintain those high standards. Even after he retired in 1991, Vito Sr. returned every year during the demanding holiday season to support his sons Vito Jr. and Salvatore, who operated Boston Fish Market until it closed in 2009. The below photograph includes, from left to right, (first row) Camille Ciaburri, Domenica Cucuzza Mousa, George Mousa, and unidentified; (second row) Rocco Ciaburri, Marilyn Cucuzza Ciaburri, Vito Sr., Vito Jr., and Salvatore Cucuzza. (Both, courtesy of the Cucuzza family.)

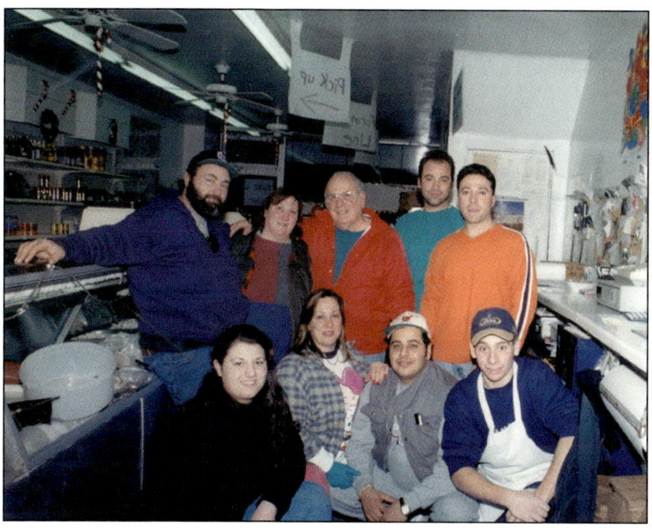

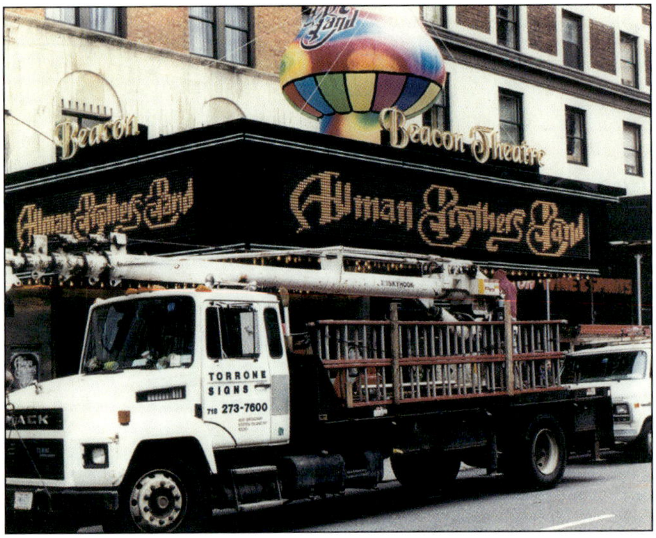

The year 2014 marks the 70th anniversary of Torrone Signs. The company began in 1944 at 794 Richmond Terrace. Since 1958, Frank Torrone & Sons, Inc. has been located at 400 Broadway. One of Torrone's specialties is theater marquee work (pictured is the Beacon Theatre in Manhattan), and the company is known for quality work such as the gate signs at the new Yankee Stadium. Other Torrone accounts include Foot Locker, Toys "R" Us, and the Peninsula Hotel. (Courtesy of Torrone Signs.)

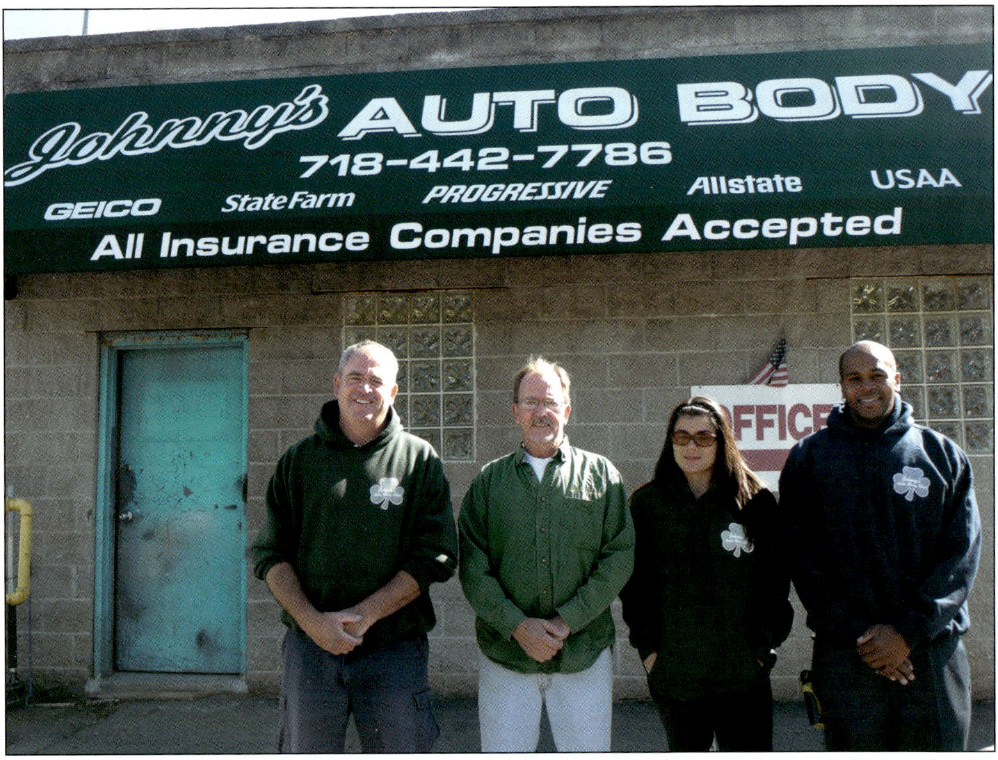

Johnny's Auto Body was established in 1948. Jimmy McConnell (second from left) bought the business in 1977 with Bruce Haggerty; McConnell assumed sole ownership in the early 1980s. Tim O'Halloran (far left) joined Johnny's Auto Body in 1992 and has since become a partner. Under his direction, the business has continued to be successful. Also pictured are longtime employees Cassandra Lista (second from right) and Myron Duncan. (Courtesy of Johnny's Auto Body.)

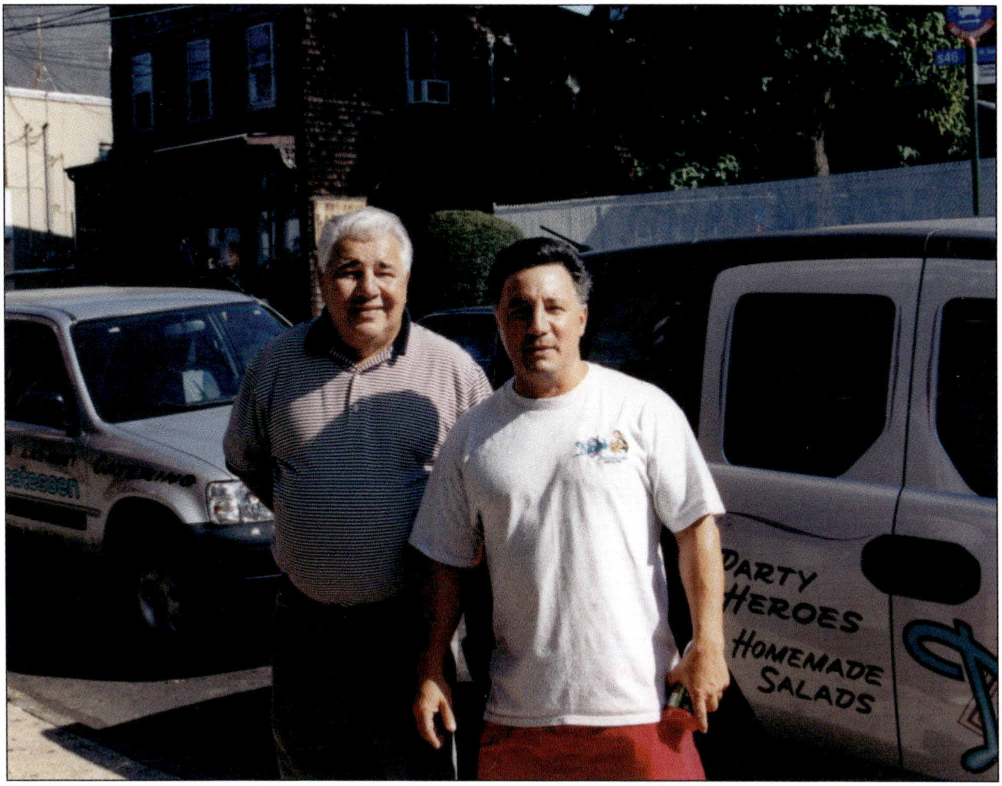

Dick's Delicatessen first opened its doors in 1928 with Eric Wholers as proprietor. Wholers served the neighborhood loyally until 1974, when he sold the business to the Benfante family. Alan (above, left) and Carolyn Benfante (below, right) along with Carolyn's sister Lena (below, left), became the new faces of the Castleton Avenue staple. With a new generation at the helm, Dick's Delicatessen continues to be a neighborhood fixture providing good food, good service, and great respect for West Brighton. Alan Benfante (above, right) is now leading the business as it celebrates its 40th anniversary in the family. Being a part of the community has become as important as the food itself. Angelina Guido is in the center in the below photograph. (Both, courtesy of Dick's Delicatessen.)

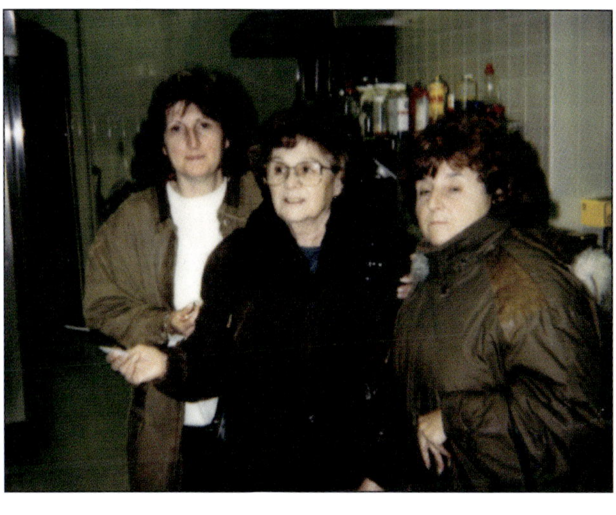

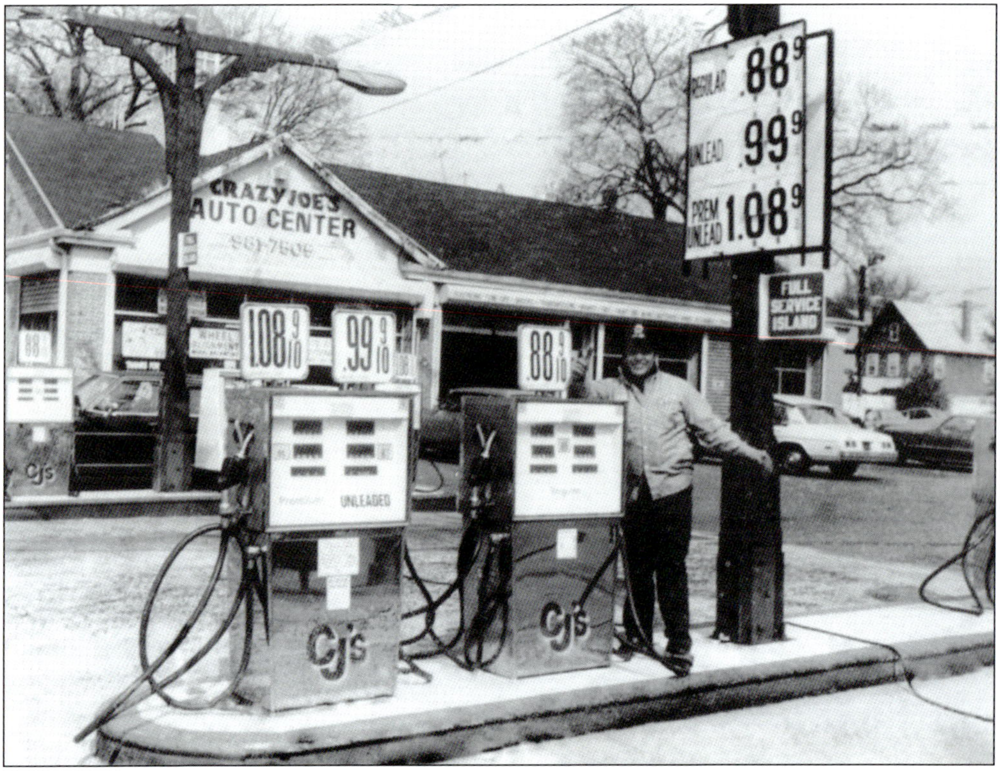

In 1971, Joseph Russo (pictured above) started doing business as J&D Auto Service at 661 Cary Avenue, selling Mobil gasoline and doing automobile repairs. In 1977, he started Crazy Joe's Auto Center, which was located at 823 Forest Avenue. He operated there until 1983, when he relocated both businesses to the current location at 685 Cary Avenue (below). Crazy Joe's Auto Sales & Service repairs all types of vehicles and sells pre-owned automobiles. (Both, courtesy of Crazy Joe's Auto Sales & Service.)

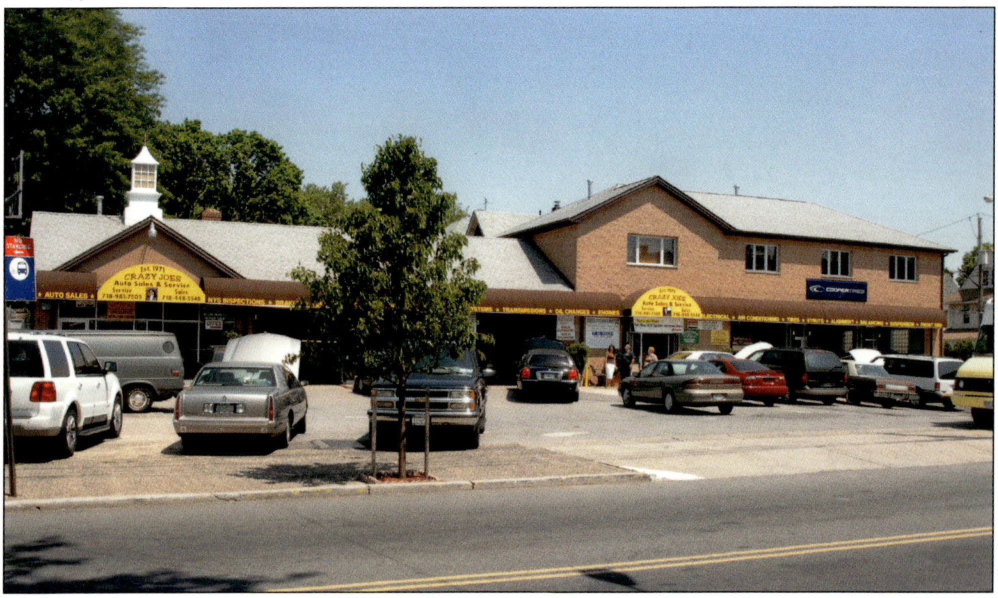

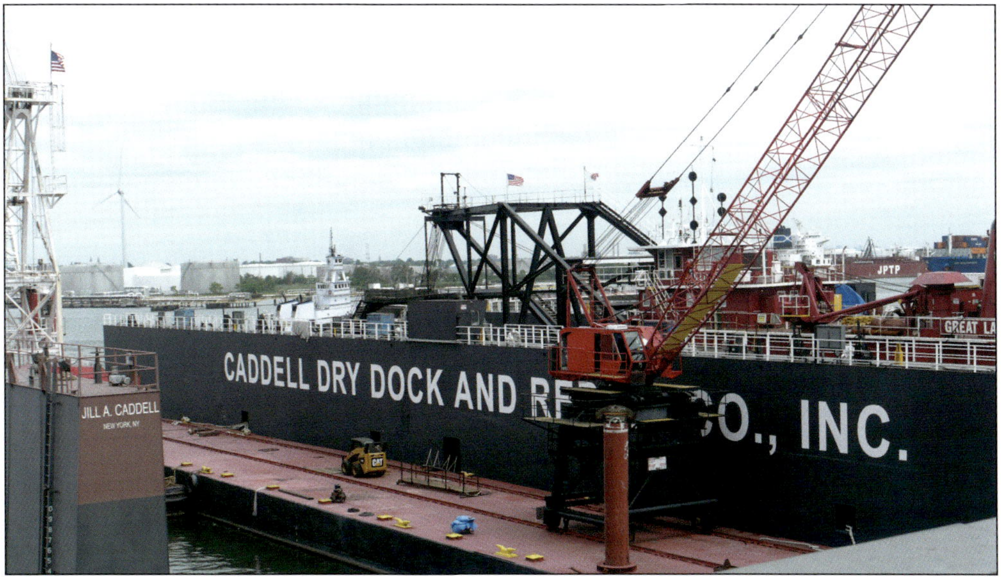

In 1888, John Bartlett Caddell left Nova Scotia to capitalize on his knowledge of shipbuilding. He came to New York and worked for a few shipyards along Richmond Terrace. In 1903, Caddell met Eugene Schuyler and John Payne and formed Schuyler, Payne & Caddell, a ship-repair company. In 1914, Caddell formed John B. Caddell Dry Dock Company. In 1916, he moved the company to Broadway, where it remains today. (Courtesy of Caddell Dry Dock.)

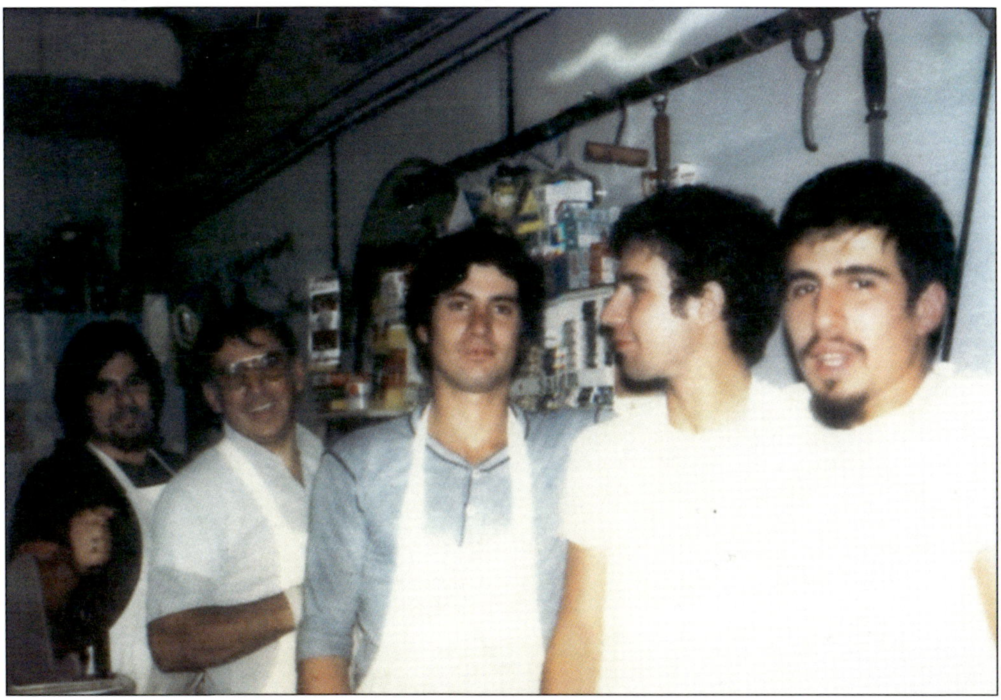
This picture was taken in the 1970s at the Henderson Meat Market, a family business that began in West Brighton in 1935 and lasted almost 60 years. Shown in their store are the Napolitano men—from left to right, Joseph, Anthony Sr., John, Anthony Jr., and Stephen. (Courtesy of Theresa Napolitano.)

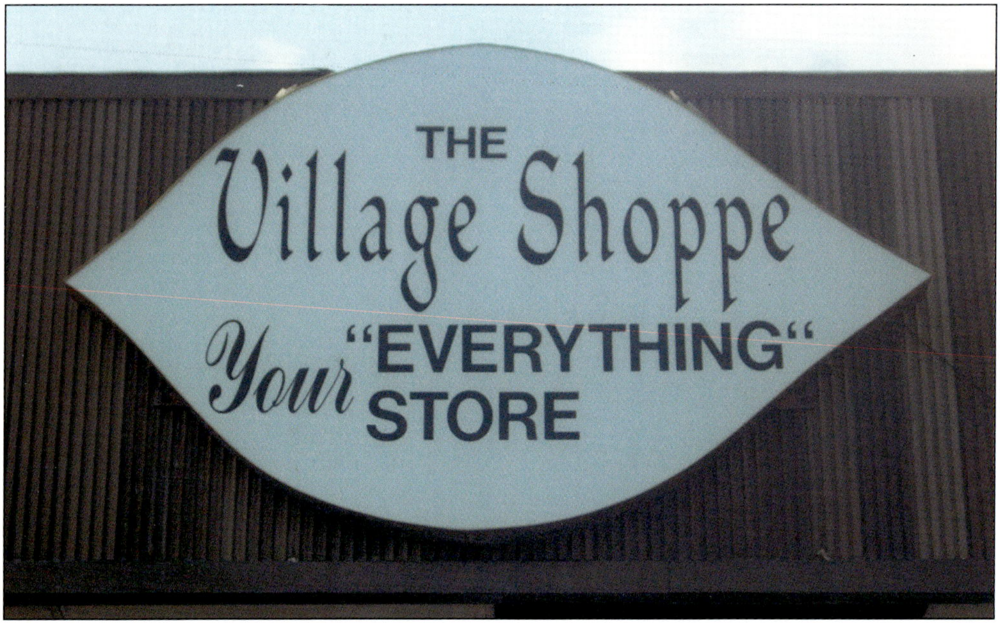

For 40 years, the Ferraiuolo family owned and operated the Village Shoppe at 748 Forest Avenue. It was always known as "Your 'Everything' Store." If a person ran out of something, he knew Village Shoppe would have it. The store's customers appreciated that Frank and Frank Ferraiuolo Jr. (pictured below) and the Village Shoppe staff always greeted them by name and with a smile—a personal touch that may be hard to find today. According to Frank Jr., "Our customers were like family to us. The West Brighton community will always be close to our hearts." Over the years, the men of the neighborhood would gather at the store to socialize and get the news of the day; they were heartbroken when the store closed in August 2013. (Both, courtesy of Ferraiuolo family.)

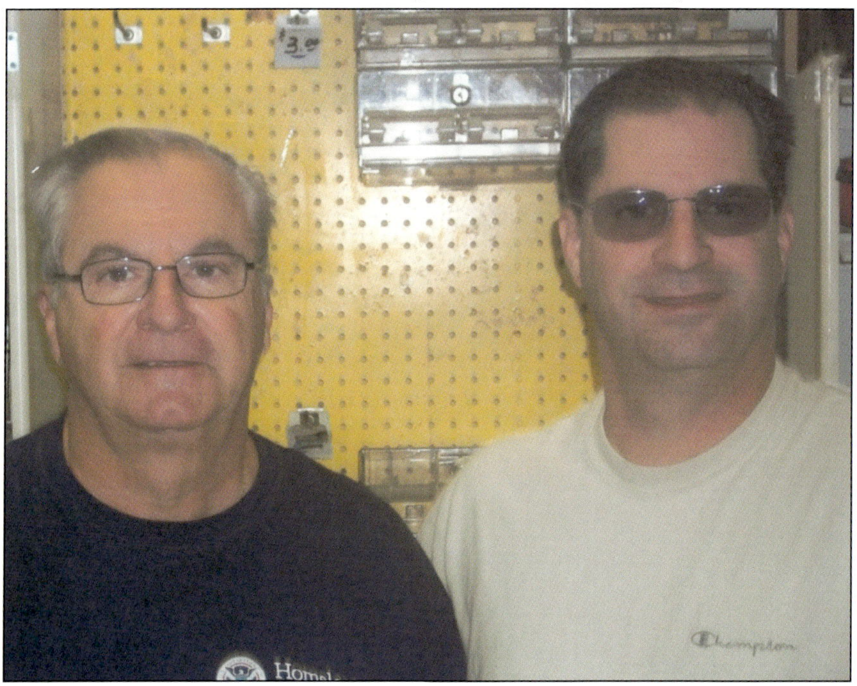

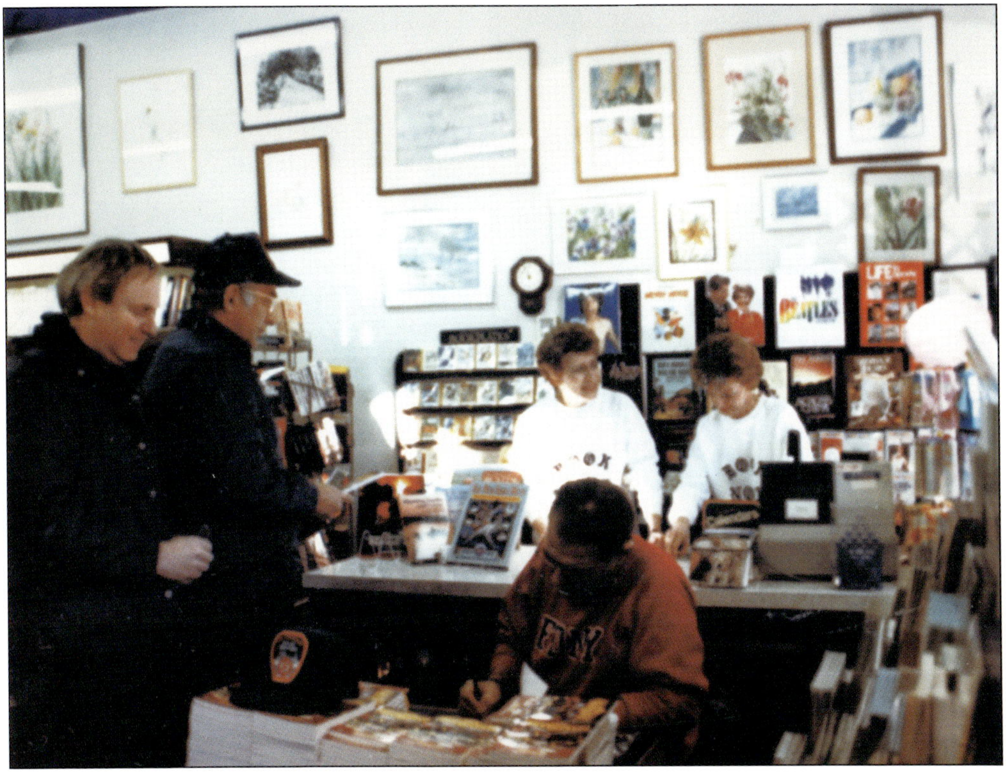

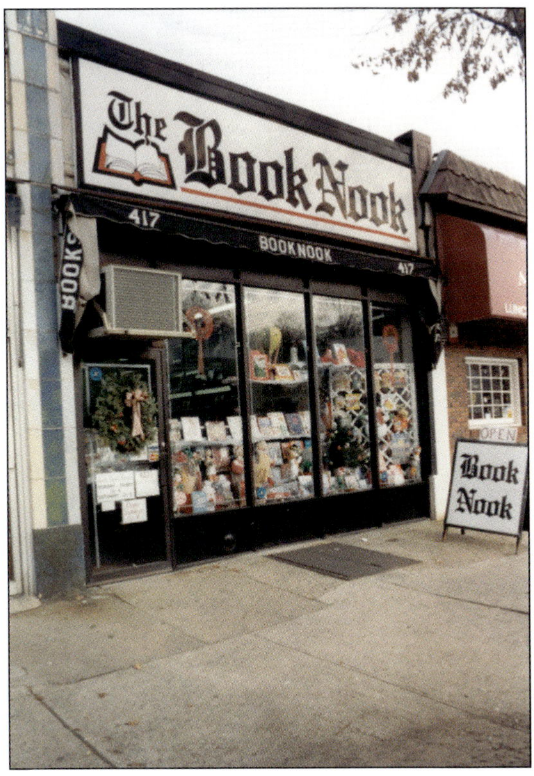

Elizabeth Trifoglio, shown in the center of the above photograph, opened The Book Nook at 417 Forest Avenue in 1974. She welcomed many readers until The Book Nook closed in 1986. Her selection of children's books was outstanding, and she provided textbooks for the Staten Island campus of St. John's University. Her stock ran the gamut from best sellers to poetry to political science. The Book Nook was a true independent book store. (Both, courtesy of the Trifoglio family.)

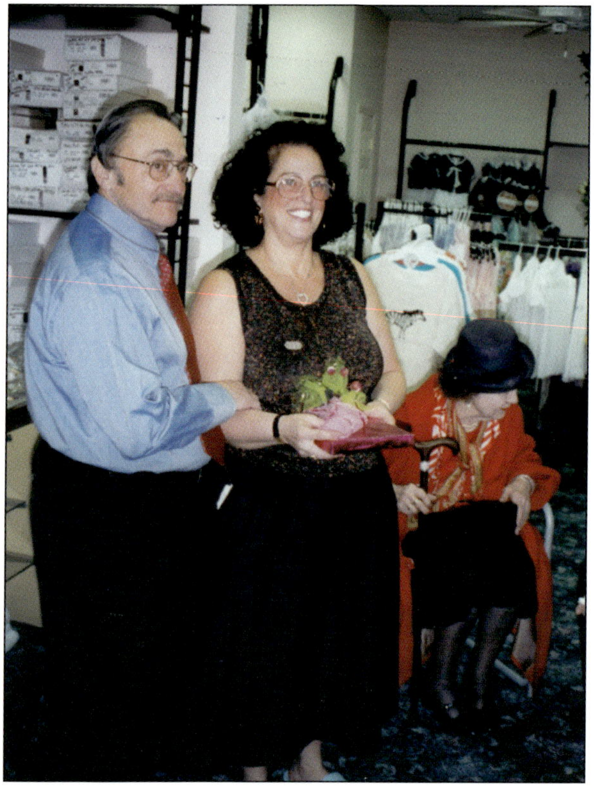

This photograph was taken during the grand opening of Suzanne's Fashion Corner on April 18, 1999. Elliot Berelson (left), Suzanne Berelson (center), and Josephine Marli are pictured here in the store at 656 Forest Avenue. Marli's husband, Lou, owned and operated the Bement Pharmacy in the same location for many years. (Courtesy of Suzanne's Fashion Corner.)

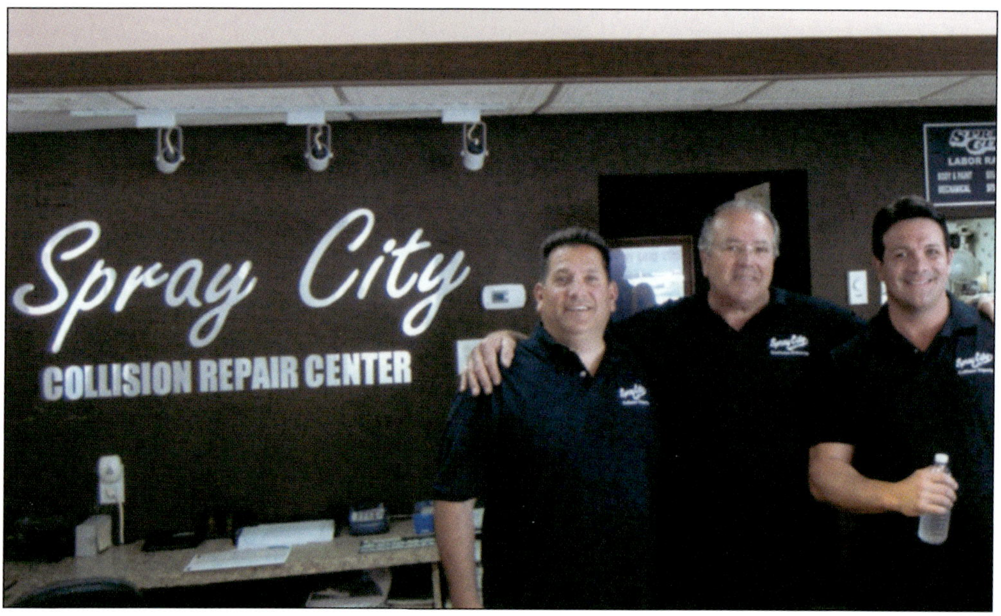

Spray City Collision has been family owned and operated and serviced over 40,000 vehicles since its founding by Gerard Maiorani Sr. in 1969. Spray City Collision built its reputation on quality automotive collision repairs. Spray City Collision has been handed over to Jerry Jr., who works to uphold the strong reputation that this business is known for, providing quality automotive services with a personal touch. (Courtesy of Spray City Collision.)

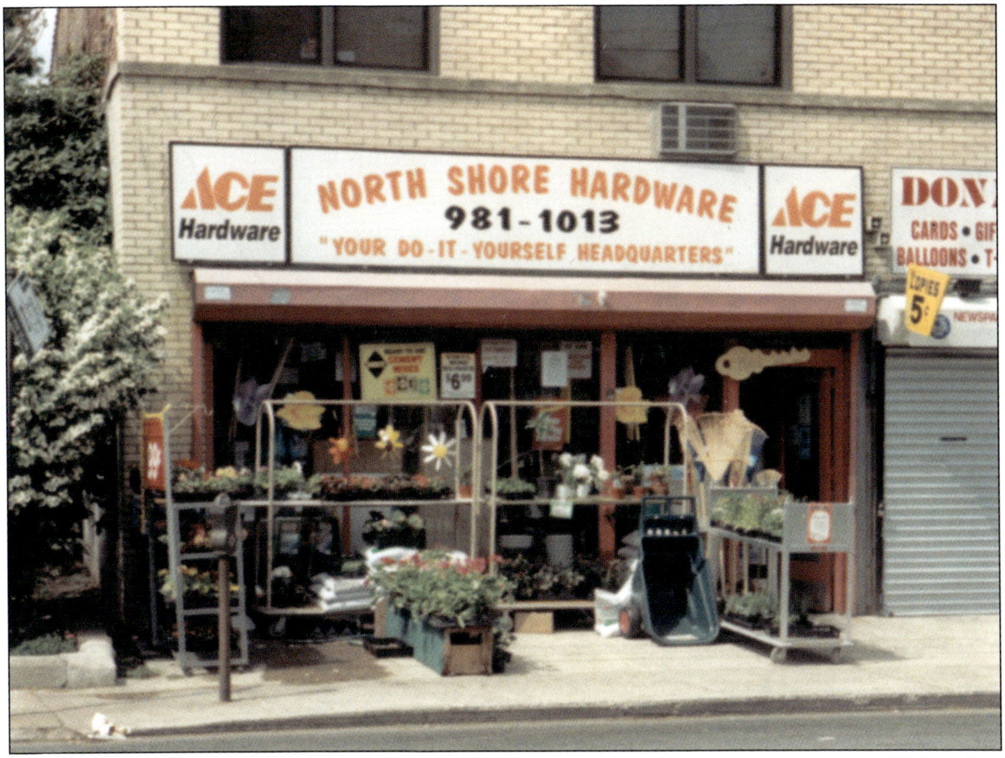

There has been a hardware store at 647 Forest Avenue in West Brighton since 1950. That tradition continued in December 1992, when Gil and Francisca Ross opened North Shore Hardware. For over 20 years, Gil and Francisca (pictured below with their daughter Coleen and Gil's mother, Mary Alice Ross), have maintained a high level of service to their loyal customers. North Shore Hardware remains a staple in the West Brighton community. (Both, courtesy of North Shore Hardware.)

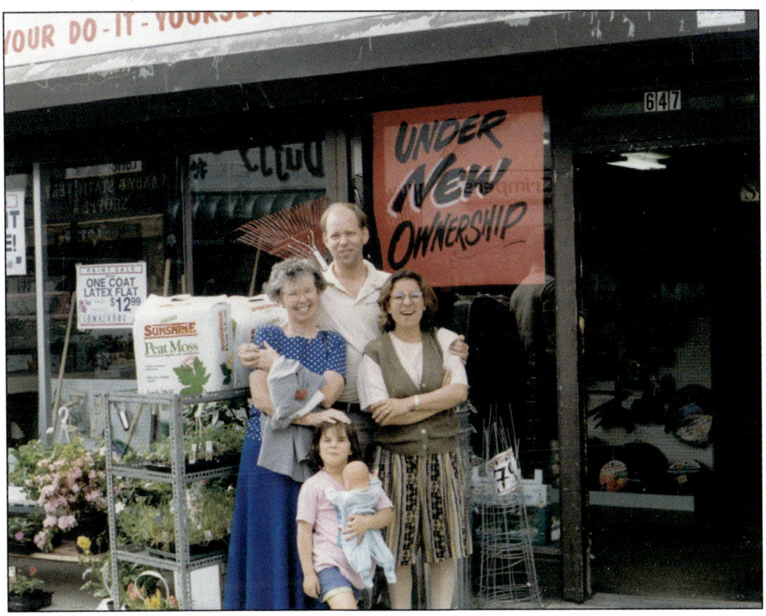

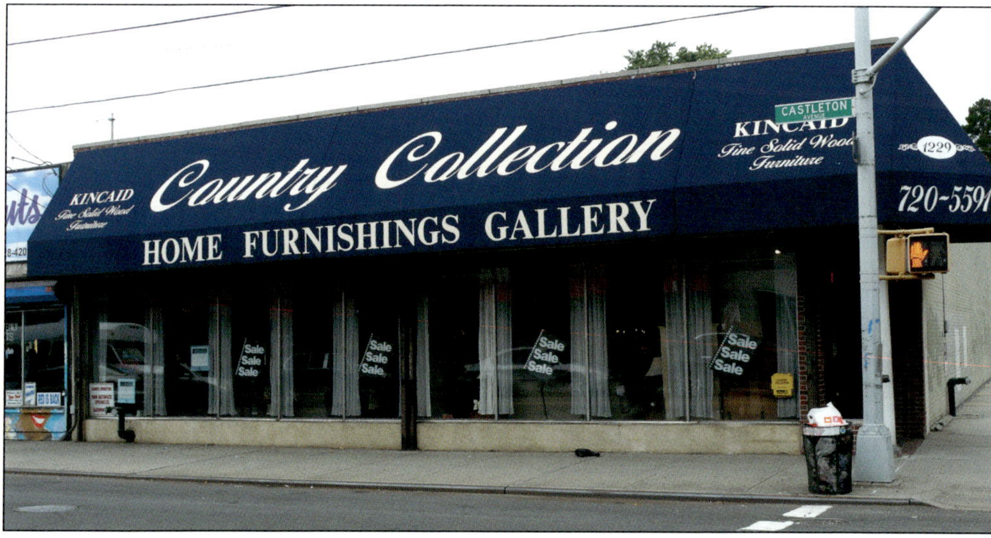

Paul Godnig opened Country Collection Furniture in 1980 on Hyatt Street in St. George. In 1987, he moved the business to 1230 Castleton Avenue in West Brighton. Ten years later, he moved across the street to 1229 Castleton Avenue. Godnig has always provided quality home furnishings backed by excellent service. (Courtesy of Paul Godnig.)

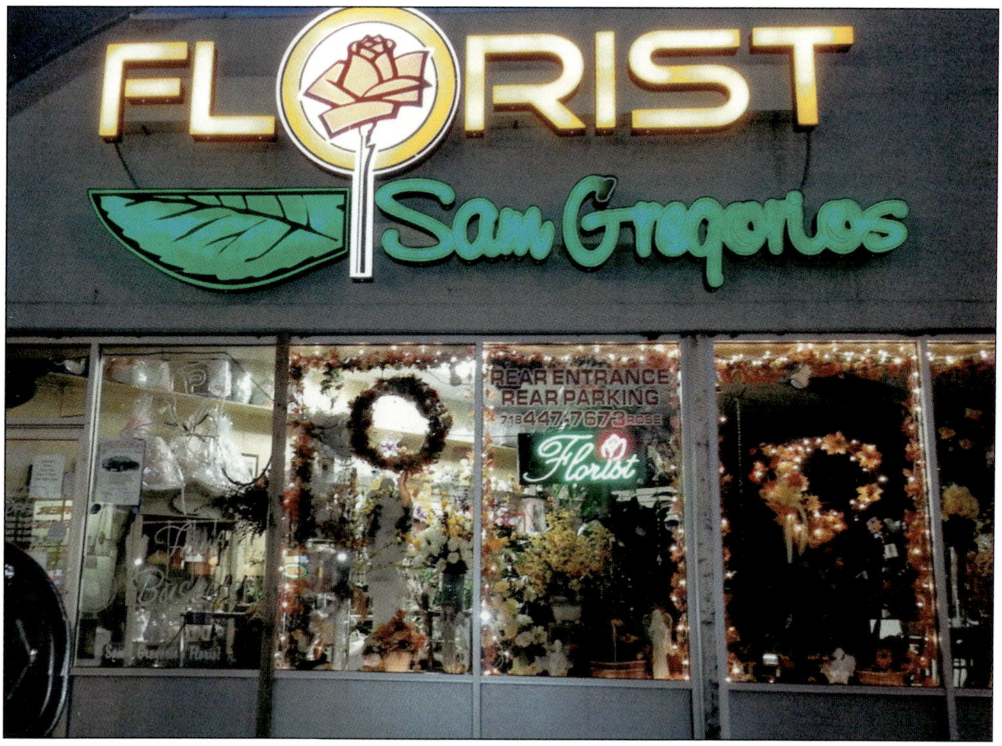

Sam Gregorio's Florist, located at 814 Forest Avenue, opened in September 2008. The Gregorio family has served West Brighton's floral needs for generations. That tradition continues with Sam's son, Sam Gregorio Jr. The family owned and operated shop has grown into a premier event planning florist that serves as house vendor to most catering halls on Staten Island and extends to the tristate area. (Courtesy of Sam T. Gregorio.)

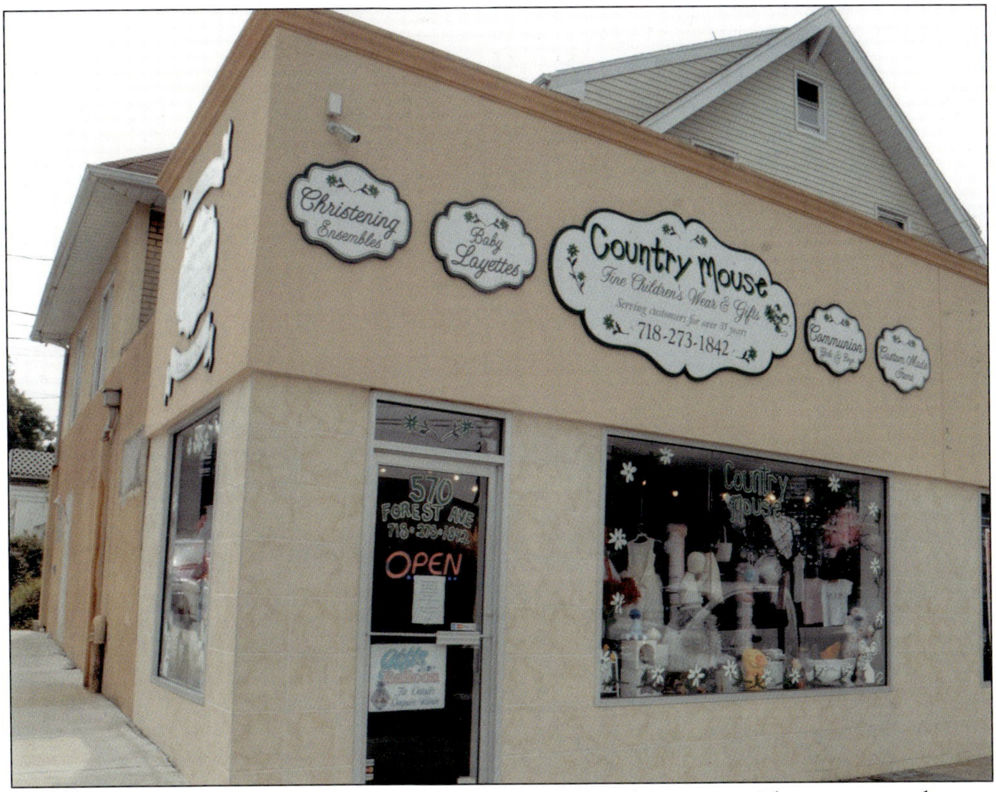

Country Mouse boutique has been serving the North Shore for 40 years. The store specializes in communion, christening, birthday, and embroidery items. It carries "take me home" outfits, layettes, and hand-knit items. Country Mouse started as a traditional baby store in West Brighton, but when Janine Detore moved the store to its current location at 570 Forest Avenue, she began to carry not only traditional items but also the newest trendy fashions. (Courtesy of Janine Detore.)

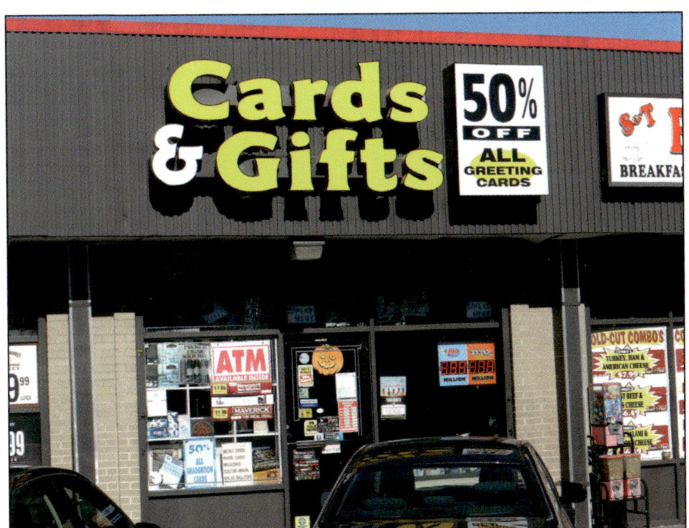

The Cards & Gifts Shop was established by Rocco Eugenio in 1987. It quickly became a friendly neighborhood store selling cards, gifts, holiday merchandise, and lottery tickets. The store has had several big winners over the years. After Eugenio passed away, the Patel family took over the Cards & Gifts Shop in 2004, and they look forward to serving the West Brighton community for many years to come. (Courtesy of the Cards & Gifts Shop.)

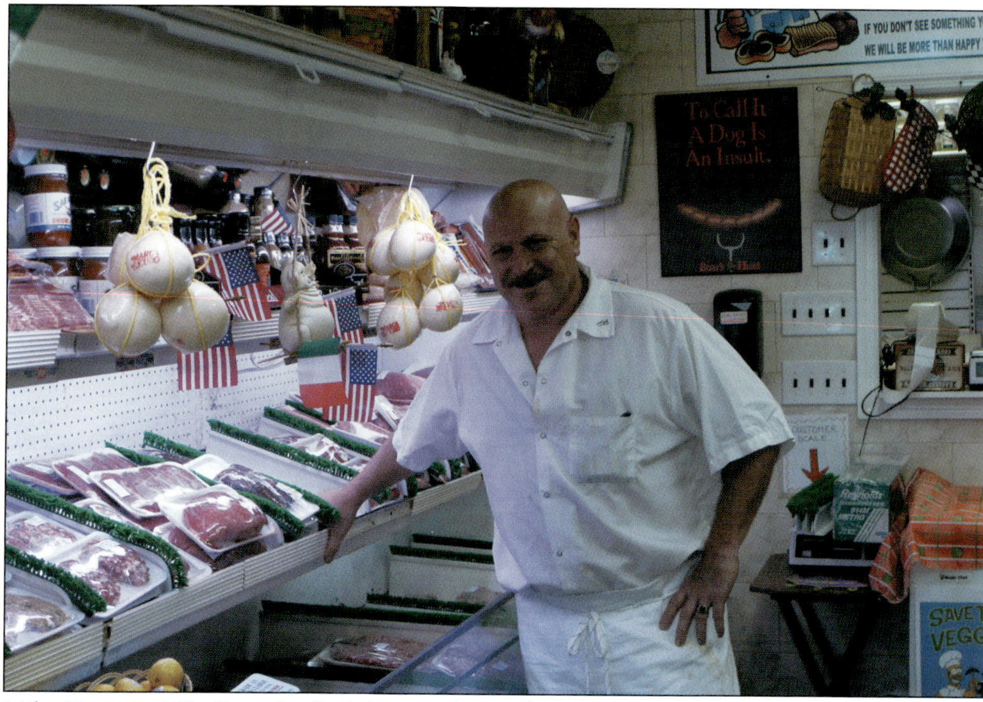

Mike Fiorito's Bella Famiglia Pork Store is located at the corner of Forest and North Burgher Avenues. Fiorito is a 45-year veteran of the meat business who has worked in Brooklyn, Lower Manhattan, and Port Richmond. He has been at the West Brighton location for three years. (Courtesy of Mike Fiorito's Bella Famiglia.)

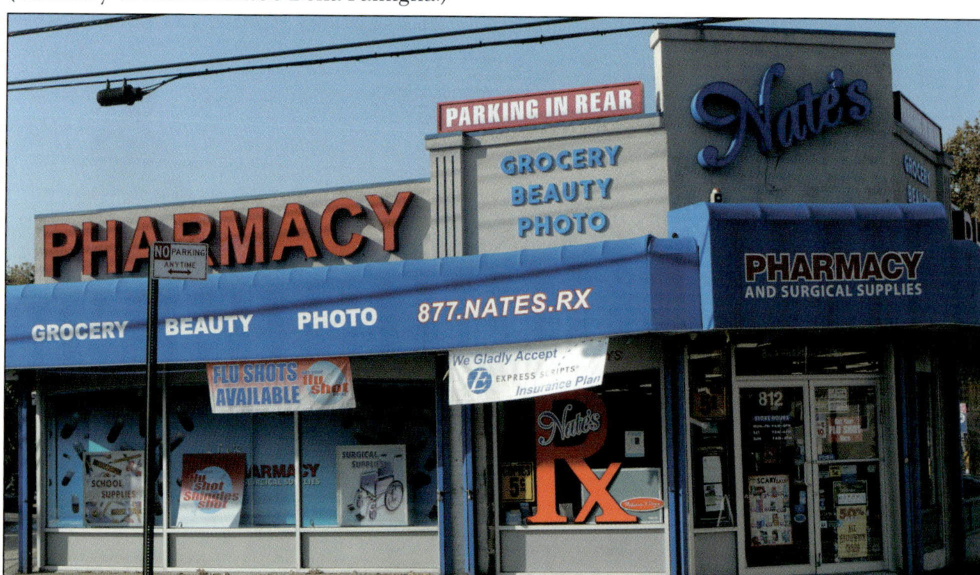

April 2014 will mark 10 years since Angela and Boris Natenzon opened Nate's Pharmacy in West Brighton. It began at 821 Forest Avenue with only three employees; two years later, it moved to its current location at 812 Forest Avenue. Nate's Pharmacy is proud to be part of this neighborhood, and it hopes to provide the community with excellent customer service for many years to come. (Courtesy of Nate's Pharmacy.)

Four

Profiles

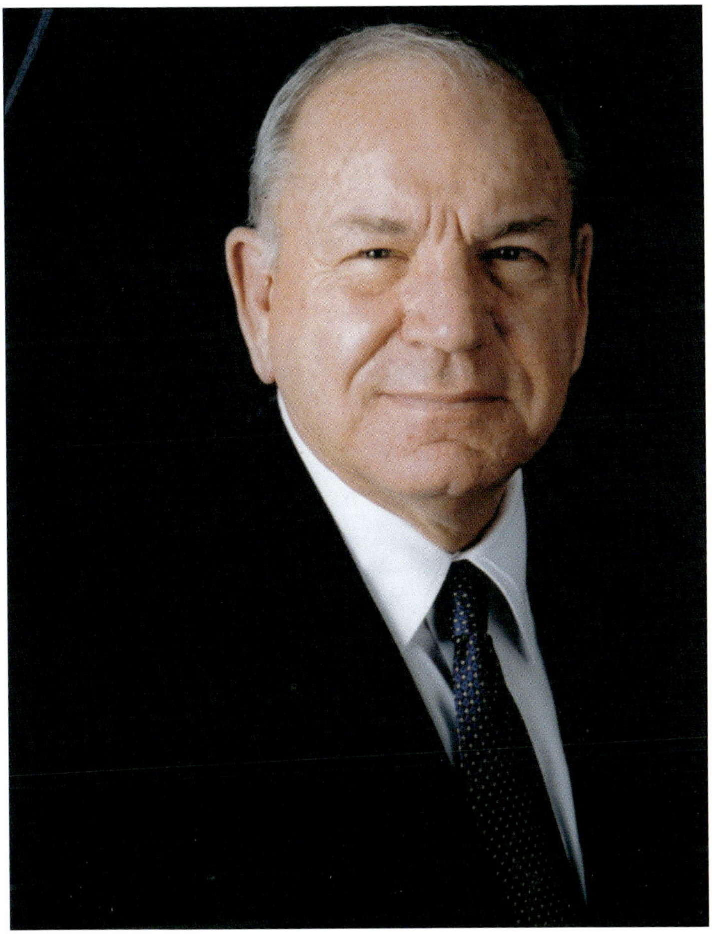

Ralph Lamberti was born and raised on Cary Avenue near Broadway and graduated from PS 18 and Curtis High School. In 1974, he was appointed Staten Island deputy borough president to Robert T. Connor and reappointed by Anthony R. Gaeta. Lamberti was elected Staten Island borough president in 1984 and served until 1990. He and his wife, Susan, have four children and five grandchildren. (Courtesy of Ralph Lamberti.)

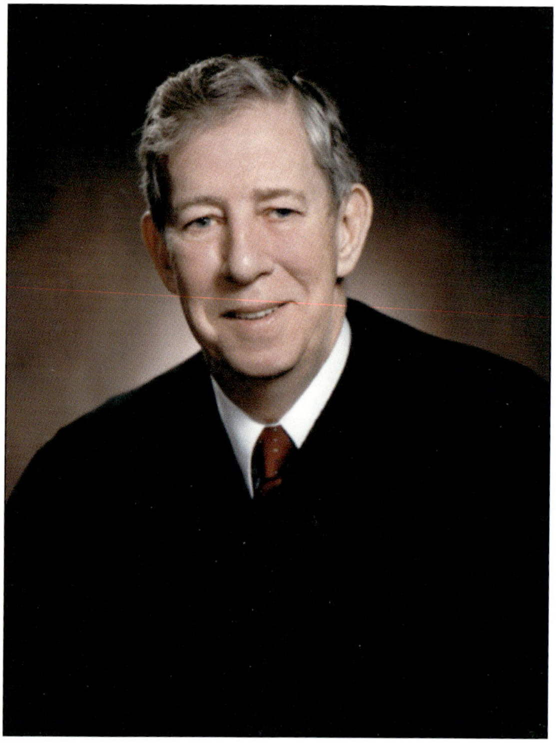

The Hon. Thomas R. Sullivan was born in West Brighton, educated at Good Counsel and the Augustinian Academy, and graduated from Villanova University, Fordham, and Brooklyn Law Schools. Sullivan began his career in public service in 1955 when newly elected district attorney John Braisted tapped him as one of his assistant district attorneys; he quickly became Braisted's chief assistant district attorney. Sullivan ran for Staten Island district attorney and won the office in 1976. The below photograph shows Sullivan, Braisted, and Judge Vito Titone. In 1982, Sullivan stepped down as district attorney to run for Supreme Court in the Staten Island–Brooklyn judicial district. He won, and in 1986, he was appointed to the appellate division by then governor Mario Cuomo. He retired from the bench in 2001 as an associate justice of the appellate division. (Both, courtesy of the Sullivan family.)

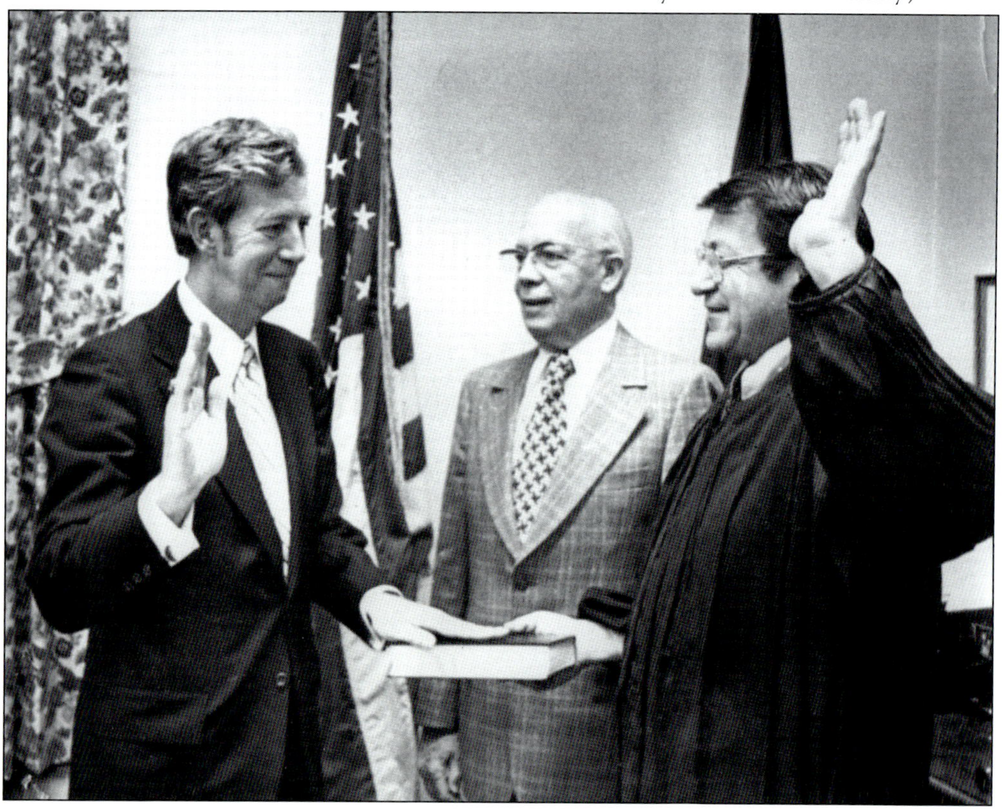

Born in West Brighton, Anthony R. Gaeta graduated from PS 18 and McKee Vocational and Technical High School. He continued his education at New York and Cornell Universities. His career as a public servant began as a tax assessor in 1949. Gaeta was elected councilman at large in 1972, then reelected to two more terms. In 1977, his fellow councilmen chose Gaeta as borough president to fill a vacancy created when Robert T. Connor left to take a job in Jimmy Carter's administration. Later that year, Gaeta was elected to a full term and served Staten Island until he retired in 1984. Gaeta is pictured below with his family—from left to right, daughter Susan, wife Ollie, Anthony, and son Robert. Gaeta passed away in 1988. (Both, courtesy of the Gaeta family.)

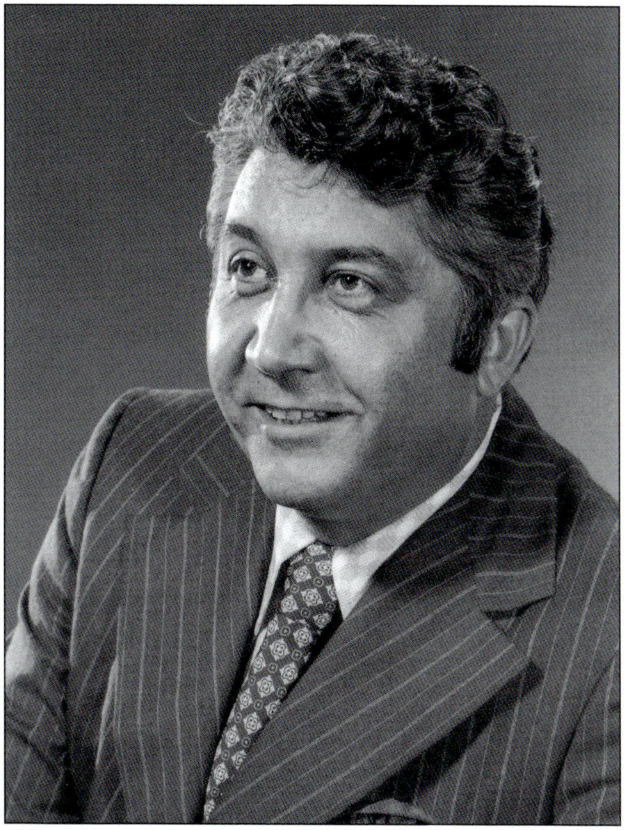

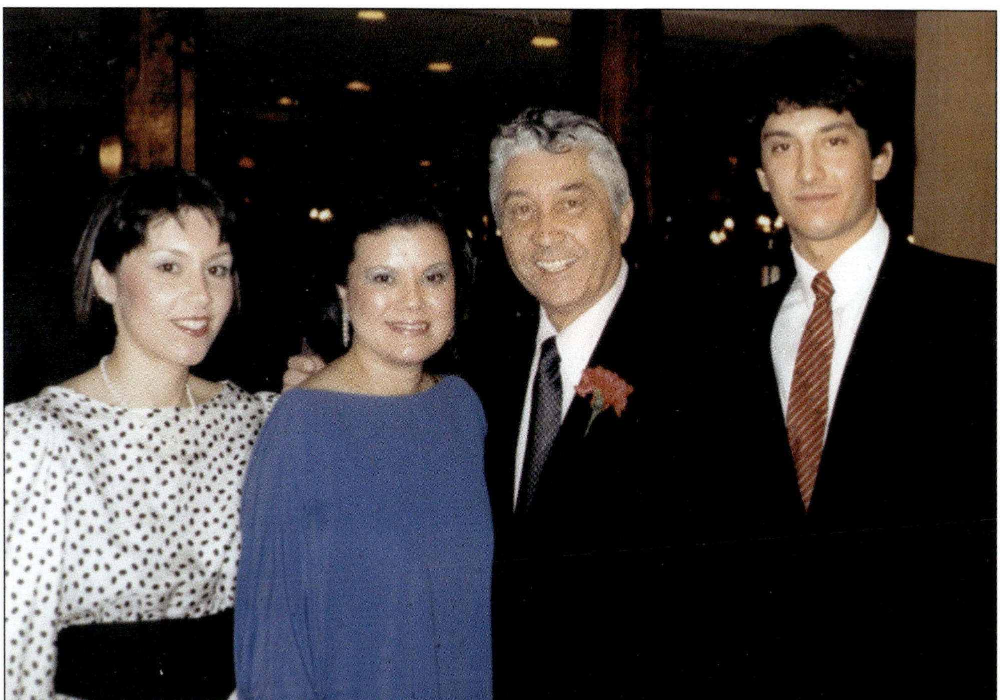

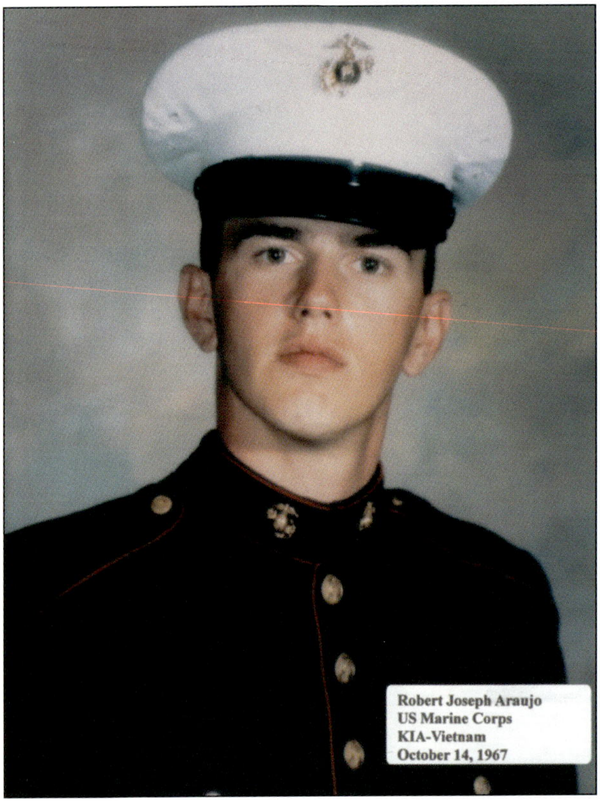

PFC Robert J. Araujo was a member of H Battery, 3rd Battalion, 12th Marines 3rd Marine Division. Araujo died on October 14, 1967; he was awarded the Purple Heart. (Courtesy of the Thomas J. Tori Vietnam Veterans Chapter 421.)

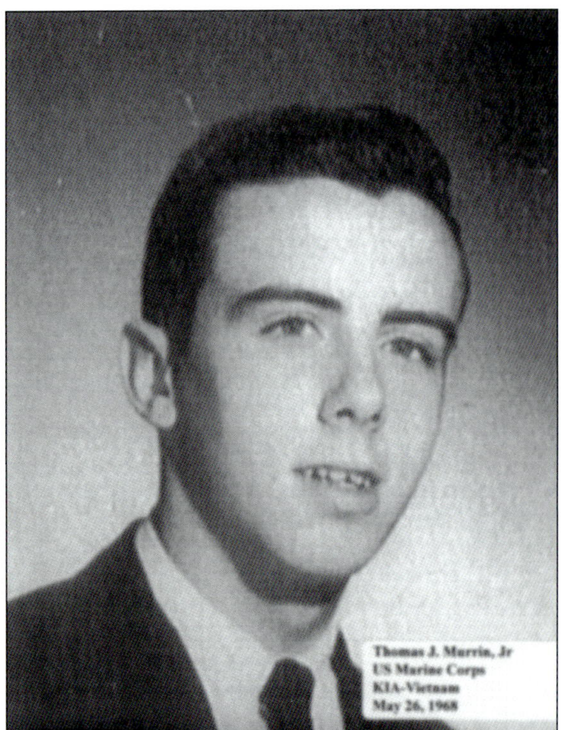

PFC Thomas F. Murrin Jr. was a member of 1st Company, 3rd Battalion, 3rd Marines, 3rd Marines Division. Murrin died on May 26, 1968; he was awarded the Purple Heart. (Courtesy of the Thomas J. Tori Vietnam Veterans Chapter 421.)

With 21 years of service, district attorney William L. Murphy (pictured at right) was the longest-serving district attorney in Staten Island's history. Gov. Mario Cuomo appointed Murphy in 1983 after his predecessor, Thomas Sullivan, was elected to the New York Supreme Court. That fall, Murphy won election to the office and was then reelected four more times over his remarkable career. Born in Chicago, he came to Staten Island at just six weeks of age. He graduated from St. Paul's School and St. Peter's High School in New Brighton. In 1966, Murphy graduated from Fordham University, and in 1969, he graduated from Harvard Law School. After starting his career as a prosecutor in the Manhattan district attorney's office, Murphy transferred to Staten Island in 1976 to serve as chief assistant under Sullivan (pictured below with Murphy). (Above, courtesy of Kathleen Murphy; below, courtesy of the Sullivan family.)

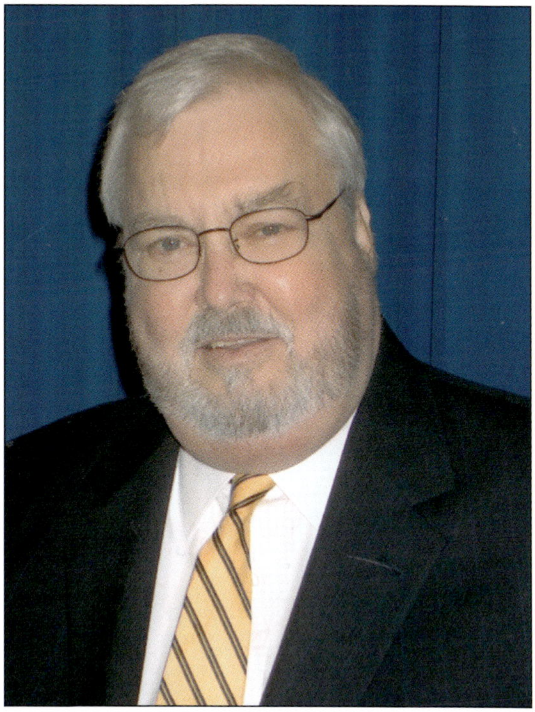

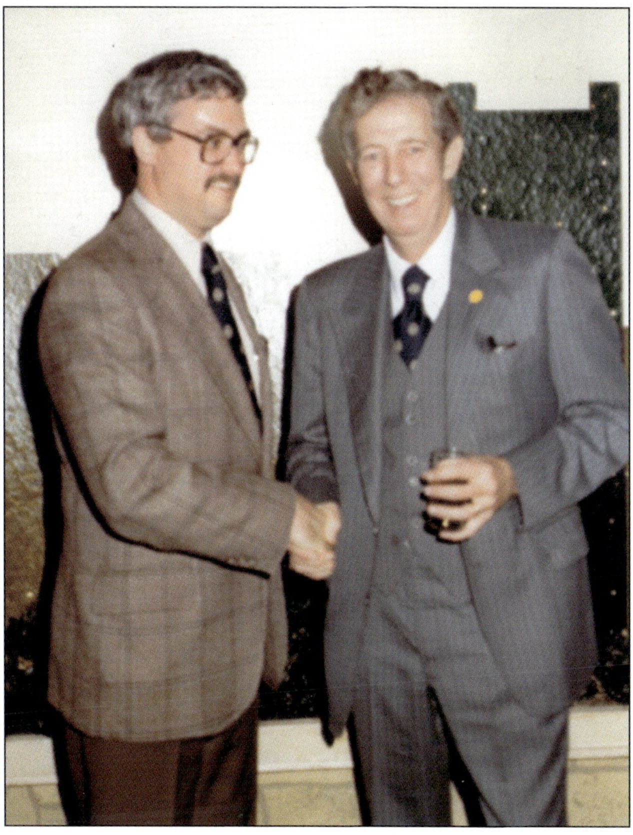

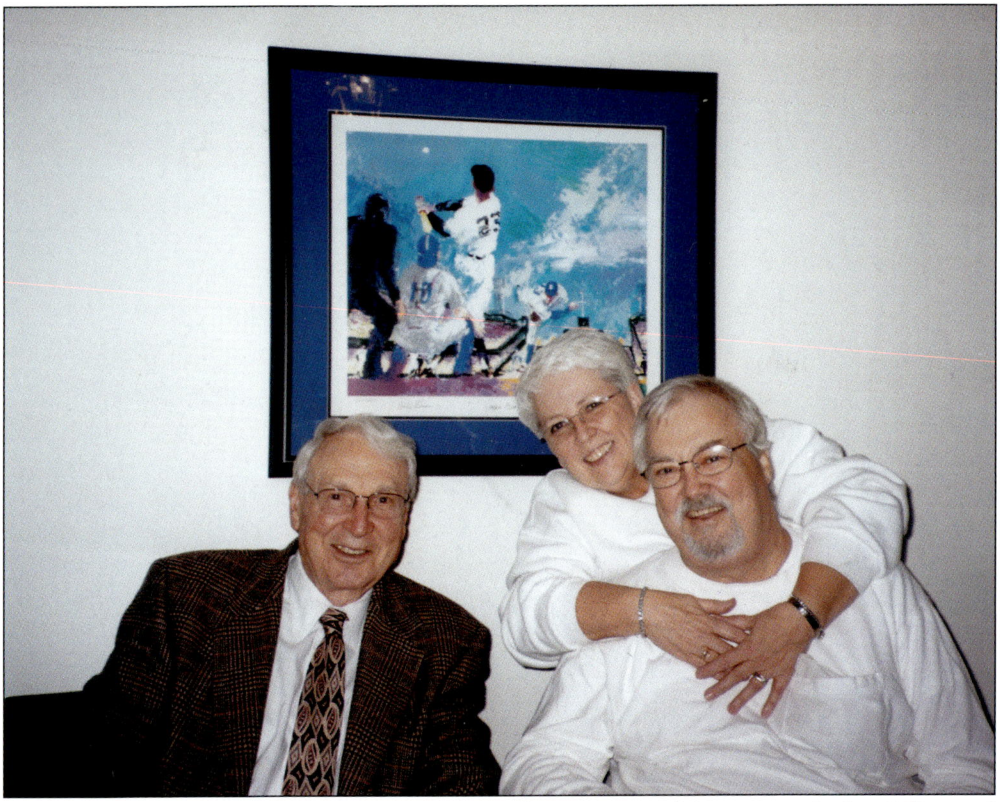

Bill Murphy (right) and his wife, Kathleen (center), were married for 41 years before Bill passed away in 2010. The couple had two daughters. Bill, a lifelong Giants baseball fan, spent the day with New York Giants and Staten Island legend Bobby Thomson (left). Behind the trio is a LeRoy Neiman painting of Thomson's "Shot Heard Round the World." The painting was given to Bill Murphy by Dr. Craig Campbell. (Courtesy of Kathleen Murphy.)

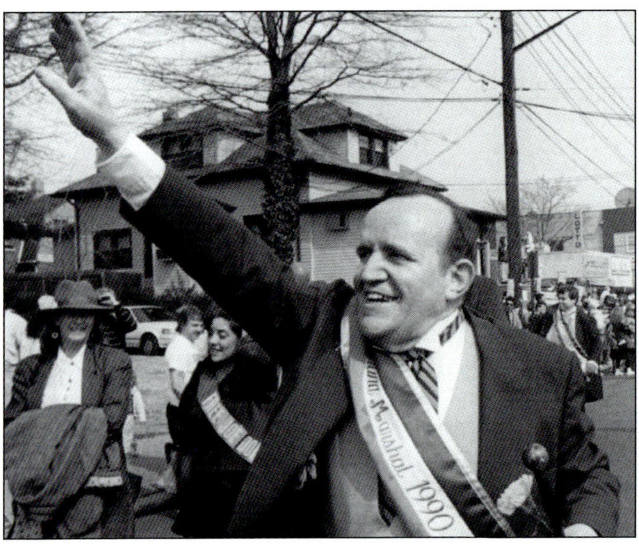

Born in West Brighton, John Kearney graduated from Good Counsel, Augustinian Academy, and Wagner College. Kearney was appointed public administrator in the early 1970s and held that position until his death in 1996. He was dedicated to the job. His sister Miriam remembered, "He was a man that made a difference." Kearney was very active in organizations such as the Ancient Order of Hibernians, Catholic Youth Organization, and the Staten Island Zoo. (Courtesy of the Cusick family.)

The Honorable State Supreme Court justice Peter P. Cusick graduated from PS 40, St. Peter's Boys High School, Manhattan College, and St. John's Law School. In 1981, Cusick was elected to the civil court. From 1986 to 2000, Cusick served in the New York State Supreme Court. He and his wife, Miriam, have three sons—Peter, Michael, and John. (Courtesy of the Cusick family.)

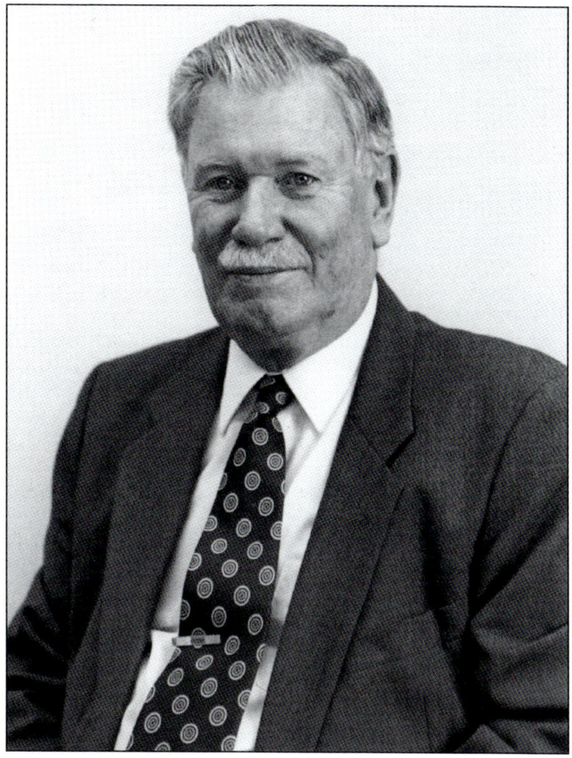

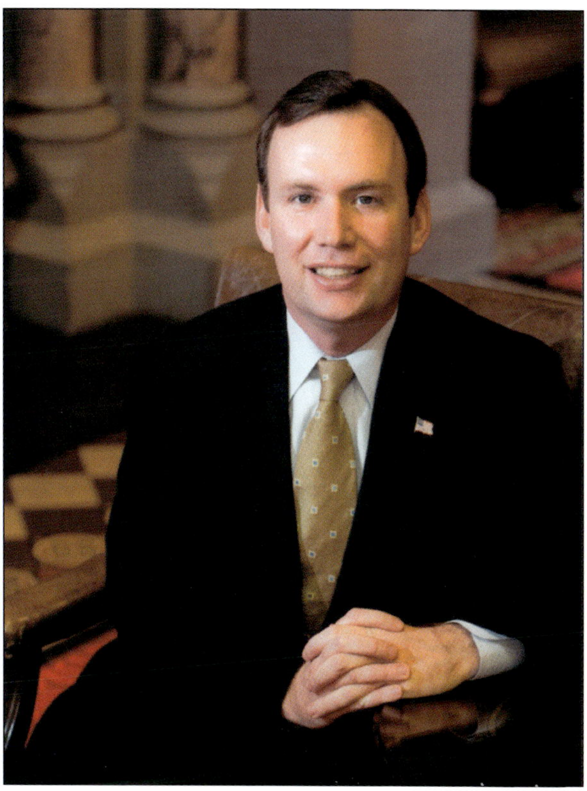

Born in West Brighton and a graduate of Villanova University, Michael J. Cusick represents the 63rd District in the New York State Assembly. Prior to his election, Cusick served as director of constituent services for US senator Charles E. Schumer and as the chief of staff for former Staten Island assemblyman Eric N. Vitaliano. He has been a member of the New York State Assembly since 2003. (Courtesy of Michael J. Cusick.)

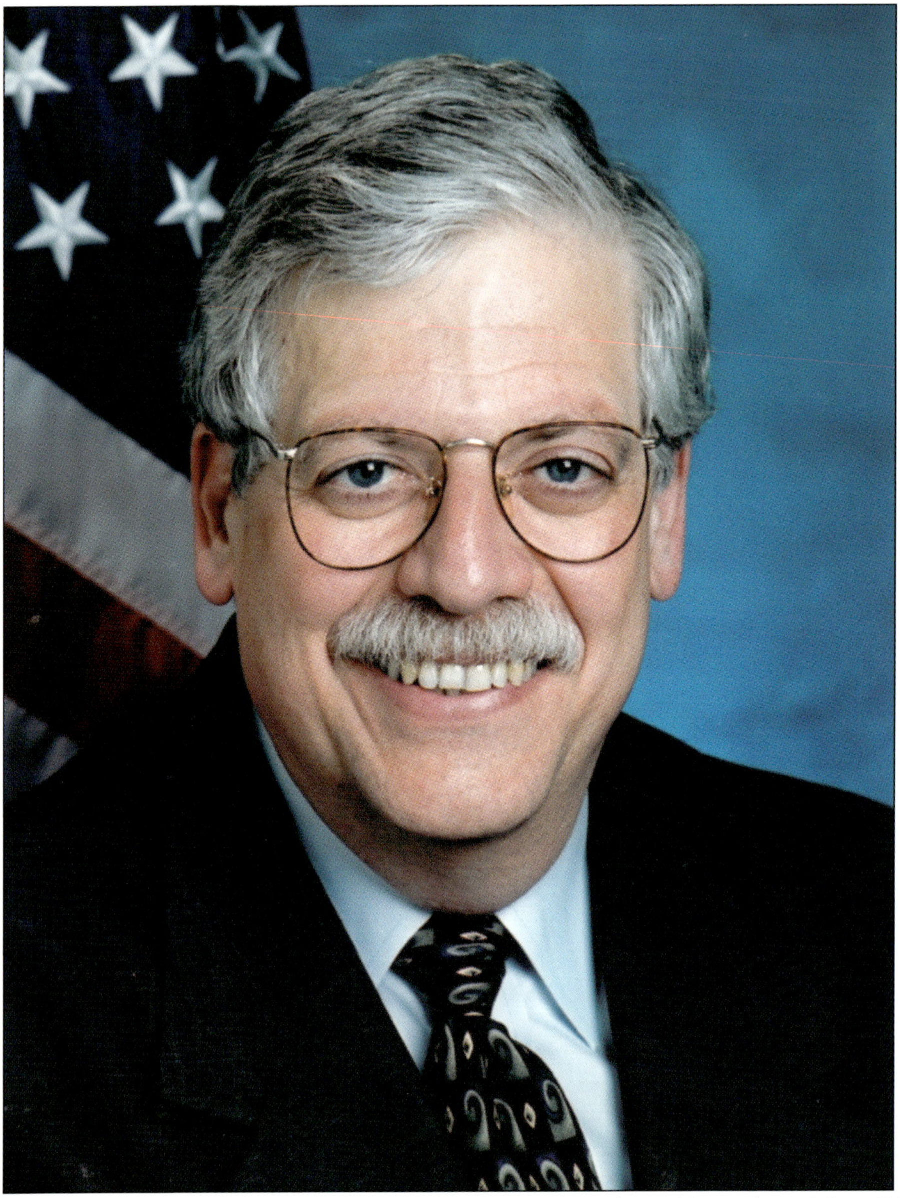

Judge Eric N. Vitaliano was born in February 1948 in West Brighton. He graduated from PS 19, St. Peter's Boys High School, Fordham College, and New York University School of Law. He is proud to be a second-generation West Brighton resident. After growing up on Taylor Street between Cary and Delafield Avenues, Vitaliano has fond memories of playing in Bodine Creek and Tompkins Department Store. Assumption Council was an important part of his life as a child and a young adult. He was first elected to the New York State Assembly in 1982 and reelected to nine consecutive two-year terms. Assemblyman Vitaliano authored more than 300 state laws, including the closing of the Fresh Kills Landfill. Vitaliano began his judicial career in 2001, when he was elected to the Civil Court of the City of New York. He entered into service as a US district judge on February 8, 2006. Judge Vitaliano is only the second Staten Island resident to attain that position. The first was the late Judge Mark A. Costantino, for whom Vitaliano served as a law clerk. He and his wife, Helen, have four children. (Courtesy of Eric N. Vitaliano.)

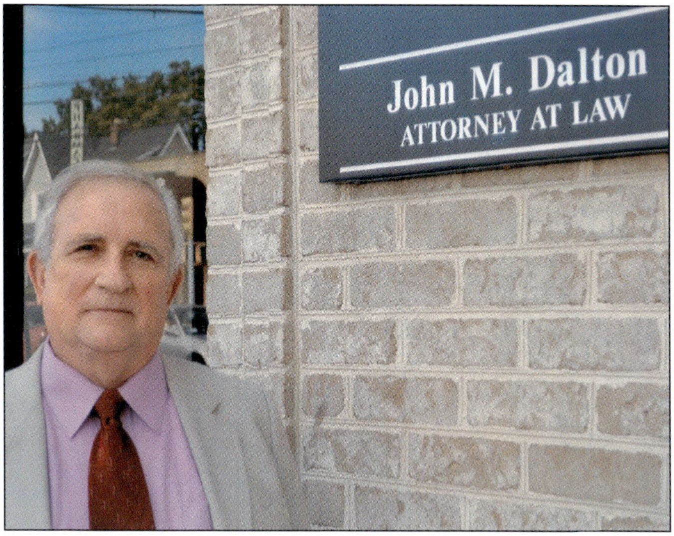

John "Jack" Dalton has practiced law in West Brighton for 31 years. He is a director of the Forest Avenue Business Improvement District. He is also a member of the Joseph F. Merrill American Legion Post; Division 1 of the Ancient Order of Hibernians; and the Warren Jaques Committee, sponsor of the prestigious boys and girls high school basketball awards, in effect since 1948. (Courtesy of Daniel Ingellis).

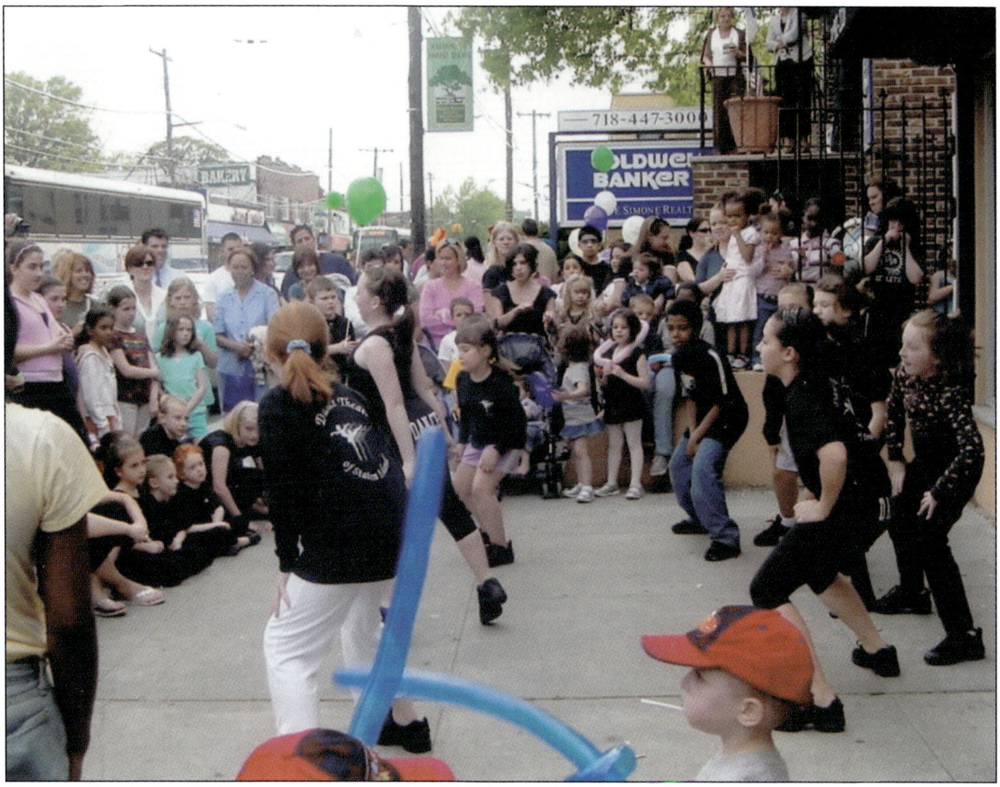

The Forest Avenue Business Improvement District (BID) in West Brighton runs along Forest Avenue from Broadway to Hart Boulevard. Since 2005, all services provided by the BID are the result of investment by merchants and property owners within the BID. Some of the services include street cleaning, graffiti removal, special events and community development, Christmas lighting, and the holiday and spring strolls (pictured). (Courtesy of the Forest Avenue Business Improvement District.)

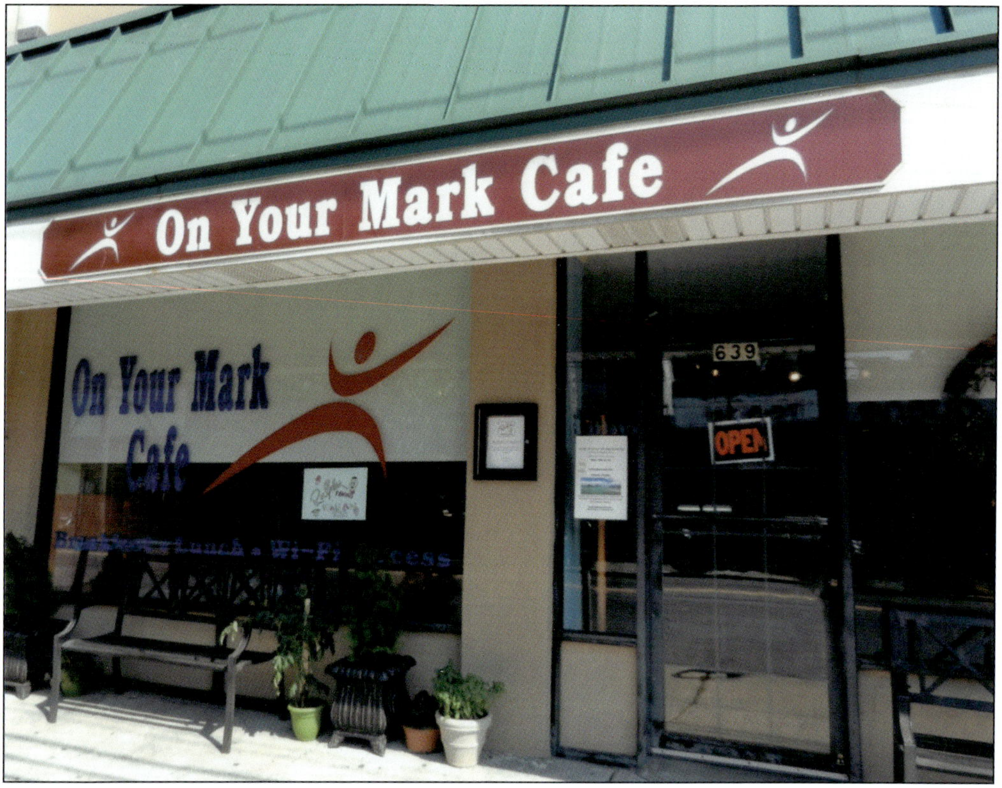

Since 1979, the mission of On Your Mark is to provide innovative and comprehensive community-based services to people with developmental disabilities, including those with autism, cerebral palsy, traumatic brain injuries, and neurological impairments. The organization is committed to helping each individual experience the highest quality of life possible by providing person-centered programs that promote community and social inclusion, health and fitness, daily activity participation, independence, self-empowerment, and productivity. (Courtesy of On Your Mark.)

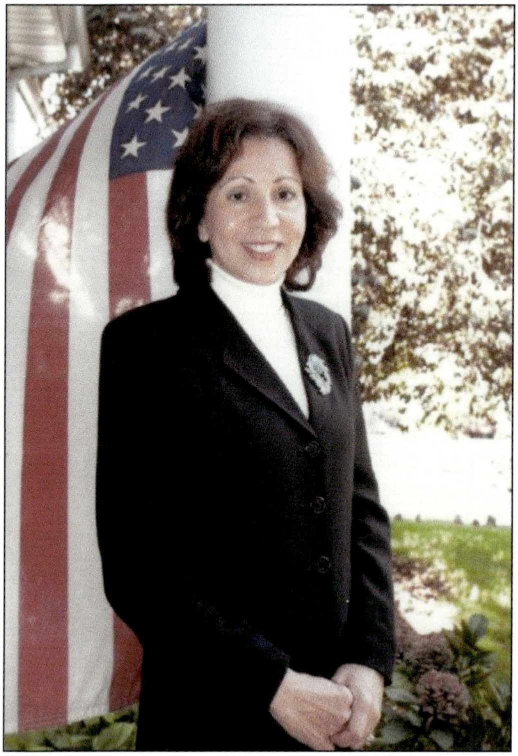

Justice Judith N. McMahon was elected to the New York City Civil Court in 2002. In 2008, Judge McMahon was the first justice to be elected to the newly created 13th Judicial District and the first female from Richmond County to be elected to the Supreme Court of New York State. She has been married for 27 years to former congressman Michael E. McMahon. The couple has two children. (Courtesy of Judge Judith N. McMahon.)

Five

Bars and Restaurants

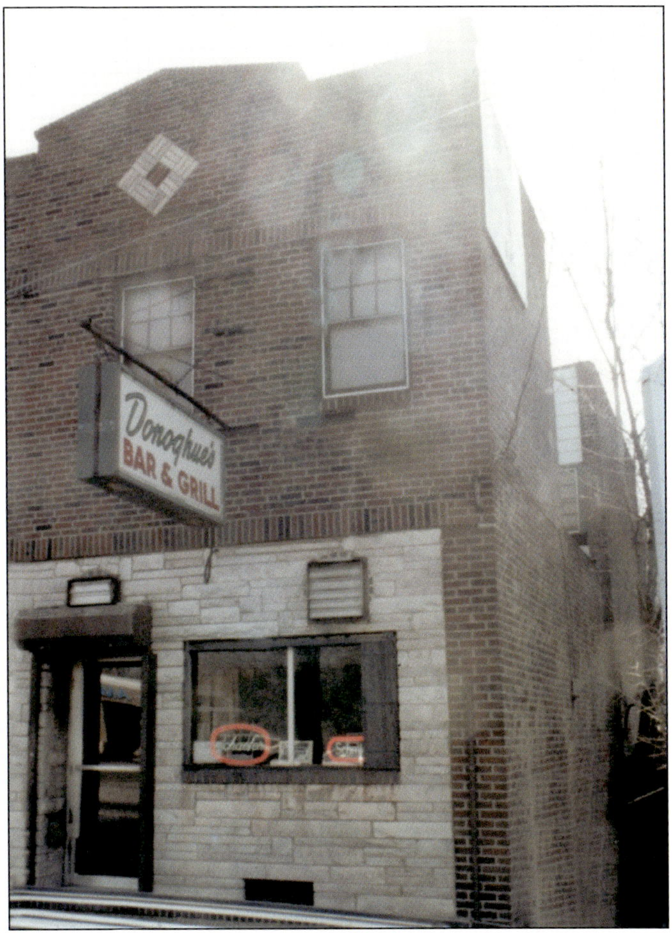

Donoghue's Bar & Grill was located at 530 Forest Avenue. John Donoghue's daughter Maureen recalled that her father bought the building in 1940, when it was a tailor shop, then opened and operated Donoghue's Bar & Grill. John sold the business in the 1960s, but it continued to be a popular West Brighton watering hole until the 1990s. (Courtesy of New York City Municipal Archives.)

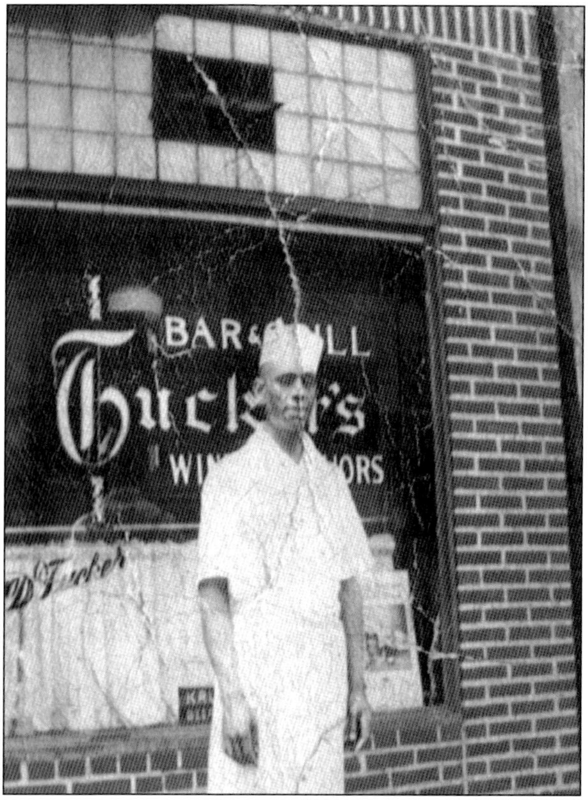

Damond Tucker stands in front of his establishment, Tucker's Bar and Grill, which was located on Broadway between Castleton and Henderson Avenues. The restaurant was at this location until 1960, when it closed to make room for the West Brighton Houses. (Courtesy of Damon Tucker.)

Al Cardone's Rhythm Rascals are pictured in the Plaza Casino in West Brighton. The band played the New York City metro area from the 1950s to the late 1970s. According to Cardone's son, Al Cardone Jr., the groups was Staten Island's "we gotta get them for our wedding" band. Pictured here are, from left to right, Matteo Cannizarro, Rocky Cetani, Al Cardone, Patty "O'Day" Rufolo, Mike Zasa, and Guy DeRosa. (Courtesy of the Cardone family.)

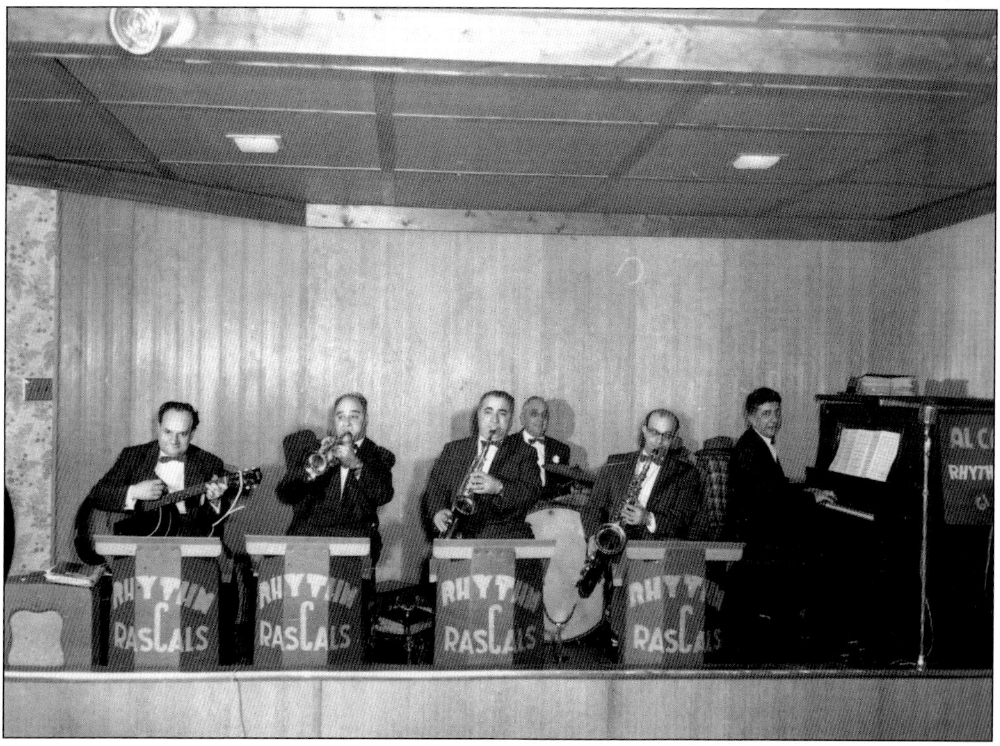

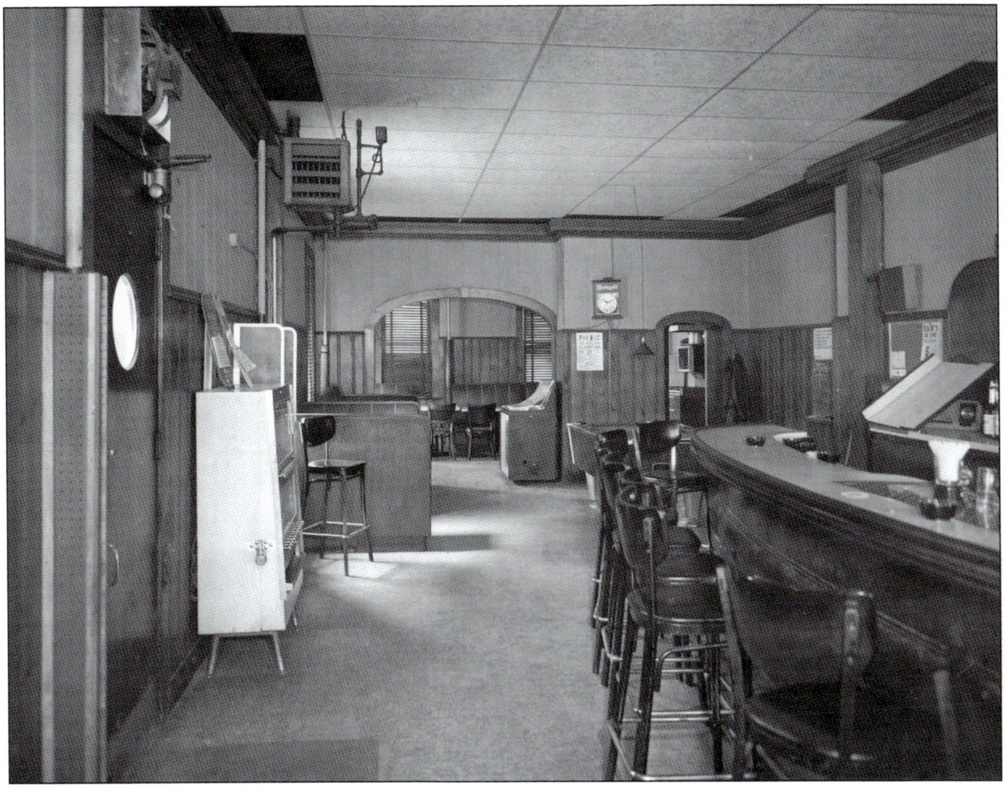

Longtime West Brighton residents will recognize this establishment—Duke Fraser's bar—at Broadway and Cary Avenue. The below photograph shows Mike Iannatto mixing a drink behind the bar in the mid-1970s. Iannatto co-owned Duke Fraser's with Tom Hollywood. Duke Fraser's may no longer be around, but the familiar "1895" date still remains on the side of the building. (Both, courtesy of Glenn Iannatto.)

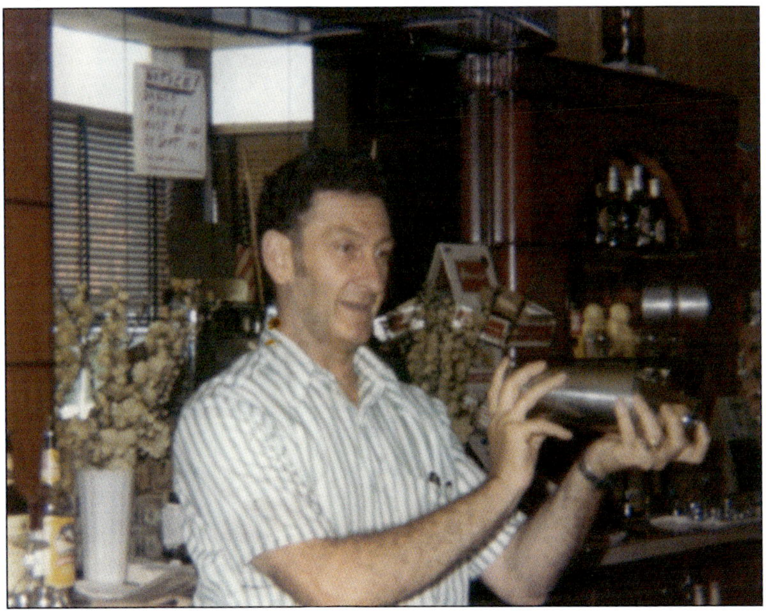

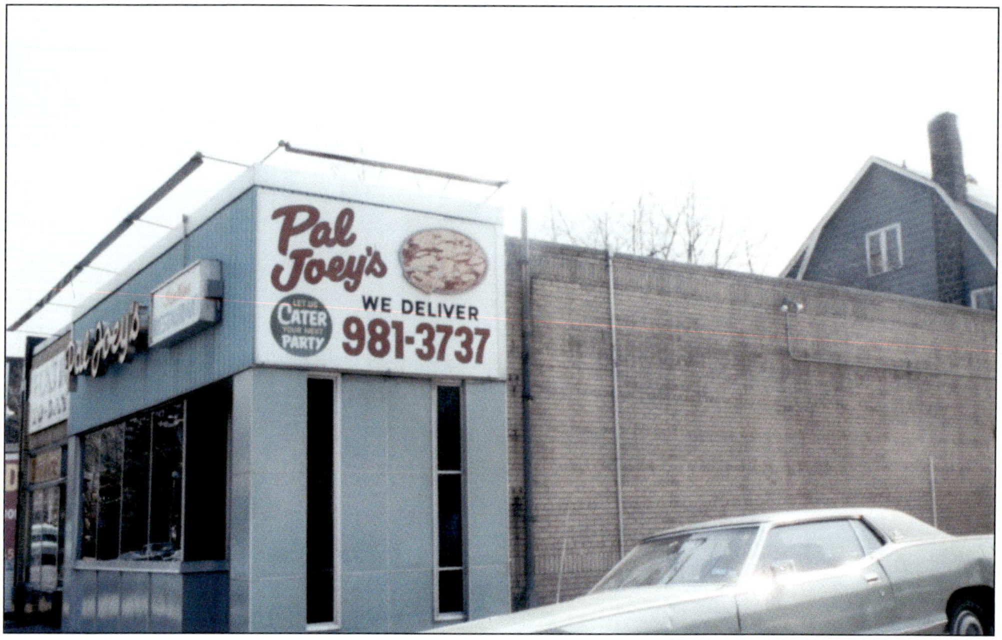

When Joseph Andreano opened his Pal Joey's pizzeria in 1958, he was excited about the business venture. He had worked at Aiello's Bakery on Henderson Avenue, where he met his wife, Lori, whose family owned the bakery. The couple wed in 1946. When the original Pal Joey's opened at 616 Forest Avenue, a customer could get a slice of pizza and a soda for 25¢, and it was the only pizzeria on Forest Avenue. The Andreanos' daughter Addie (below with longtime Pal Joey's employee Bobby Smith) recalled that when her parents moved to the second Pal Joey's location at 538 Forest Avenue (above), they simply wheeled the pizza oven down the street. Pal Joey's was always very active in the West Brighton community and sponsored many sports teams. The Andreanos retired from the business in the 1970s. (Both, courtesy of the Andreano family.)

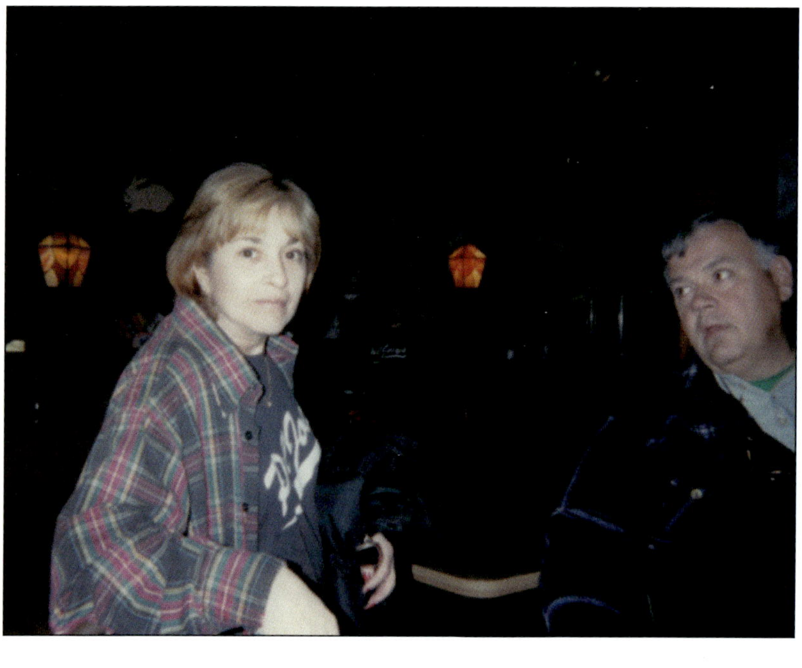

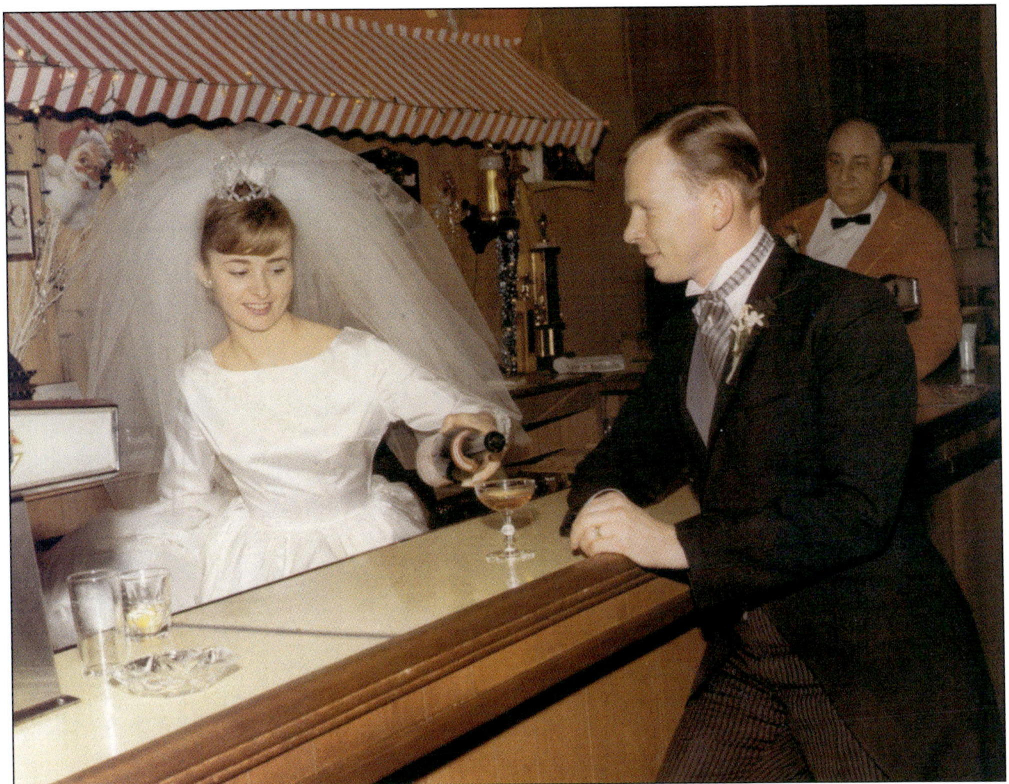

On January 29, 1967, Elizabeth A. Carinci and Edward Morand were married in St. Peter's Church. In the image above, Elizabeth and Edward are enjoying their reception in the Red and Gold Room of the Columbian Lyceum on Clove Road. Behind Edward is Joseph "Wimpy" Fabisinski, a well known bartender at the Knights of Columbus. Pictured below are, from left to right, Elizabeth's father, Paul Carinci; Elizabeth and Edward; Elizabeth's mother, Lillian; and Elizabeth's younger brother, Paul Jr. "P.J." (Both, courtesy of the Morand family.)

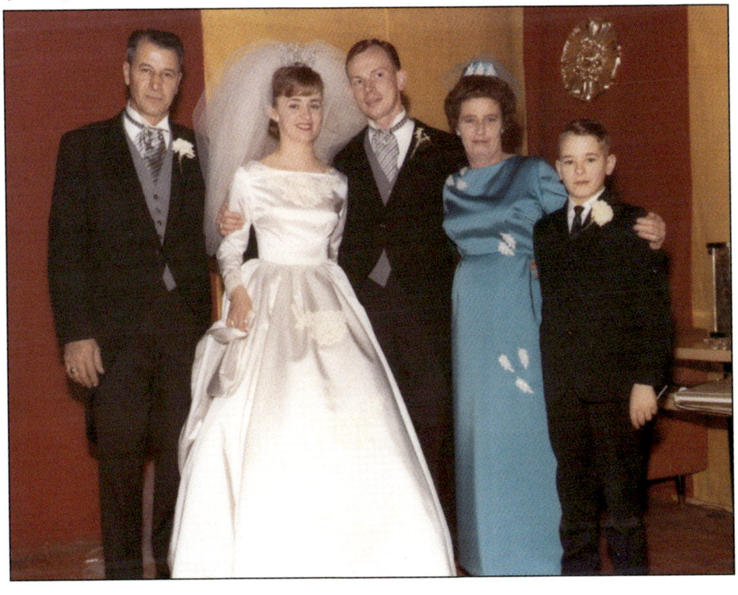

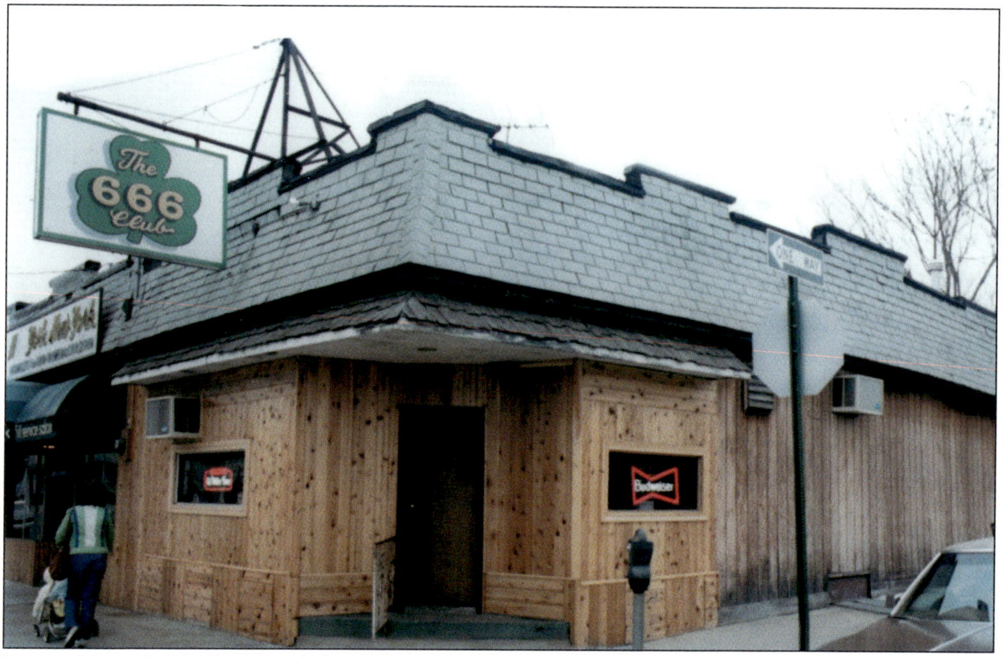

Ina and Joseph Clark opened the original 666 Club in the 1940s at 666 Forest Avenue on the corner of Bement Avenue. Sometime in the 1950s, it moved to 618 Forest Avenue on the corner of Oakland Avenue. Some of the owners through the years include Frank Burke, Charles Burton, and John Joe Conroy. Richard "Richie" Emde bought the club from Conroy in 1976, and the 666 Club closed in 1988. (Courtesy of New York City Municipal Archives.)

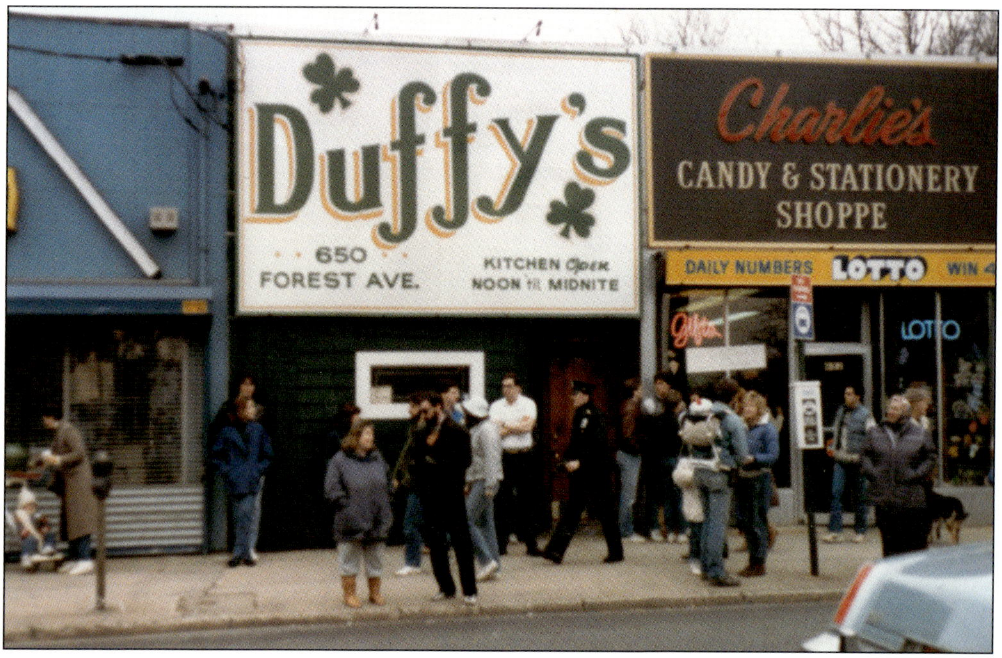

Duffy's opened in March 1985. George Froehlich and John Duffy, who bought it from Danny Blaine and Brian Noone, still own and operate Duffy's today. It is famous for having Staten Island's best burgers. (Courtesy of George and Michele Froehlich.)

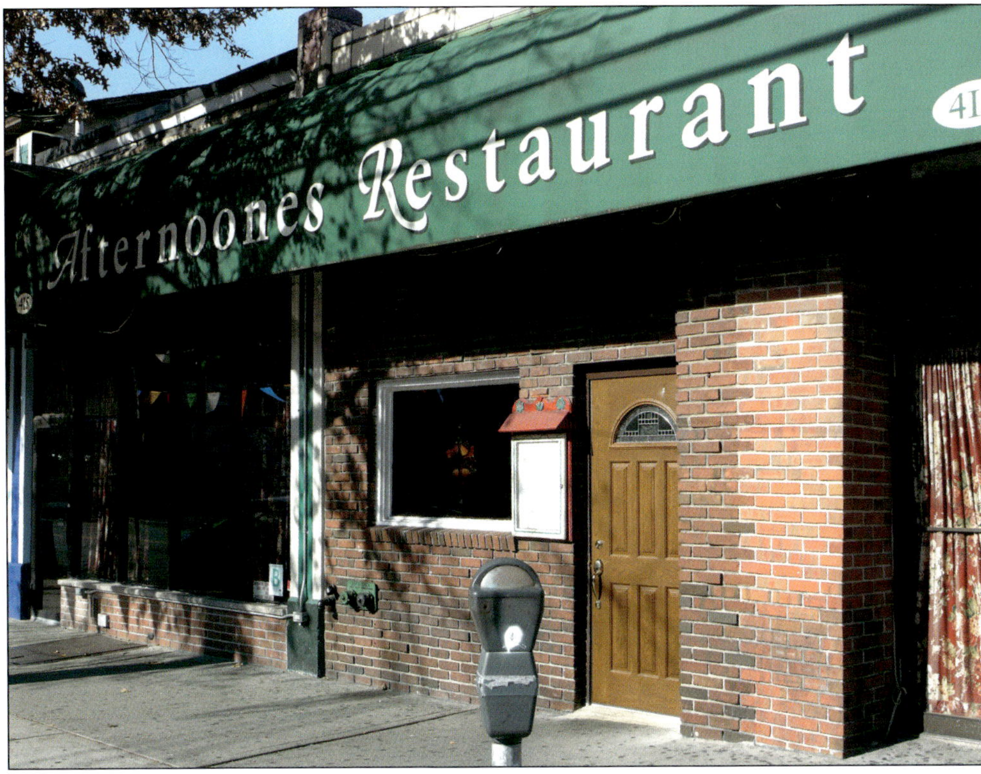

Afternoones Restaurant, located at 415 Forest Avenue, was established in October 1992. Joe Territo purchased the restaurant from Brian Noone. According to Territo, "That's why we spell it 'Afternoones,' with the 'es' at the end." The restaurant has been serving the West Brighton neighborhood for 21 years with a friendly atmosphere where people can come and feel at home. (Courtesy of Joe Territo.)

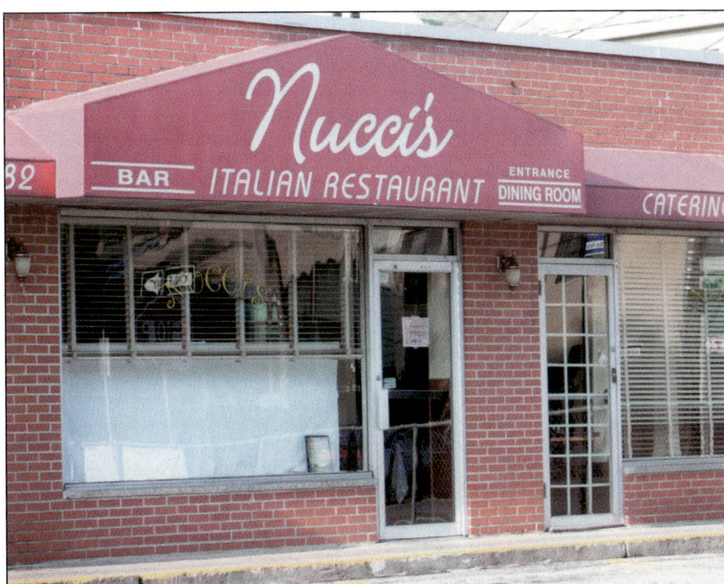

Nucci's Italian Restaurant, located on Forest Avenue between Pelton and Oakland Avenues, has been serving West Brighton since December 1999. Owners Paul Montella, Ronnie Martinucci, and Dr. Peter Montella consider their loyal patrons more like an extended family than just customers. (Courtesy of Nucci's Italian Restaurant.)

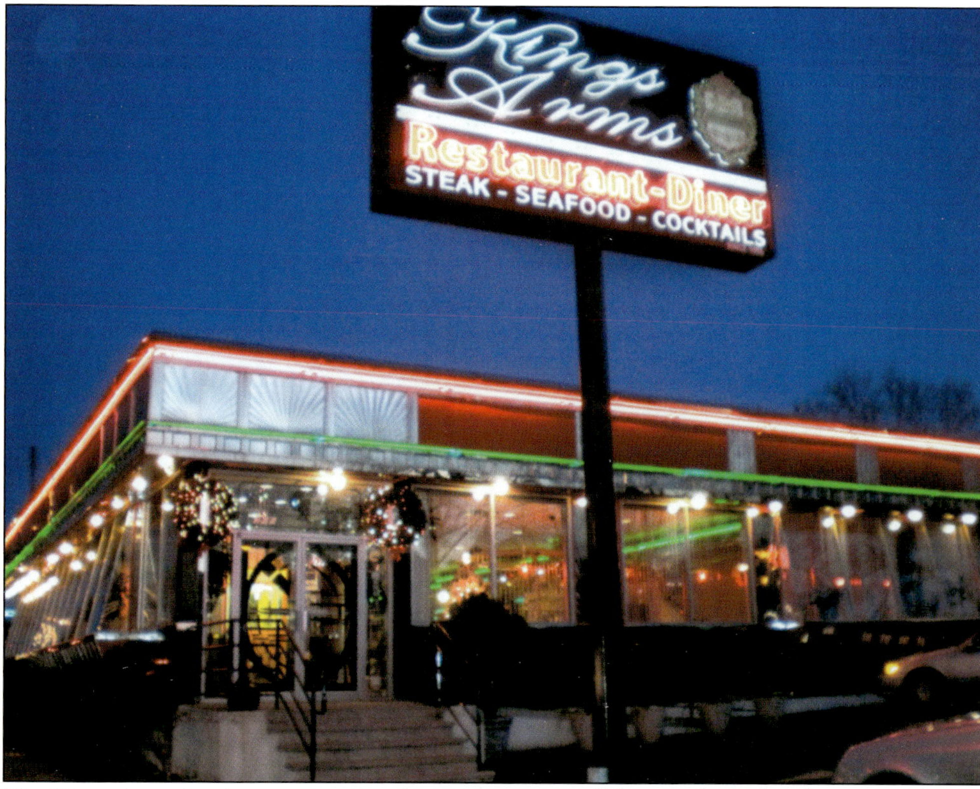

The Kings Arms has been a very popular restaurant—well known for its hamburgers—in West Brighton for decades. Dimitrios "Jimmy" Koutsovasilis purchased the diner in 1982 with two partners. Koutsovasilis came from Greece in 1973. He worked hard as a dishwasher, grill man, cook, and more. Today, he is the sole owner of the King's Arms, which he renovated in 1996. The Koutsovasilis family is pictured below: from left to right, daughter Aliki, Jimmy, daughter Gia, and Toula (Jimmy's wife). (Both, courtesy of the Koutsovasilis family.)

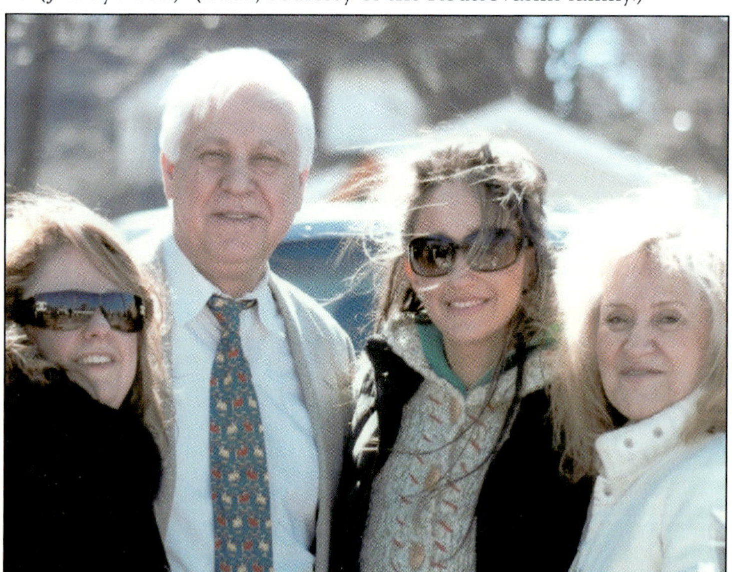

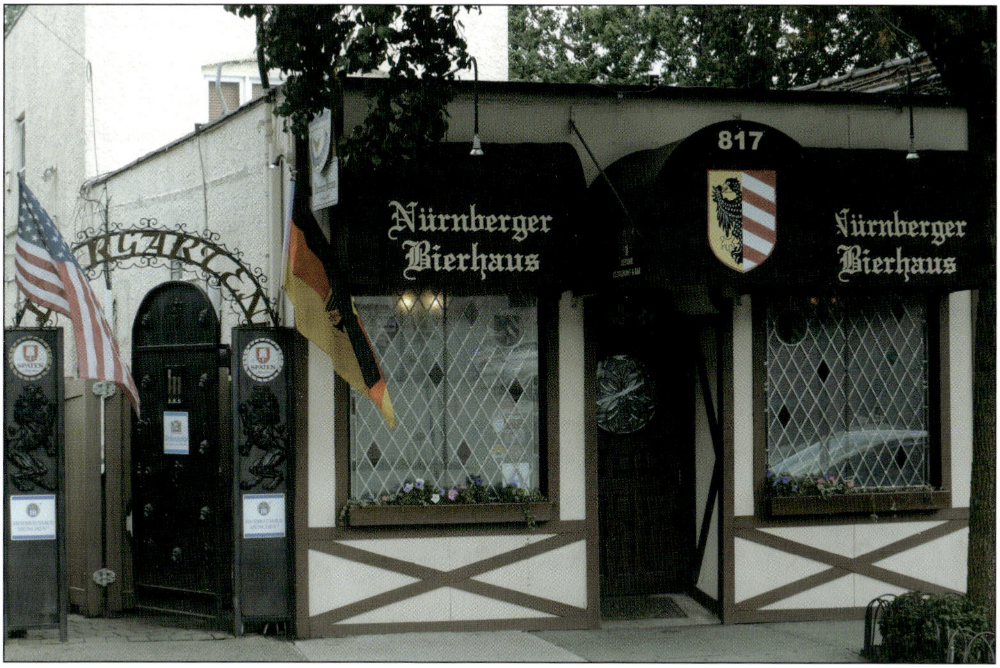

After working for the New York Police Department for 20 years, Detective Robert Karl Kelly decided to open a business following his retirement. As an ode to his mother, Irma Weberndorfer, and his arrival in the United States at age 11, Kelly opened the Nurnberger Bierhaus in 2005 with his wife, Barbara, and daughter, Monica. After eight successful years, Robert expanded next door with the addition of the Nurnberger Bierhalle. (Courtesy of Robert Karl Kelly.)

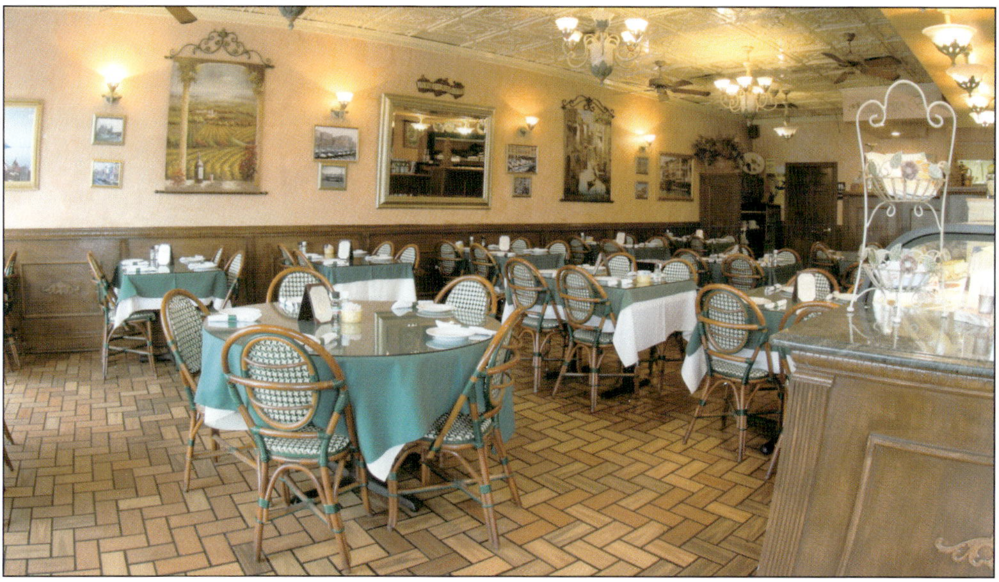

Vincent Laurino, a native Staten Islander, opened Panini Grill in 2002 at 538 Forest Avenue. The restaurant, with its large sliding front doors opening to the street, is designed to give the feeling of eating in a café in Italy. The restaurant sells paninis (pressed hot sandwiches), Old World pizza, pasta, and other creations based on Sicilian recipes Laurino inherited from his grandmother. (Courtesy of Vincent Laurino.)

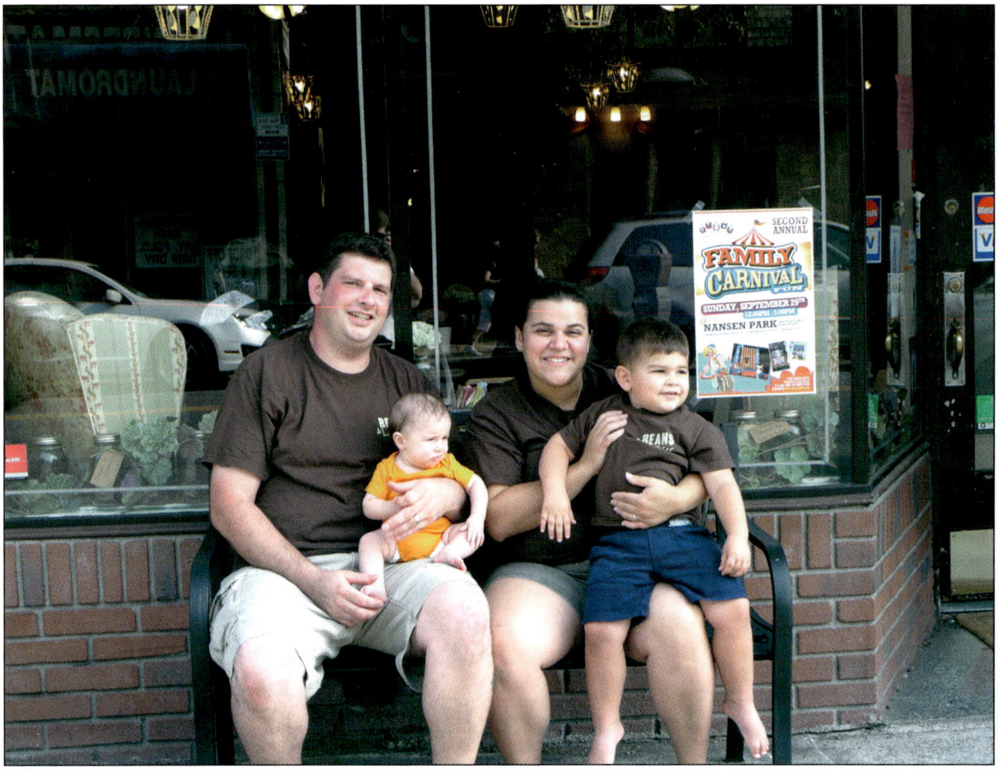

After Coffee and Tea Market closed its doors following a 14-year run, Megan and Christian Coppola (pictured above with their children, John, left, and Christian) took on the venture that is now Beans and Leaves. Megan had worked for the original coffee shop owner, Angela Matalas, for over six years to gain knowledge and training. To pay homage to her grandmother, Claire Rotunno, who was born in Paris, France, the store was resurrected with a homey French Country feel. In an interesting turn of events, Megan's grandmother had worked in the very same space when it was Kennedy's Men's Store. (Both, courtesy of Beans & Leaves.)

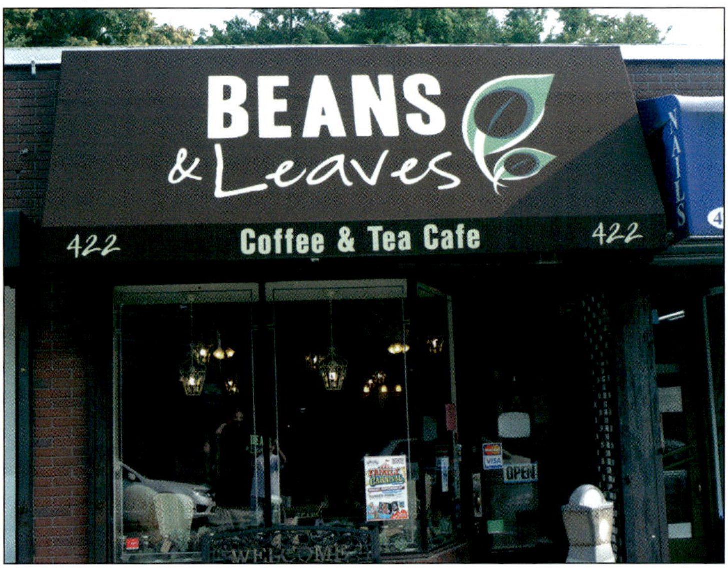

Six

Churches and Schools

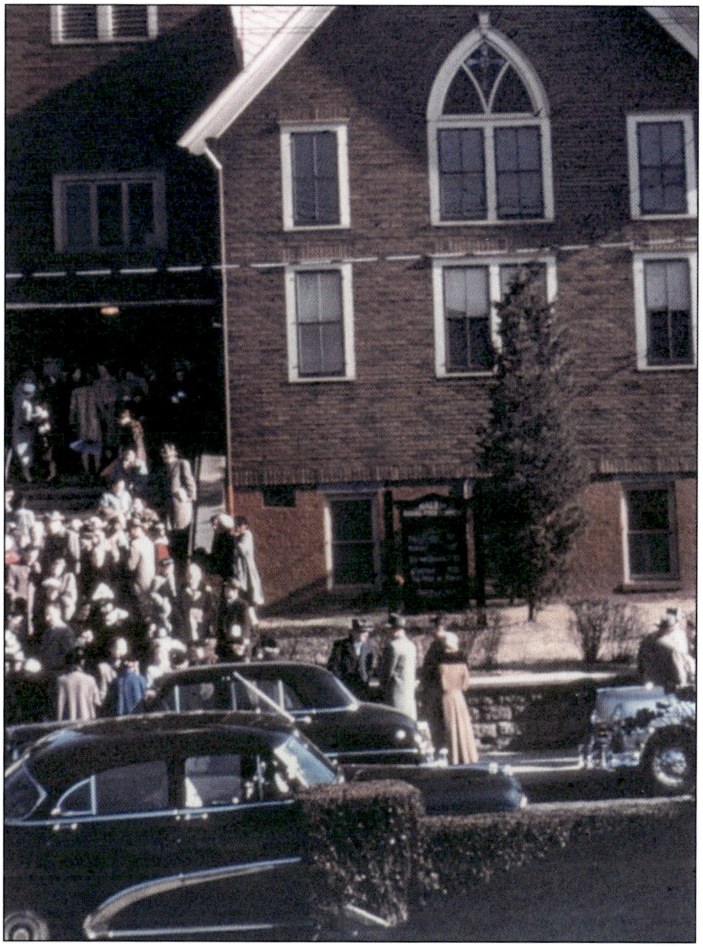

Salem Evangelical Free Church was organized on November 27, 1905, under the name Norwegian Evangelical Free Church Mission, and all services were conducted in Norwegian. The church purchased property at 179 Clove Road (then called Columbia Street). Prior to the construction of the church, the congregation met on the second-floor auditorium of Starin Hose Hall, a firehouse on Taylor Street. The church was occupied until 1954. (Courtesy of Ralph H. Johnson.)

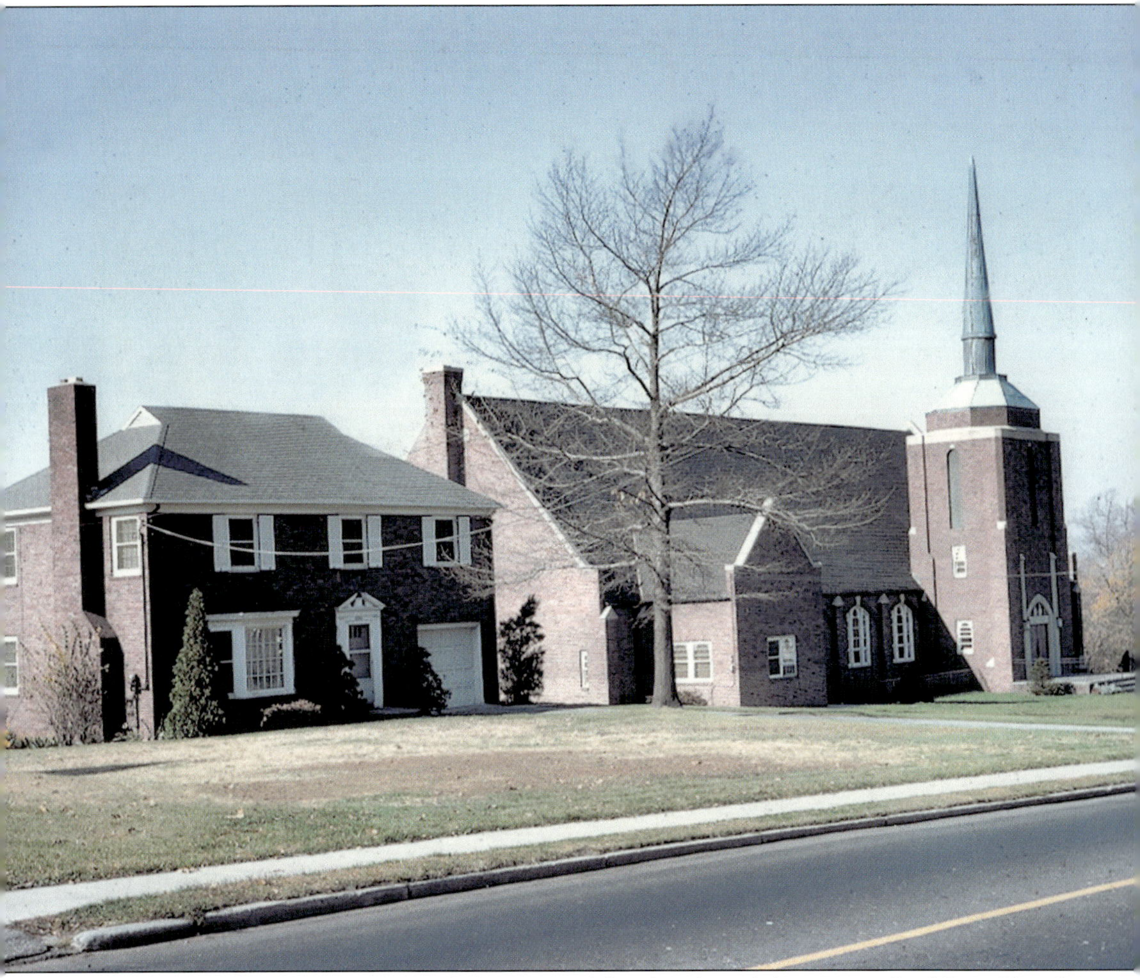

In 1935, the congregation changed the name of the church to Salem Evangelical Free Church, and by 1941, almost all meetings were conducted in English. The church began to construct a new building in 1948 after purchasing property adjacent to the park at 634 Clove Road. In May 1953, the church held ground-breaking ceremonies for the new church. Members of the Building Committee included Ole Simonsen, Dr. Lester Westlund, Pastor Ole Odegaad, Alf Abrahamsen, and Sten Johnsen. The first Sunday services were held in the new building on July 11, 1954. On November 28, 1954, the church held formal dedication services with over 1,000 people in attendance. This 1964 photograph shows the church and the parsonage and their great front lawn prior to the widening of Clove Road. Salem's ministries at the time included Sunday school for children and adults, a choir, a male chorus, five women's groups, the Tract Society, and the Missions Committee. The church also offered religious afterschool instruction and Boy and Girl Scouts activities for young people. (Courtesy of Salem Evangelical Free Church.)

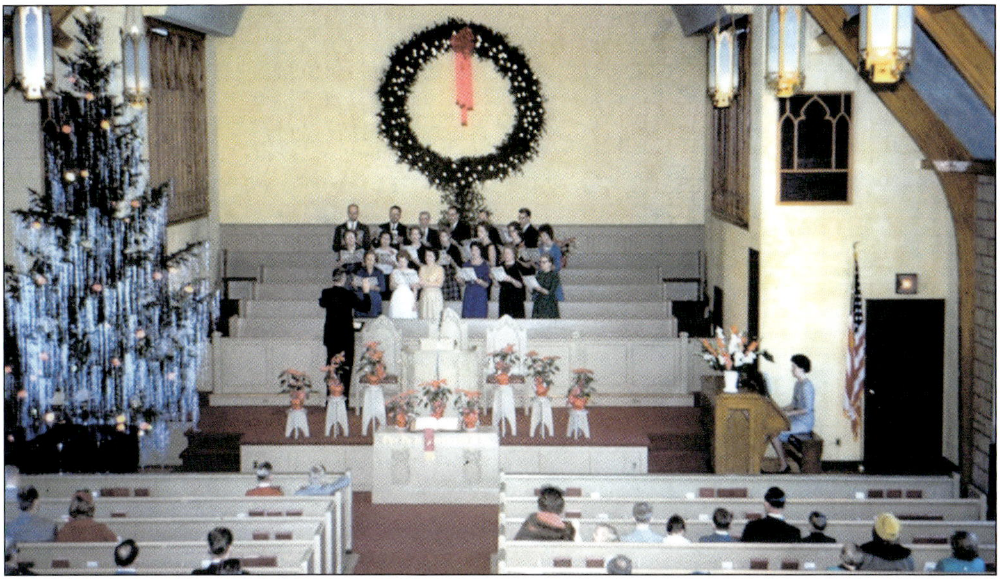

In 1962, the Salem Evangelical Free Church continued its tradition of a live Christmas tree embellished with lengthy, heavy, leaded tinsel (as was customary for the times). Poinsettias adorned the front of the platform and were later distributed to shut-ins or those in hospitals. The choir performed an annual Christmas concert and, under the direction of Stanley Ottosen, sang selections from *The Messiah*. (Courtesy of Salem Evangelical Free Church.)

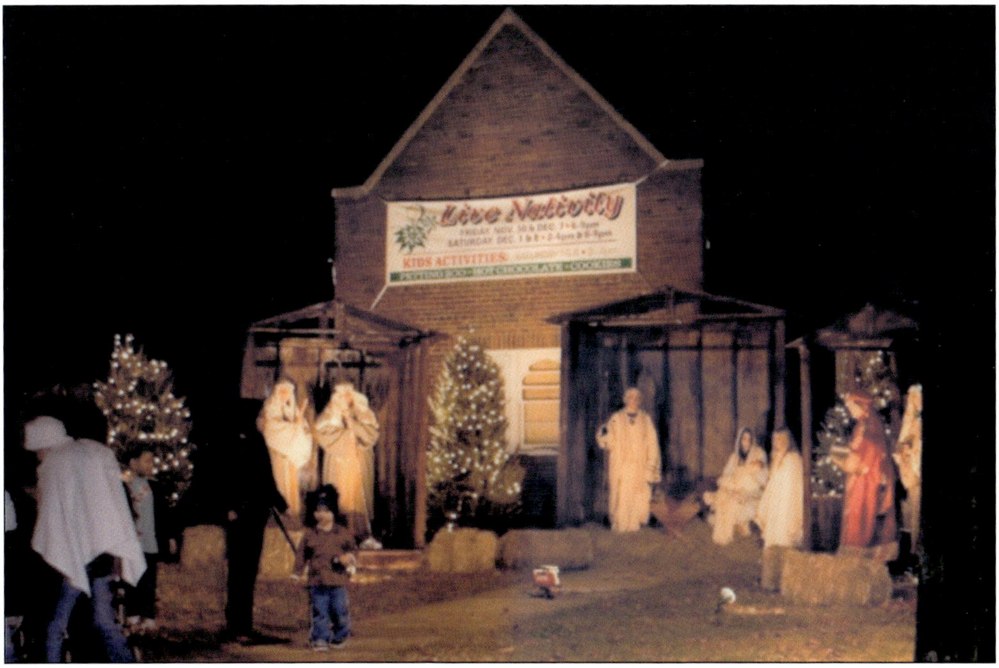

Salem Evangelical Free Church hosts a "Live Nativity" for the community each Christmas season on the front lawn. The Christmas story, as told in chapter 2 of Luke, is read by Rev. Dr. Eddie Cole. The choir sings Christmas carols on the lawn as Joseph, Mary, and the baby Jesus are ministered to by the angels with animals nearby. The wise men attend in adoration as they present their gifts to the babe. (Courtesy of Salem Evangelical Free Church.)

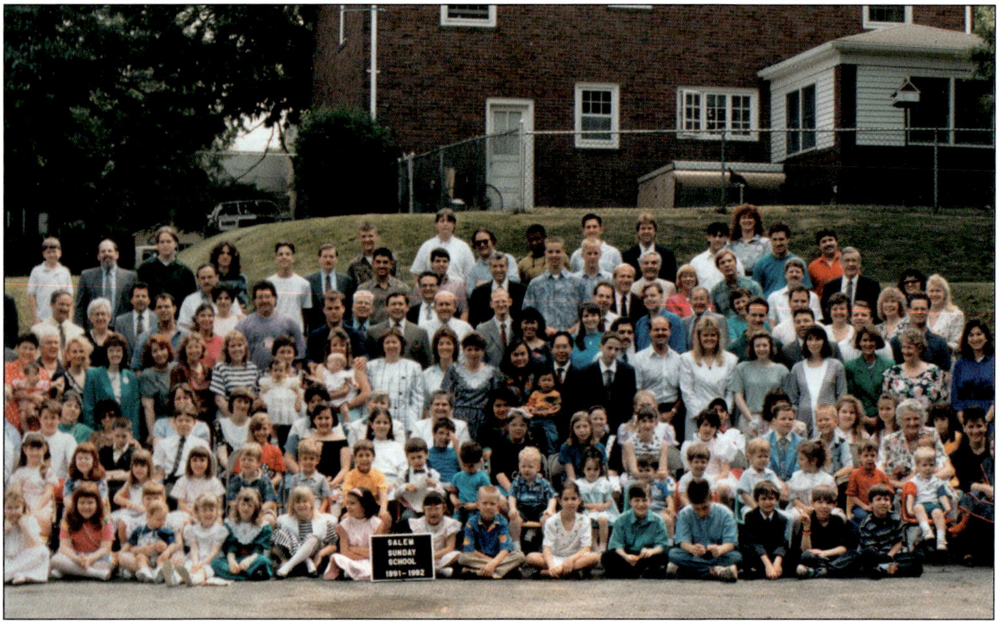

This photograph was taken in June 1992 to memorialize those who were active participants in the Salem Evangelical Free Church Sunday school. At that time, the majority of the congregation still included descendants from the original church body. A few years later, a gym was constructed where this photograph was taken. Outreach ministries, including the "Upward Basketball" program, have attracted those in the surrounding community to call Salem their church. (Courtesy of Salem Evangelical Free Church.)

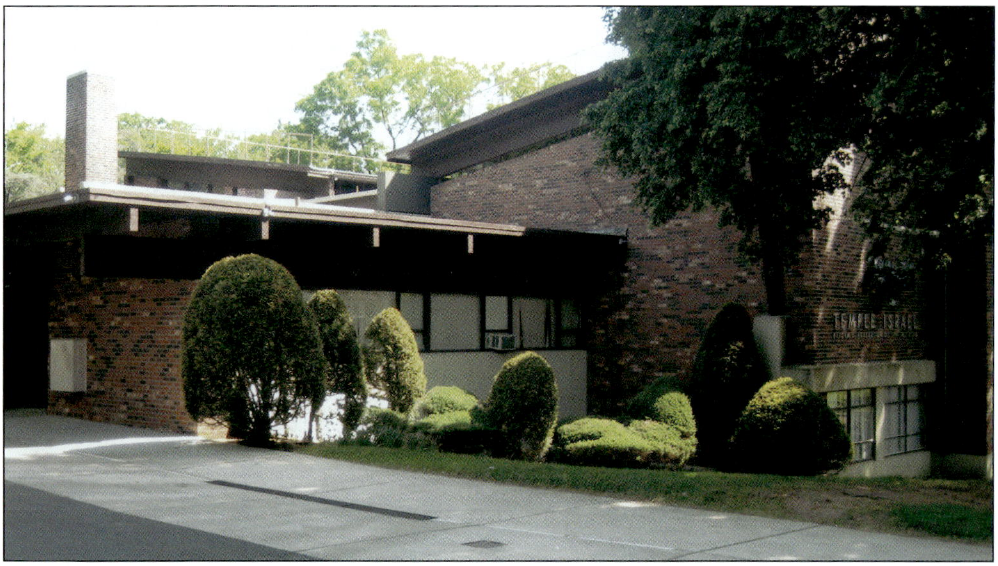

Percival Goodman, renowned religious architect, designed the Temple Israel Reform Congregation building, which overlooks a stream and is surrounded by trees. It was dedicated on September 27, 1964, five years after a fire destroyed the previous location on Victory Boulevard. Miraculously, the Torah scrolls, pulpit bible, and electric chanukiah from the 1956 Confirmation class survived the fire and were placed in their new home at 315 Forest Avenue. (Courtesy of Temple Israel Reform Congregation.)

The parish history of Our Lady of Mount Carmel–St. Benedicta is actually that of two Roman Catholic churches intertwined. The church of Our Lady of Mount Carmel was founded by Rev. Louis Riccio in 1913. The parish was created for Italian families who migrated in great numbers to Staten Island. In 1922, St. Benedicta's (pictured at right) was established as a mission to Our Lady of Mount Carmel. In 1924, it became an independent parish and remained as such until 1957, when the New York Archdiocese decided to demolish St. Benedicta in favor of the West Brighton Houses. Pictured below are members of the St. Benedicta's Holy Name Society. (Right, courtesy of Joseph Yaccarino; below courtesy of the Bruno family.)

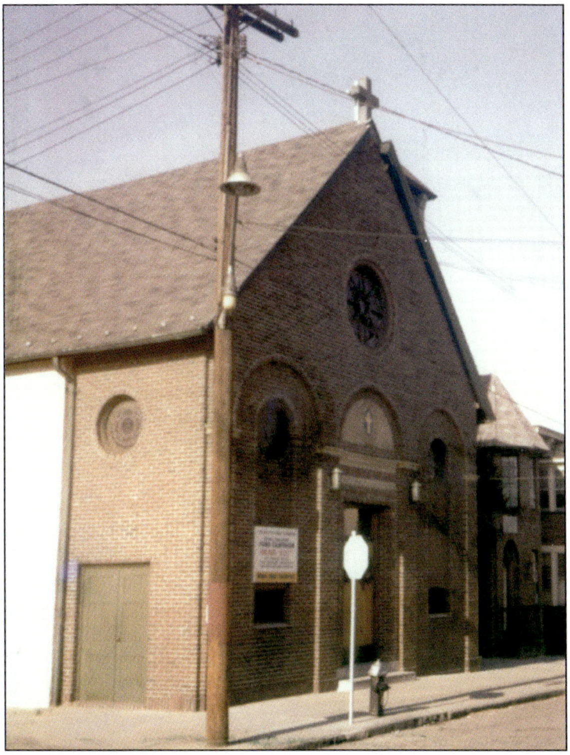

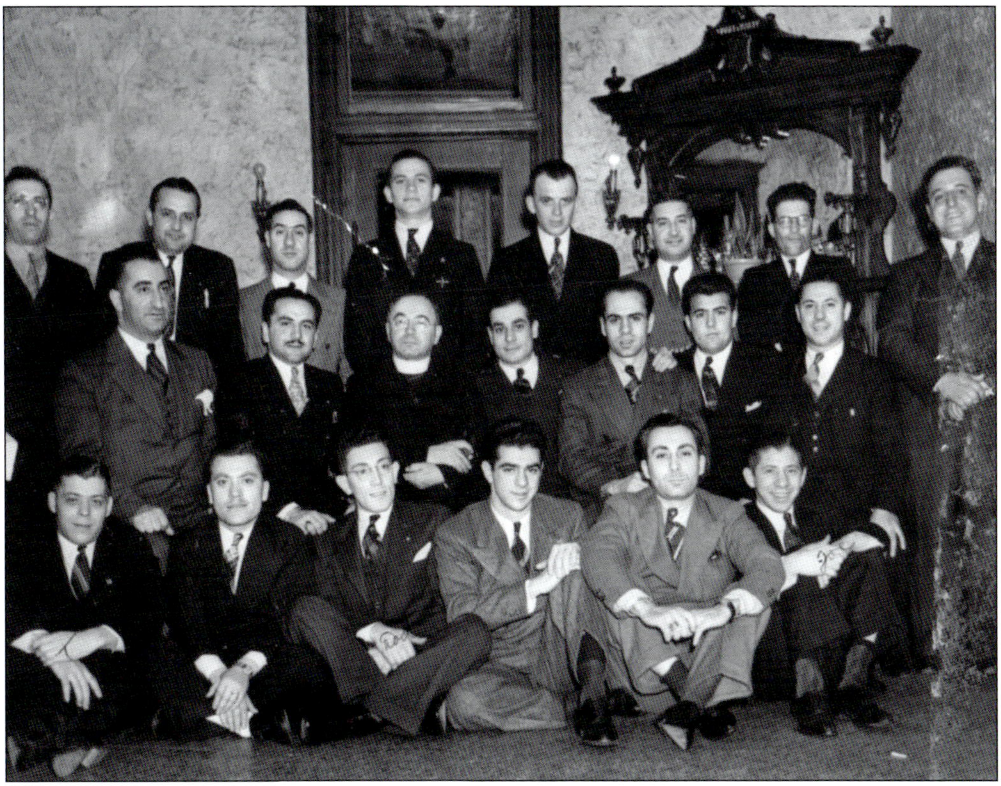

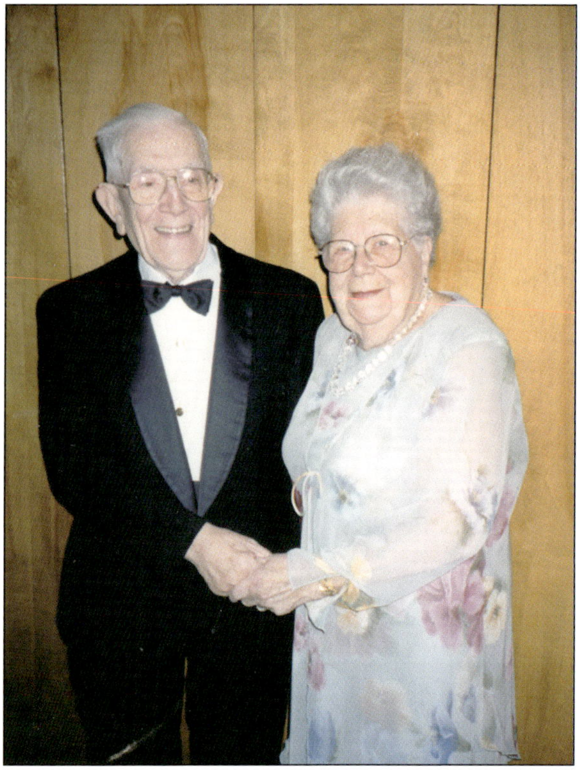

The last mass was held at St. Benedicta on January 17, 1960. Years later, longtime parishioner John Bruno (pictured at left with his wife, Josephine) reflected on that solemn day: "People were crying. After all, the church was part of their lives and their neighborhood for more than 40 years." John and Josie, as she was known, were active church volunteers at St. Benedicta's. Josie was a member of St. Benedicta's Society and was one of the original workers at the society's famous annual spaghetti dinner. She continued to work on the spaghetti dinner for 50 years. When the church merged with Our Lady of Mount Carmel, the Brunos' volunteerism continued. In 2002, they were honored by the church for almost 80 years of financial support. Pictured below is Our Lady of Mount Carmel–St. Benedicta School. (Both, courtesy of the Bruno family.)

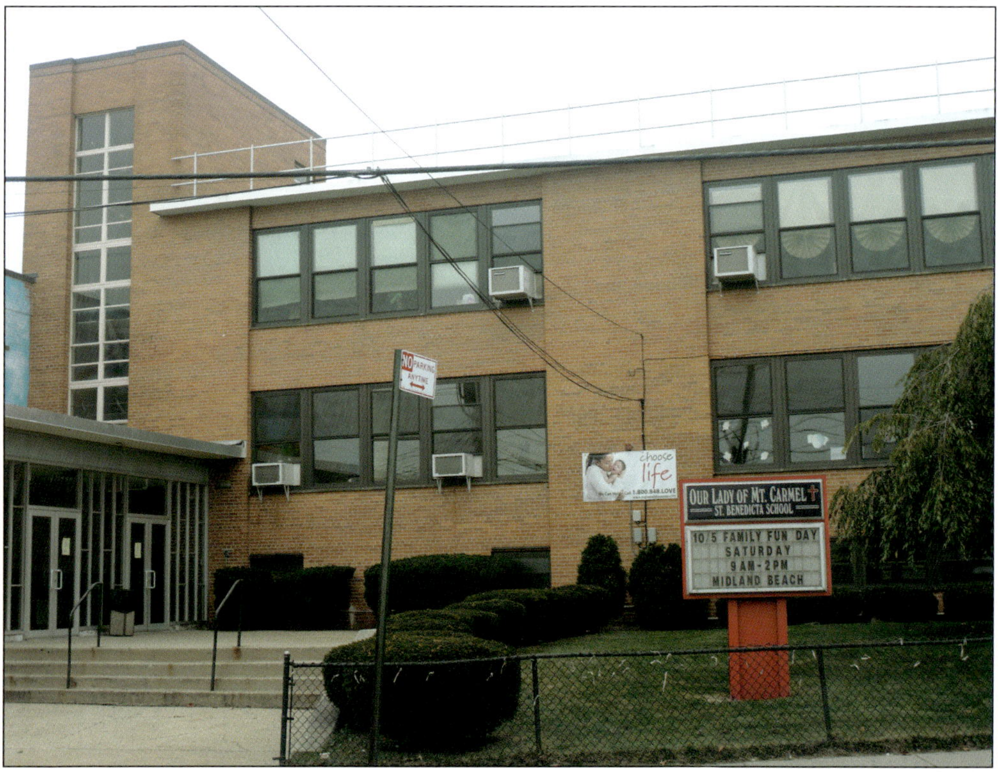

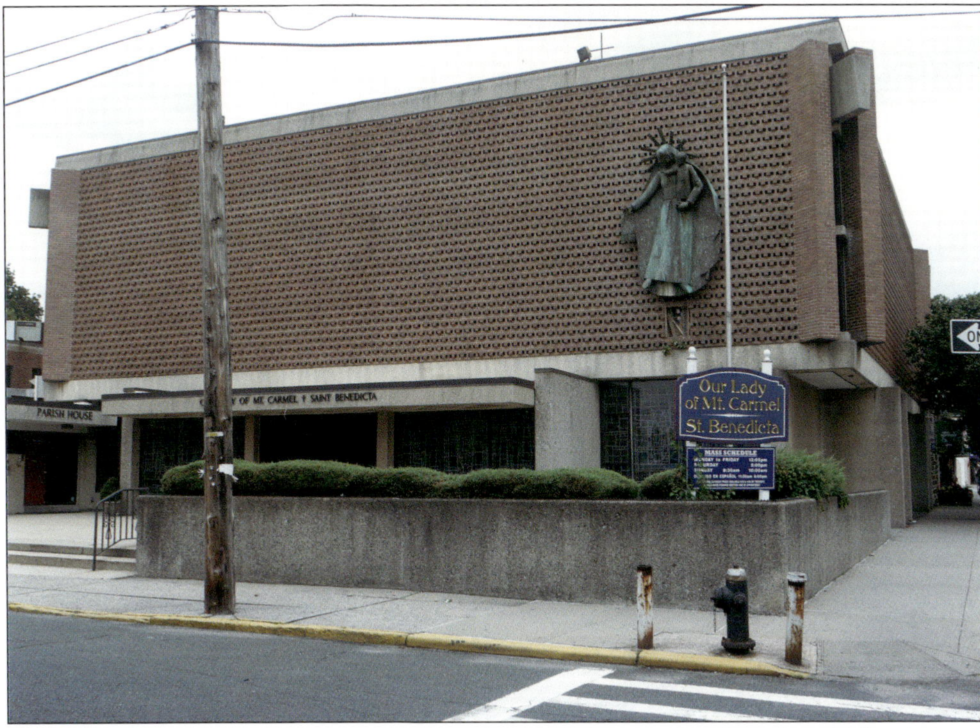

In 1957, under Rev. Charles Vecchini, the two parishes merged to form Our Lady of Mount Carmel–St. Benedicta. Plans were made for a new church to handle the increased number of parishioners. In 1961, *Staten Island Advance* publisher Samuel I. Newhouse donated the newspaper's old building, located at 1267 Castleton Avenue and Bodine Street, to the church. In 1966, a devastating fire destroyed the original Mount Carmel Church on the corner of Castleton Avenue and Clove Road. The following year, the cornerstone for the new church was in place on the site of the old *Advance* building, and the building (pictured in both images) was dedicated two years later. For a century, Our Lady of Mount Carmel–St. Benedicta has remained a vital part of West Brighton. (Both, courtesy of Our Lady of Mount Carmel–St. Benedicta.)

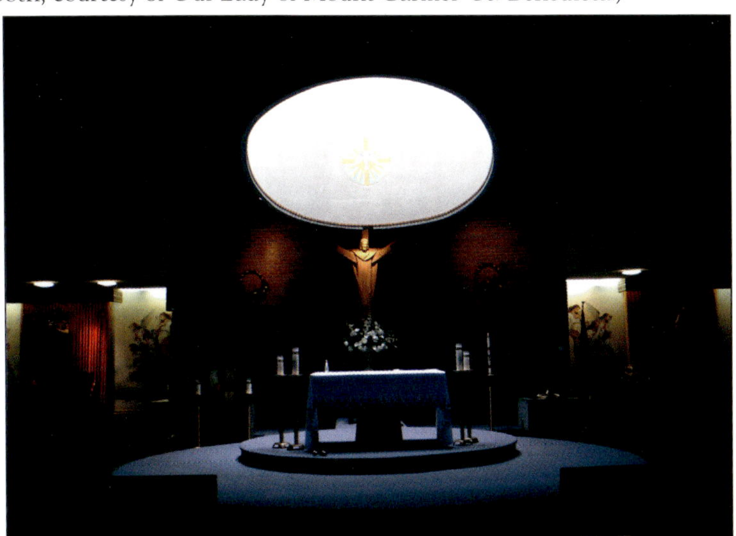

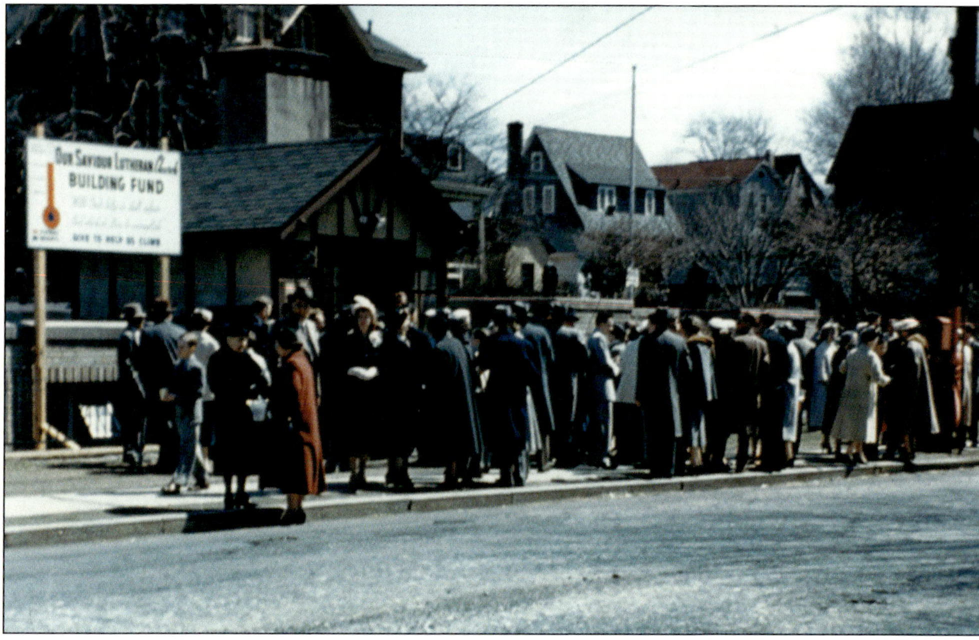

Our Saviour Lutheran Church, located on the corner of Bard and Forest Avenues, was founded in 1893. It was originally located on Nicholas Avenue in Port Richmond. The property in West Brighton was purchased in 1928, and the "basement" church (shown above) was dedicated in June 1930. The "top" section (shown below) was completed and dedicated in November 1958. Our Saviour was originally a Scandinavian congregation, with roots in Norway, but is now as multicultural as the great city it is located in. (Both, courtesy of Our Saviour Lutheran Church.)

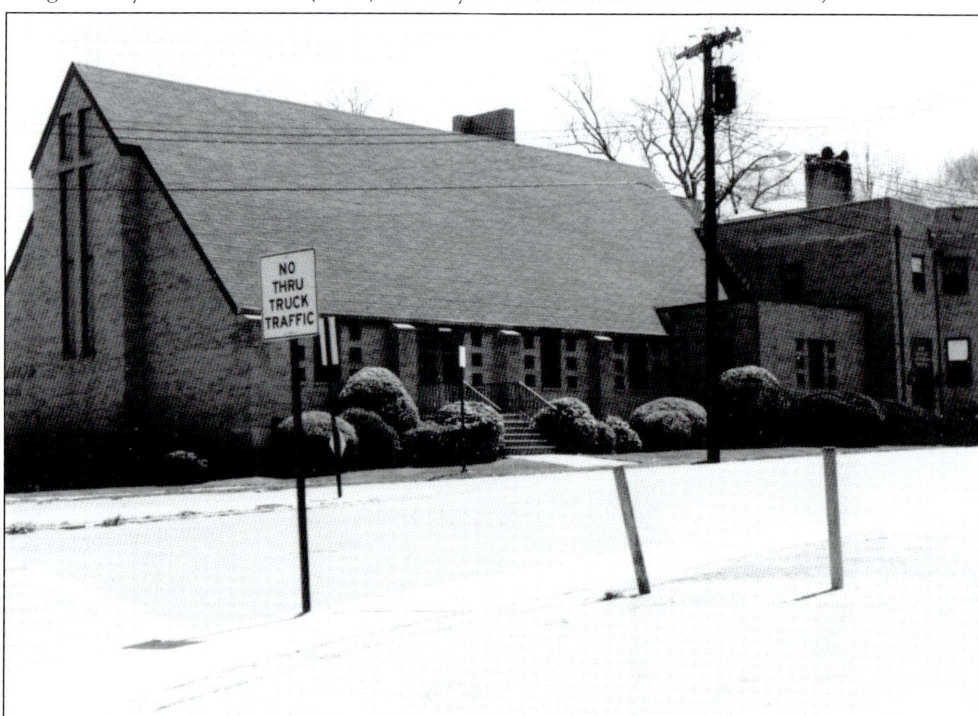

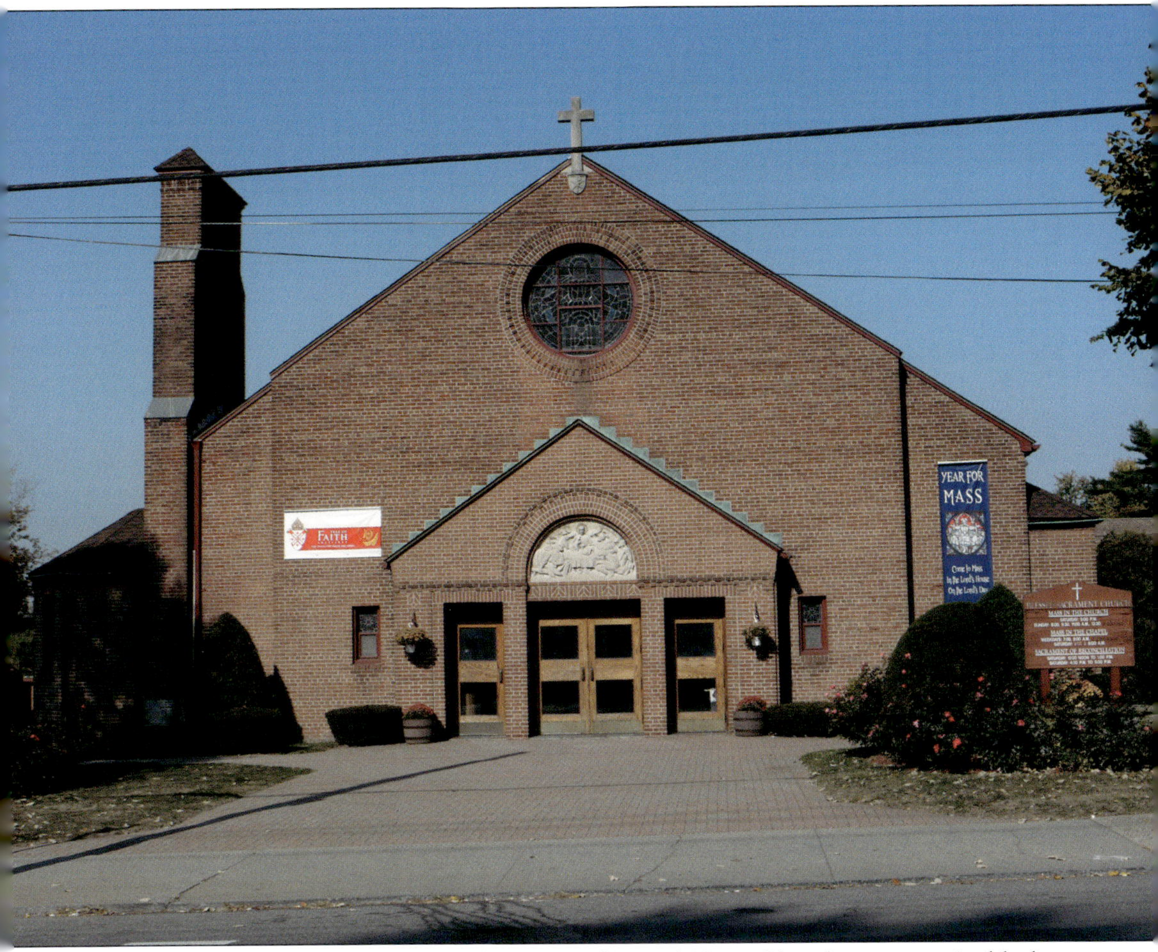

In the spring of 1910, Fr. William Poole, pastor of Sacred Heart Church, wrote to Archbishop John Farley to express that he could no longer minister to the growing number of Sacred Heart parishioners. He suggested the need for a new parish in the West Brighton area and recommended his energetic assistant, Rev. William J. Mulcahy, as the pastor of the new parish. Farley agreed, and Mulcahy became the founding pastor of the parish he named the Church of Blessed Sacrament. Father Mulcahy took residence in the DuBois House at the corner of Manor Road and Cherry Lane (later Forest Avenue), holding mass for 150 people on the first floor. Then, Father Mulcahy set to work building the first Blessed Sacrament Church. Blessed Sacrament School opened in 1917 with only a dozen pupils in the first four grades. Father Mulcahy died in August 1919, and Archbishop Hayes appointed Rev. Francis J. Heaney to succeed him. Father Heaney is remembered for building the school on Delafield Avenue at a cost of $200,000. The new Blessed Sacrament School opened in September 1928. (Courtesy of Blessed Sacrament Church.)

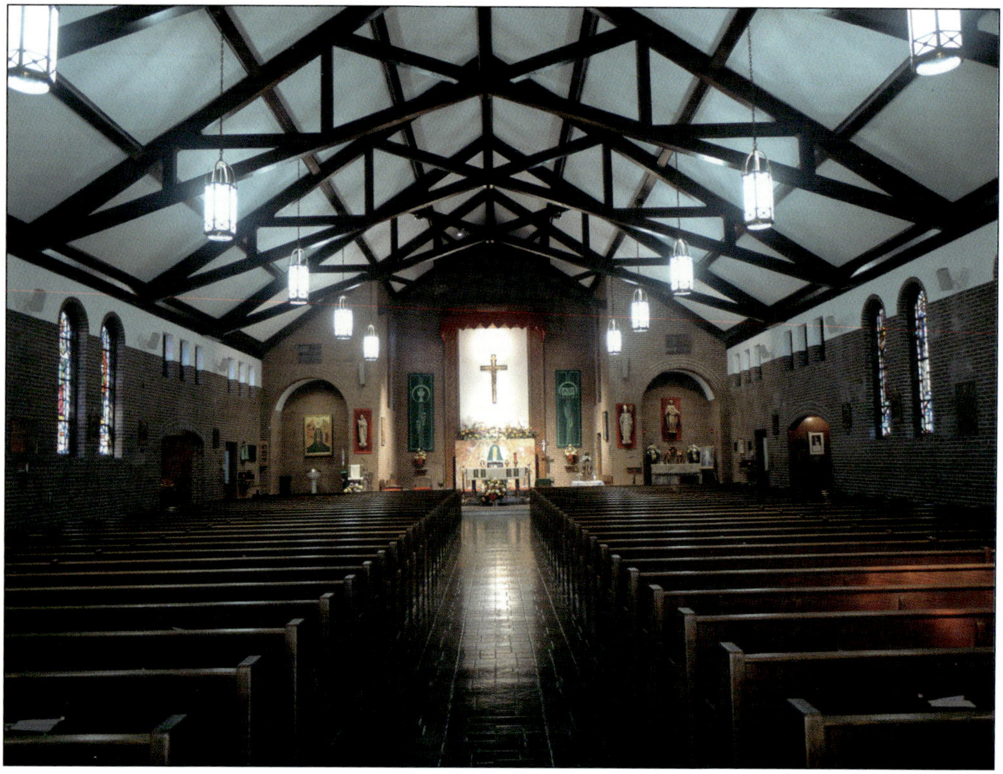

Rev. Vincent A. Julian arrived at Blessed Sacrament in June 1930 and began a 30-year association with the parish. In 1949, a new church (pictured above), with a seating capacity of 755, was constructed on Forest Avenue between Manor Road and Greenleaf Avenue. The cornerstone of the new building was laid in April 1952, and the church was completed in December 1952. Francis Cardinal Spellman presided at its dedication, and Msgr. Charles McAuliffe rejoiced with his people in a magnificent dream come true. In 1966, Msgr. John Paul Haverty arrived at Blessed Sacrament. Haverty (pictured below) is fourth from right at the July 1967 wedding of James and Mary Beth McCarthy. Also shown is Fr. Peter Finn (later a monsignor), the current pastor of Blessed Sacrament Church. (Above, courtesy of Blessed Sacrament Church; below, courtesy of the McCarthy family.)

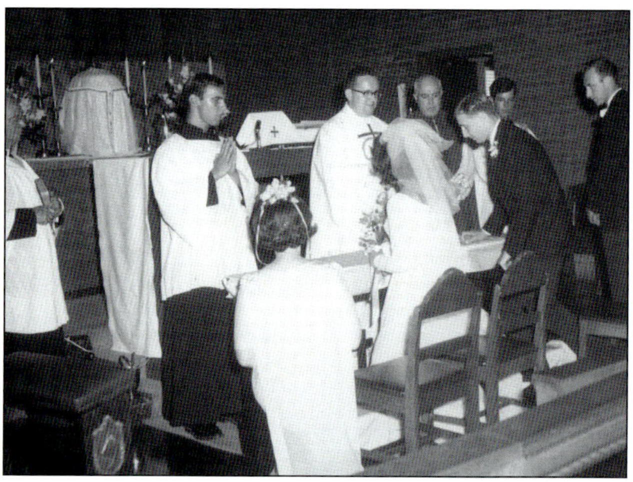

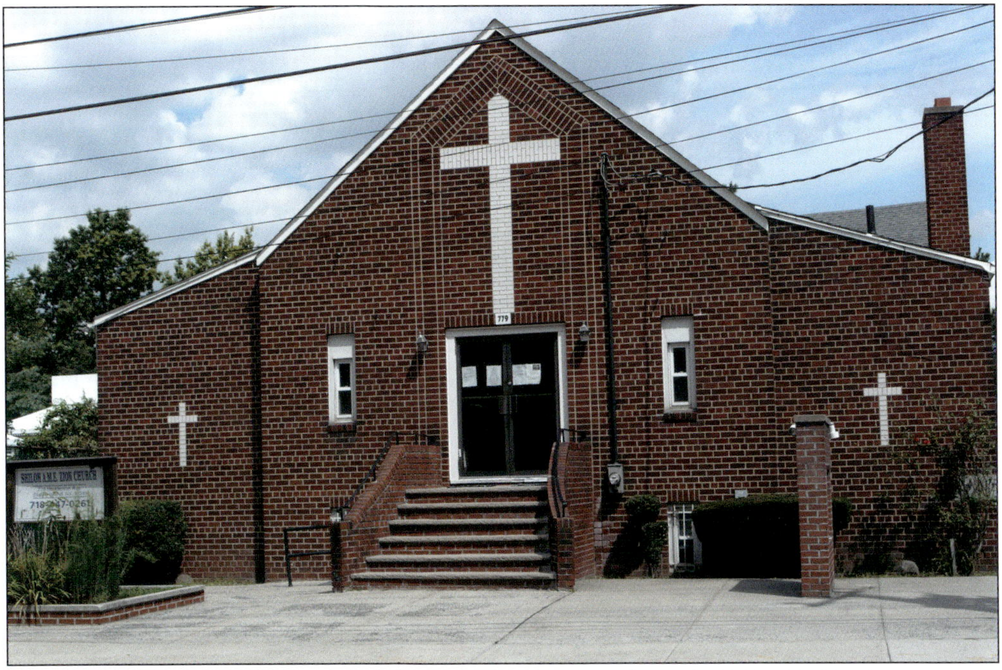

Shiloh A.M.E. Zion Church, pictured above, was a mission in the early 1900s. On Sunday mornings, a group would gather at the home of Dennis Riddick on Barker Street in West New Brighton. He would cut hair and have discussions about the need for a church. Those present included Johnson Jones, William Morris, Eliza Fox, John Elliot, William Hunter, William Pedro, Cinderella Story, Mary Cooke, Armenta Buck, and Rev. Peter Perkins and his wife, Minnie. Shiloh A.M.E. Zion Church is located at 779 Henderson Avenue on property deeded to the church by Mr. and Mrs. William Wilcox, members of a prominent West Brighton family. The below photograph shows the Shiloh congregation assembling for Easter services in the 1980s. (Both, courtesy of Shiloh A.M.E. Zion Church.)

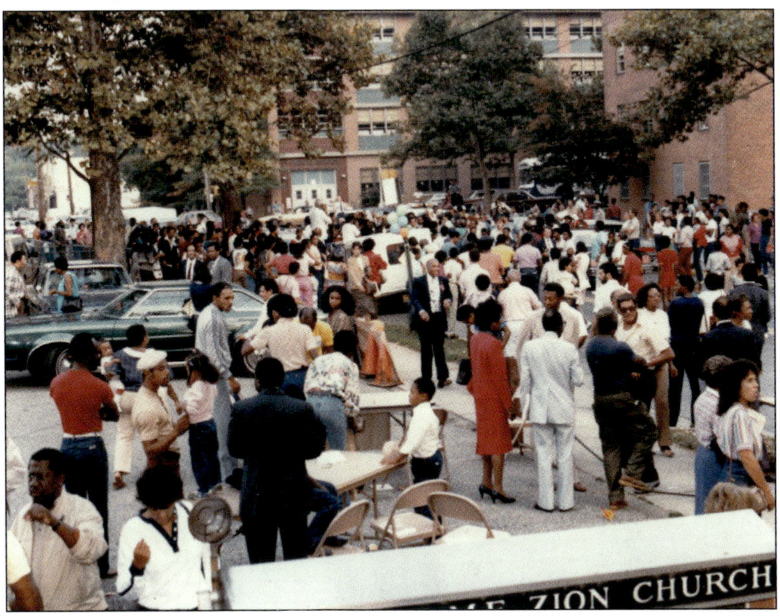

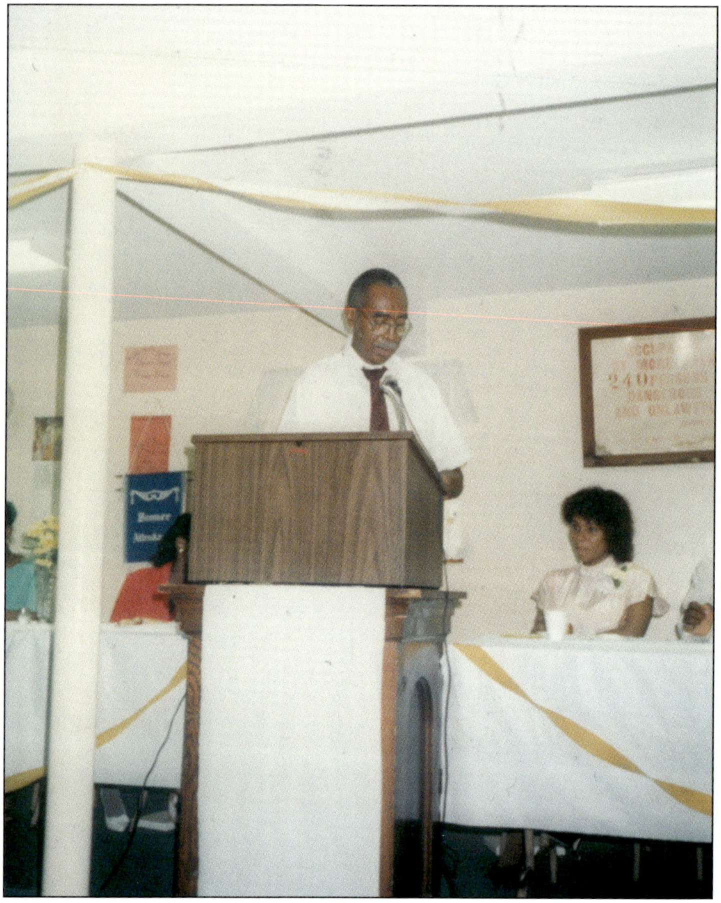

Damon Tucker, pictured at left, presents a Shiloh A.M.E. Zion Church scholarship after the Ebony Fashion Show in September 1988. The scholarship, started by Tucker with the approval of Rev. Louis Richardson and the trustee board of the church, has been in existence for more than 30 years and mostly helps students to buy books for college. The below photograph shows the Women's Day Celebration in the 1980s. The Shiloh Women's Day fundraiser began in the 1950s. (Both, courtesy of Shiloh A.M.E. Zion Church.)

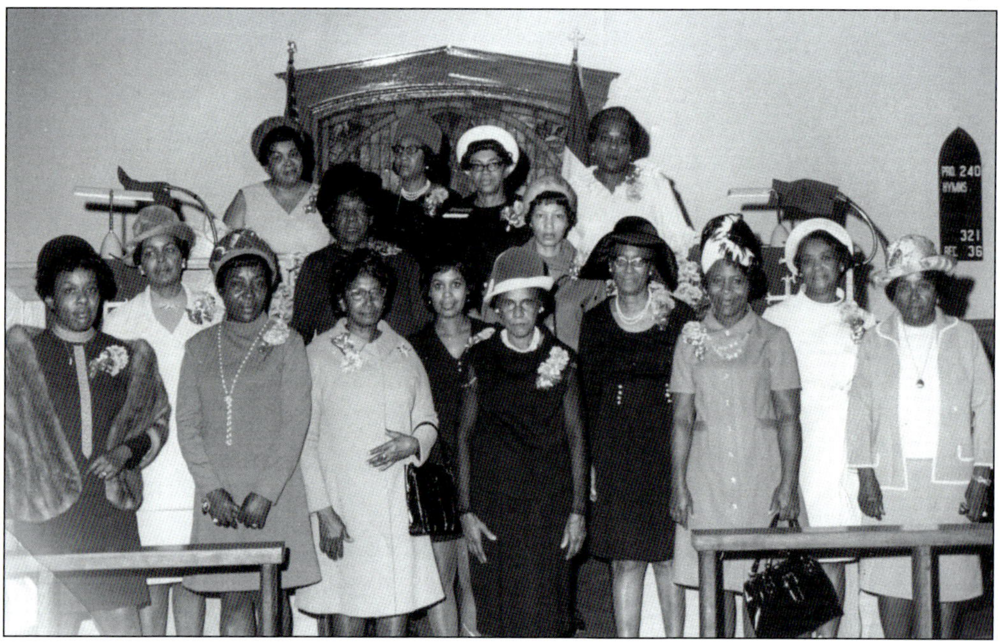

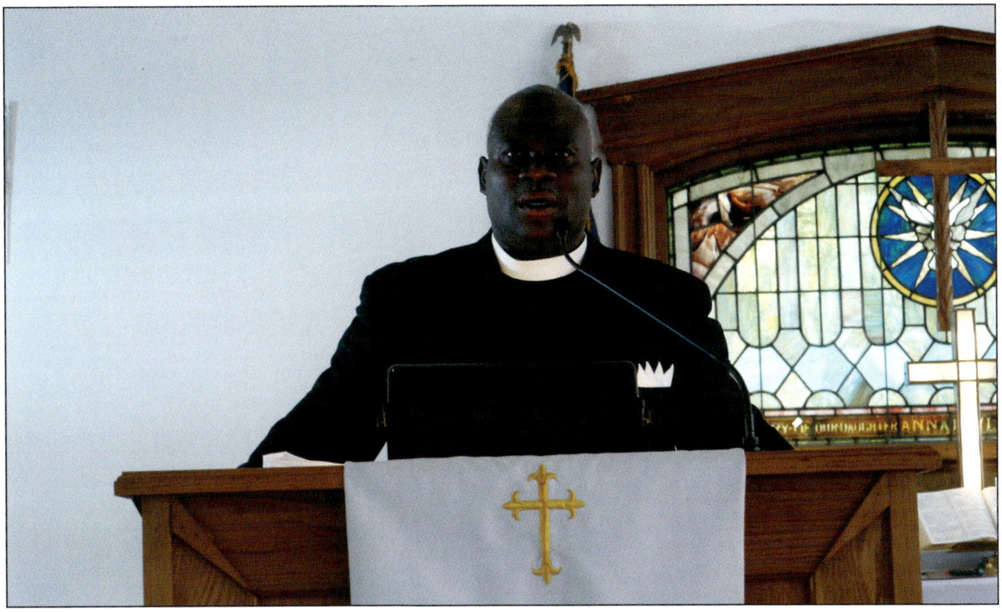

Born and raised in Kinston, North Carolina, Rev. Eli D. Smith came to Shiloh A.M.E. Zion Church in 1993. The passionate pastor has worked hard to encourage the members to improve their lives, church, and community. For over 20 years, Reverend Smith has continued to create programs to keep Shiloh an important part of the West Brighton neighborhood. Reverend Smith and his wife, Dale, have three children. (Courtesy of Shiloh A.M.E. Zion Church.)

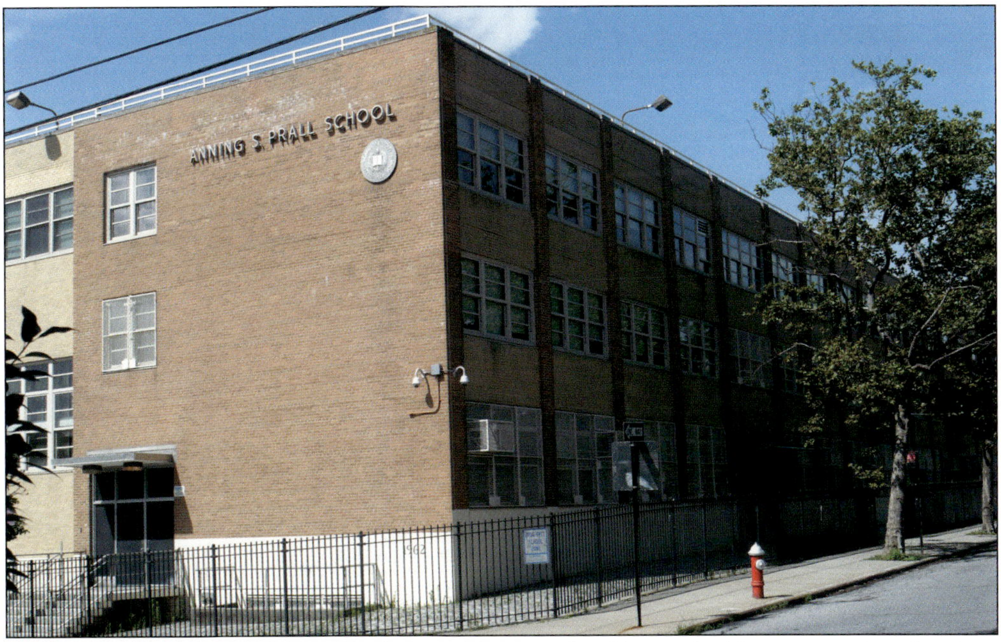

Anning S. Prall Intermediate School 27 is a magnet school for applied learning with technology integration. It houses three unique academies: Engineering, Enterprise, and Journalism. Their mission is to provide a nurturing environment in a small school setting that will enable students to perform competitively as innovative leaders in today's advanced society. (Courtesy of Anning S. Prall Intermediate School 27.)

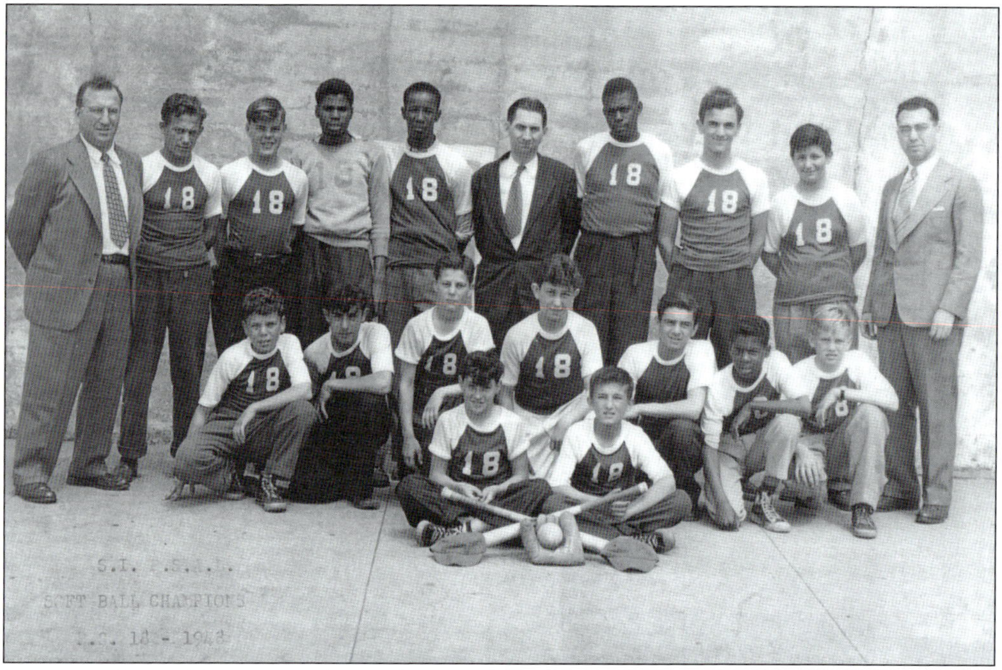

Longtime Staten Island sports fans will recognize a familiar face in the above photograph from PS 18 in the late 1940s. Ralph Lamberti (far left in the second row) points out that the coach of this 1948 softball championship team was Andy Barberi, the legendary Curtis High School football coach (far left in the third row). Lamberti also played football for Barberi at Curtis High School. Years later, when Lamberti became Staten Island borough president, he was able to get one of the ferryboats named after Barberi to honor the coach who influenced so many young people. Pictured below is Mrs. Kinsley's 1973 third-grade class at PS 18. (Above, courtesy of Ralph Lamberti; below, courtesy of Domenica Cucuzza Mousa.)

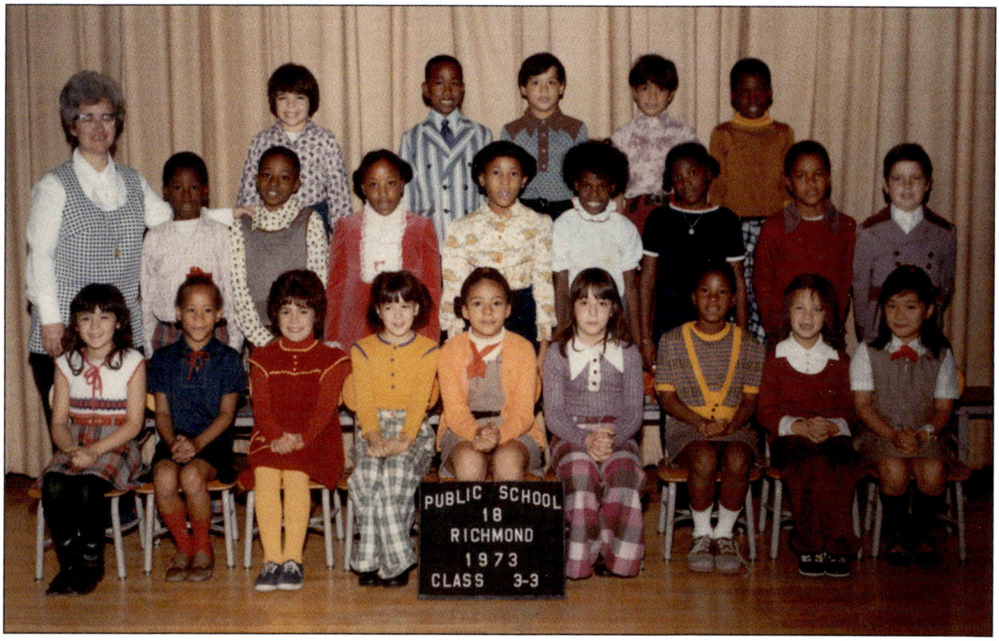

William M. Beveridge came to PS 45 in 1966 after teaching for 19 years at PS 44. He served as assistant principal at PS 45, as well as one year as principal. He is remembered by his former pupils as "Mister Piano." Beveridge played for every kindergarten and fifth-grade graduation. He retired in 1986 after 19 years at PS 45 but returned to play piano for the graduations of his four grandsons. (Courtesy of the Beveridge family.)

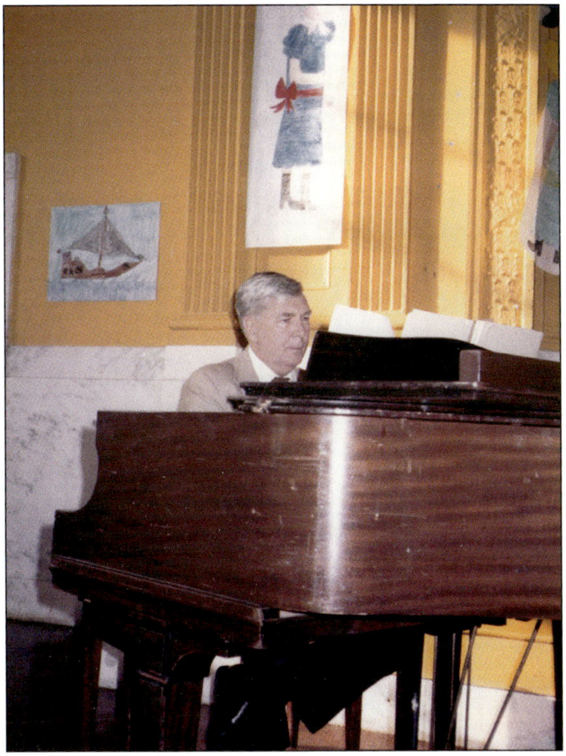

Karin Kirchin Rooney had some fond memories of attending PS 45 in West Brighton, especially of her sixth-grade class shown in this photograph. Their teacher was Robert Dizard—according to Rooney, he was the greatest teacher of all time. Even now, more than 50 years later, Rooney and her classmates recall how much Dizard meant to them. (Courtesy of Karin Kirchin Rooney.)

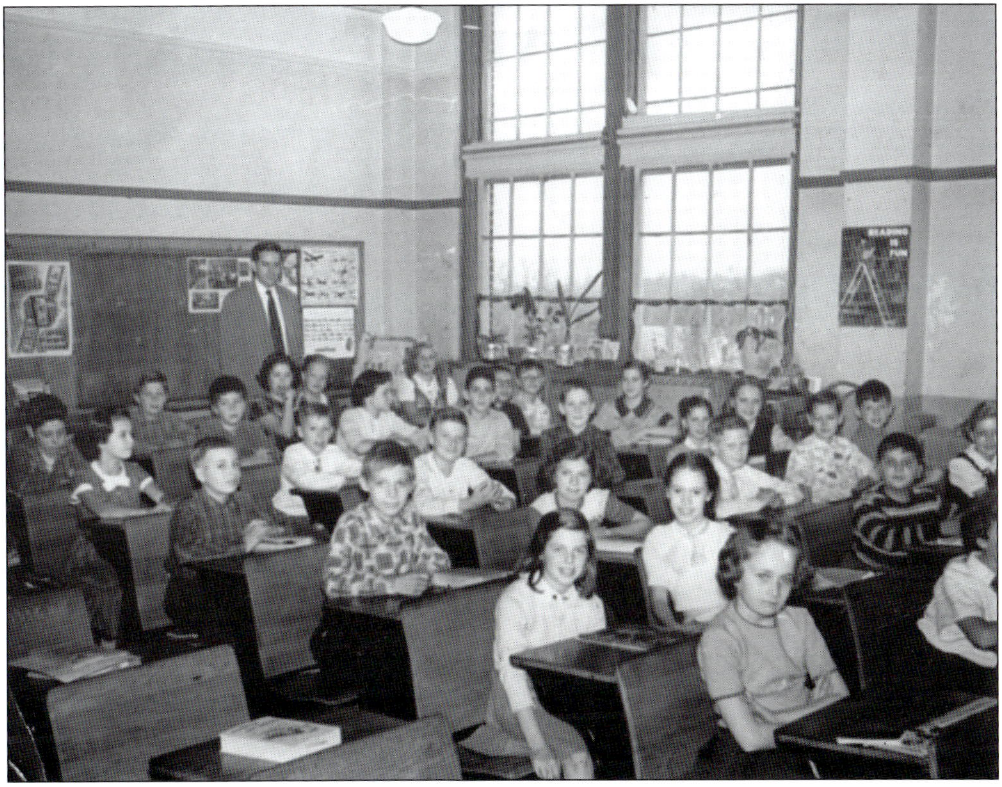

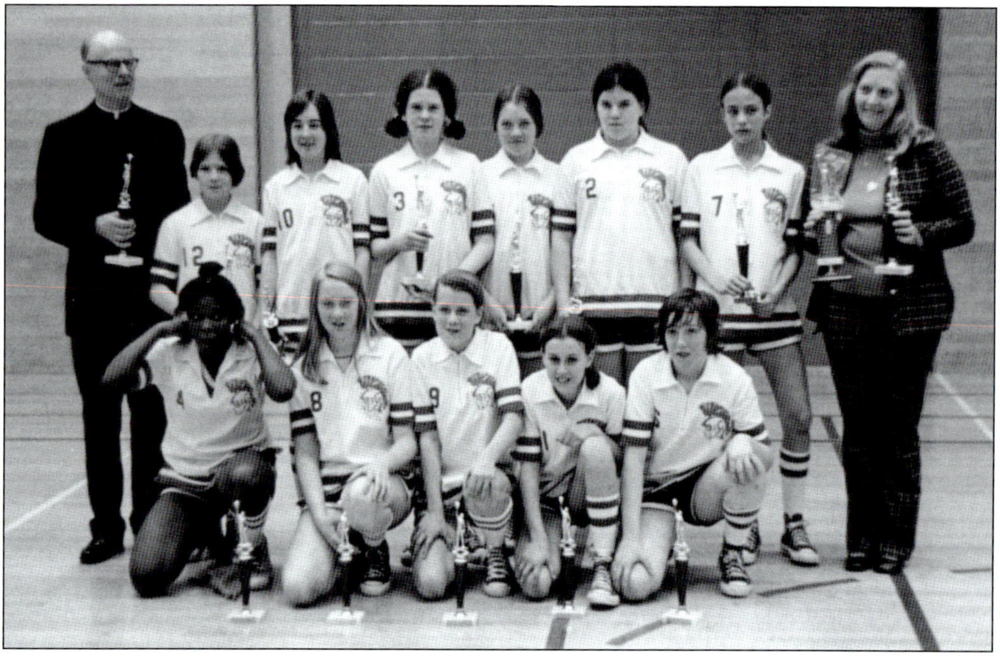

This is the Sacred Heart girls' varsity basketball team, which became the Diocean championship team in 1975. Pictured here are, from left to right, (first row) Michele Walker, Ellen Stoebling, Geri Walsh, Tracy Jackus, and Anne Wilson; (second row) Msgr. Andrew Quinn, Doreen Bossert, Laura O'Shea, Patti Bossert, Eileen Walsh, Erin Gillen, Christian Conroy, and coach Dawn Walsh. (Courtesy of Jeanne Walsh Panzarino.)

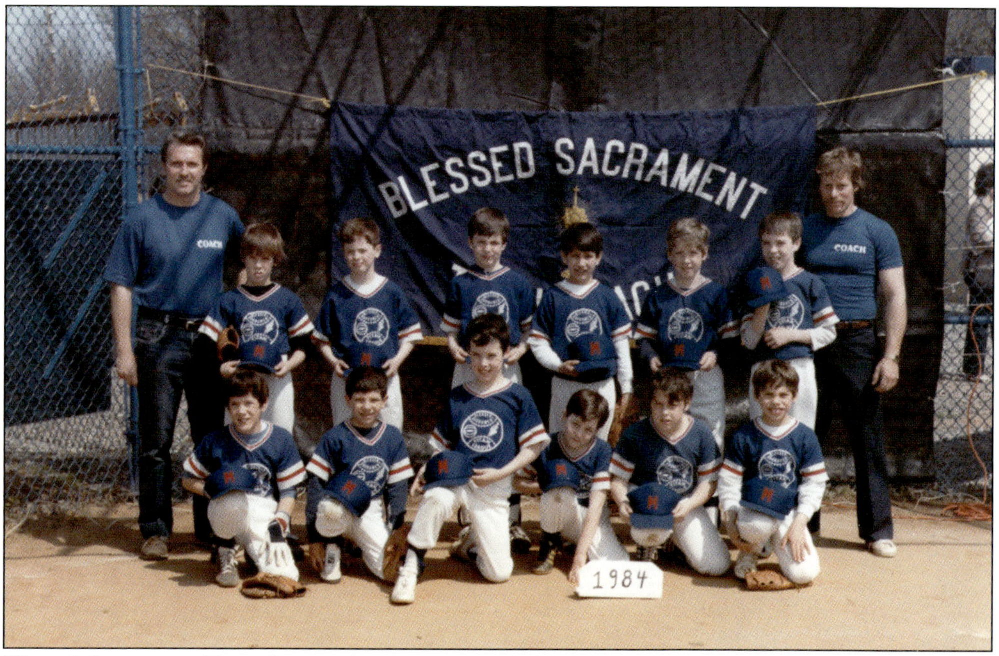

Blessed Sacrament Titan League began in 1958. The sports program was started by Fr. Robert Grogan and Fr. Kenneth Gerathy. It included basketball, baseball, and track-and-field events. This is a 1984 Blessed Sacrament Titan League baseball team. (Courtesy of Eileen Hayes.)

Seven

Generations

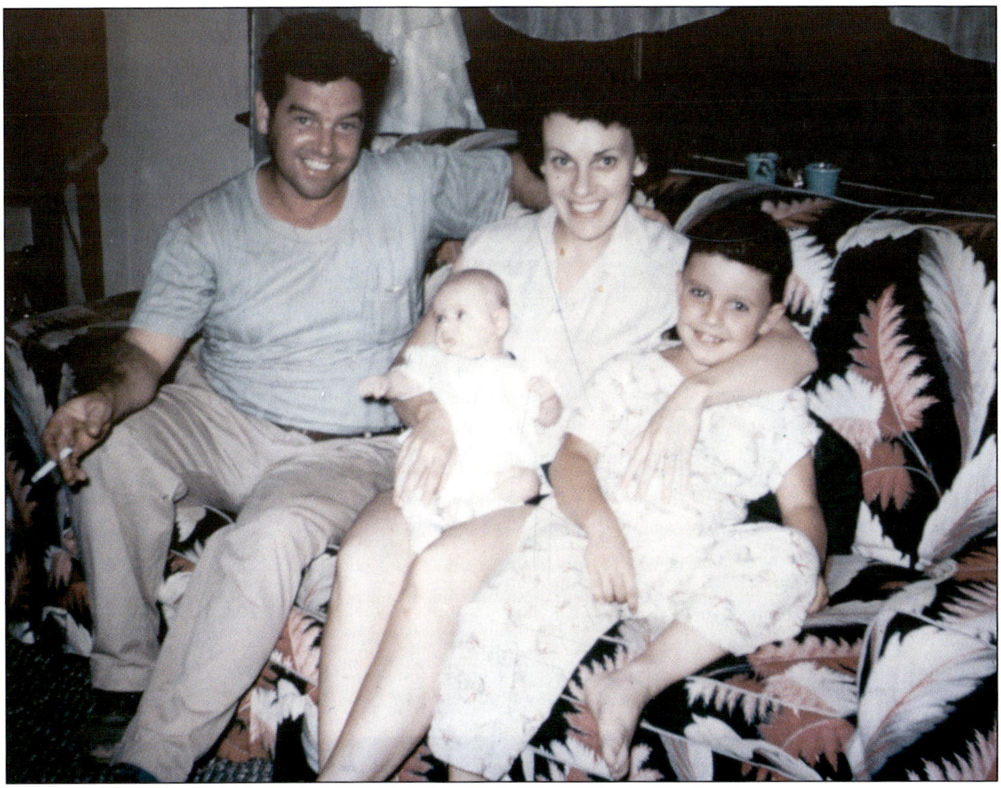

The Vanderbilt family, of Pelton Avenue, has a long association with Staten Island. Pictured here are, from left to right, David Vanderbilt, Rosemary (his wife), their baby daughter Nancy, and Russell Allen. David was a cement truck driver for Vanbro. Rosemary's father, Thomas Mullusky, played halfback for the Staten Island Stapes in the 1920s. Rosemary recalled of her father's football career, "They said he could run like the wind." (Courtesy of the Vanderbilt family.)

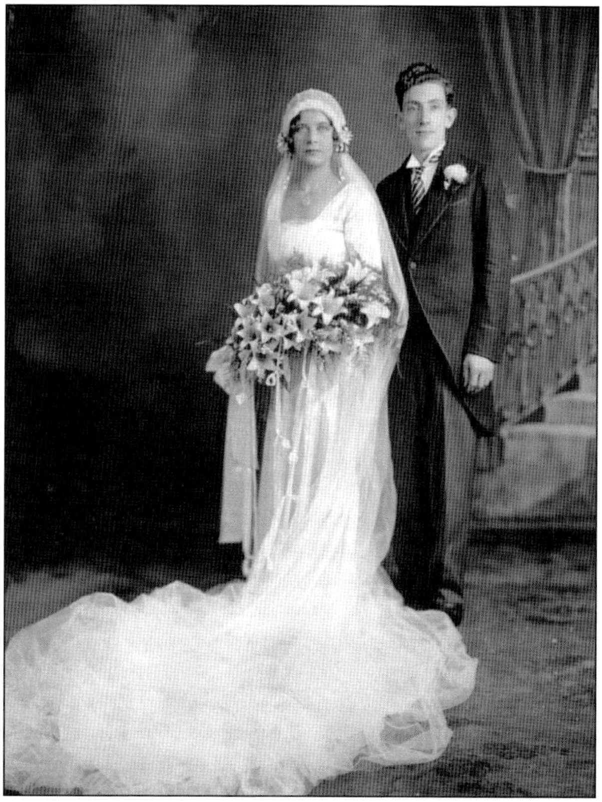

Josephine Maglio married John Bruno on September 13, 1931, in St. Benedicta Church. The West Brighton couple were wed for 72 years. John worked for the *Staten Island Advance* for 79 years. He always found time to volunteer at his beloved church, Our Lady of Mount Carmel–St. Benedicta, as president of the Holy Name Society, Sunday school teacher, or a campaign worker for Catholic Charities; he also headed up many fundraising events. The Bruno family is pictured below; they are, clockwise from left, Rita, John, John, Josephine, Mary, and Barbara. (Both, courtesy of the Bruno family.)

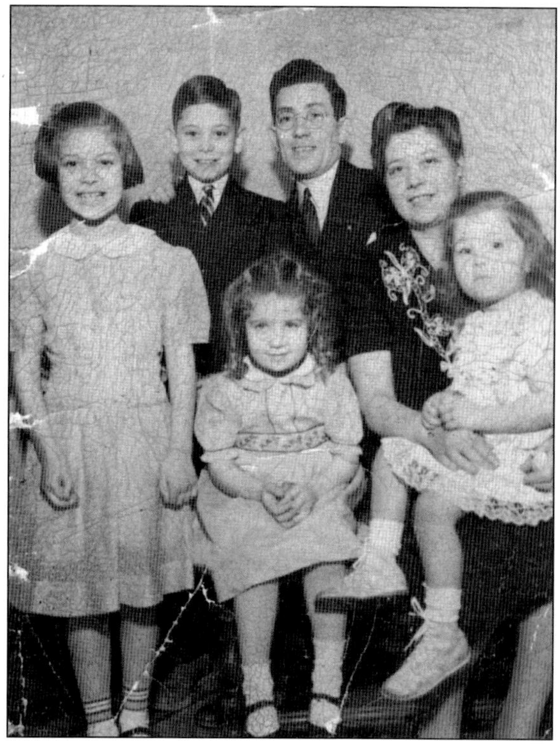

These two photographs represent several generations of the Tucker family of West Brighton. The photograph at right shows Lula Tucker (center) and her daughters, clockwise from left, Dora Jones, Elizabeth Etheridge, and Marjorie Reed. The below photograph is from the 1971 wedding of Michael Tucker. Michael is Lula's grandson. Pictured are, from left to right, Michael Tucker, his parents Shirley and Damon, and his sister Shirleen. Shirley and Damon Tucker wed in Shiloh A.M.E. Zion Church in 1946 and were married for 50 years. (Both, courtesy of the Tucker family.)

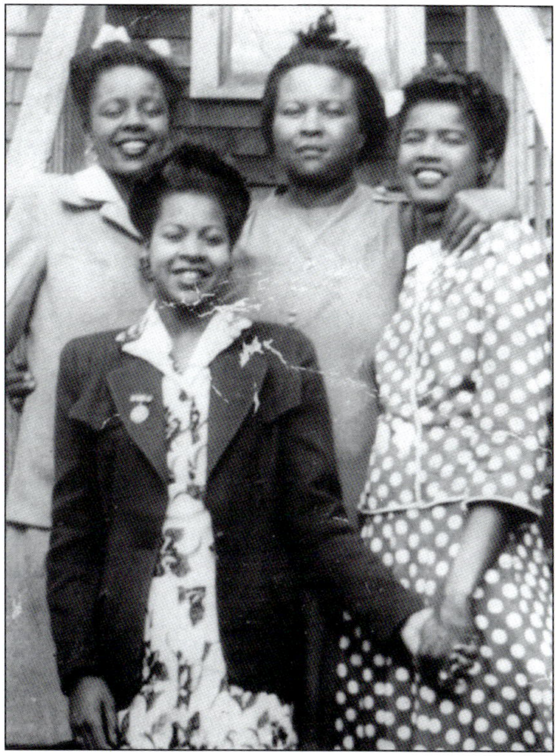

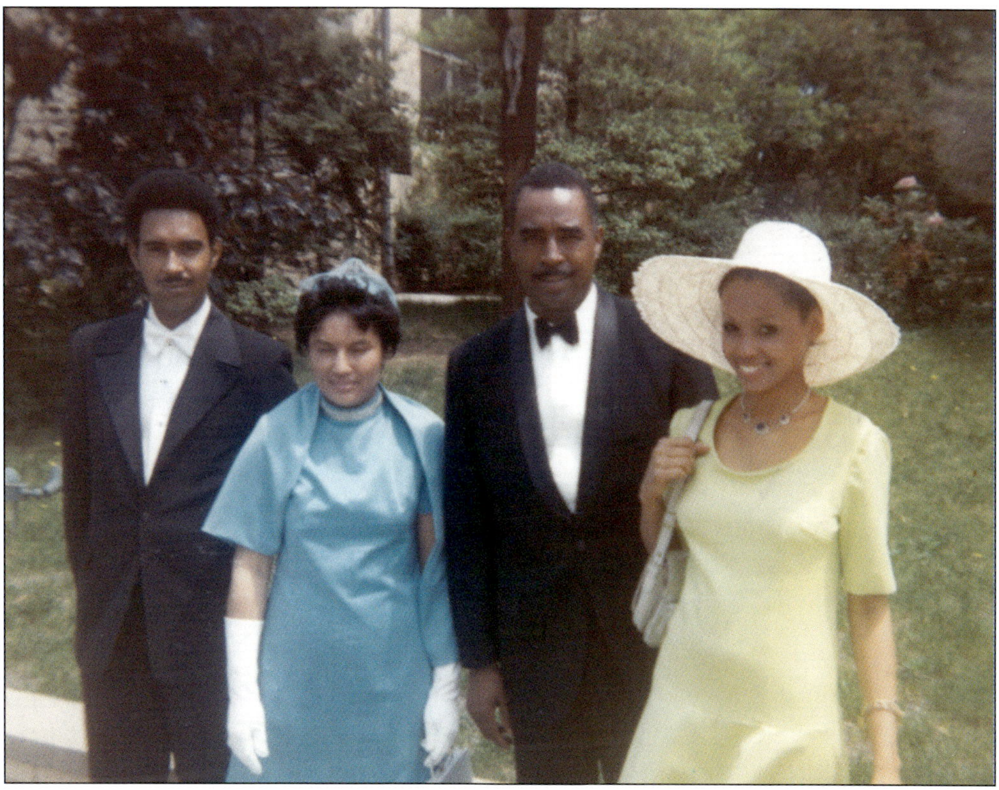

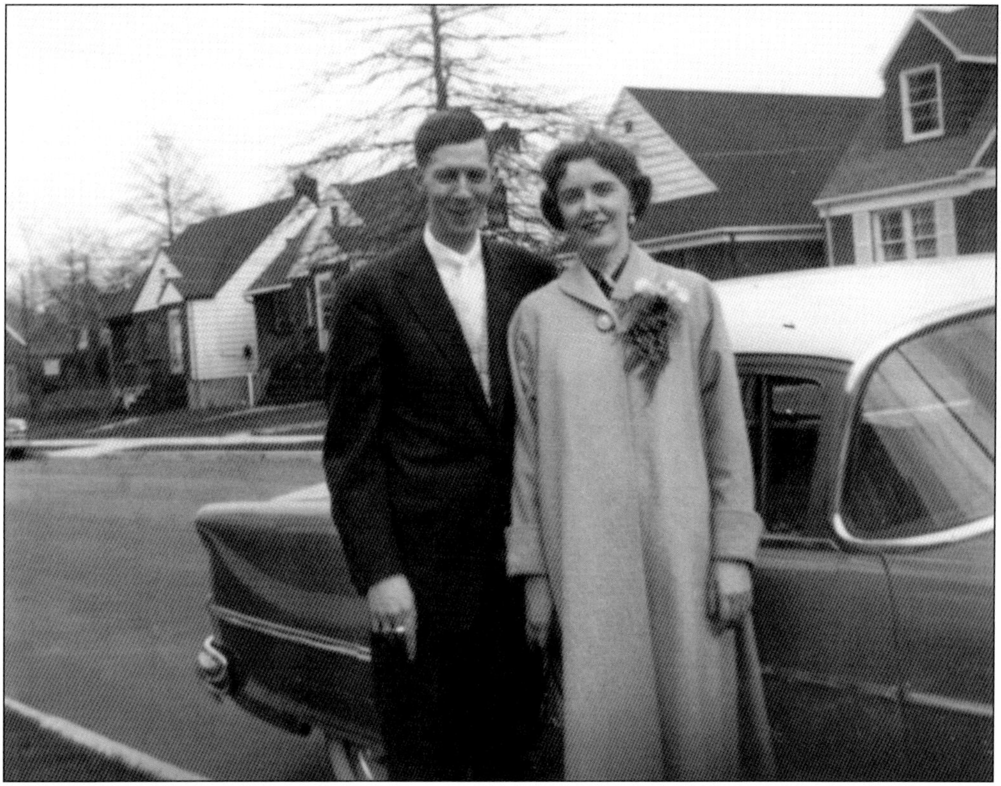

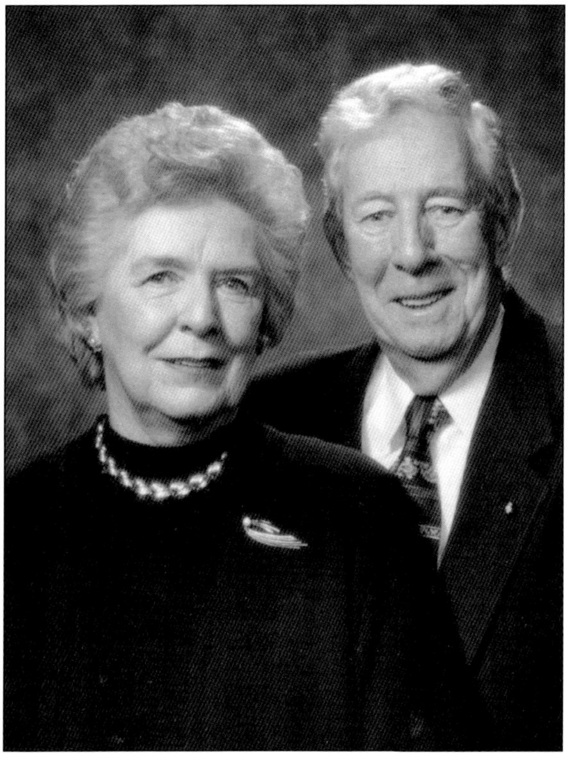

Jane Stilwell recalled the romantic courtship of her parents, Thomas Sullivan and Rita McCarthy. Thomas lived on Morrison Avenue, and Rita lived on Forest Avenue in West Brighton. Both of their grandmothers wanted to match the young couple, and the backyards to their respective homes met, so they put in a gate to get them together. When Thomas was in the Army during World War II, Rita would send him homemade fudge. The couple was married on June 24, 1950, in Sacred Heart Church. Rita was a staunch supporter of her husband's legal career that spanned more than a half a century. He was known for his wisdom, fairness, and Irish wit. Justice Sullivan served as Staten Island's district attorney for seven years before taking the bench in 1983. The Sullivans were married for 61 years. (Both, courtesy of the Sullivan family.)

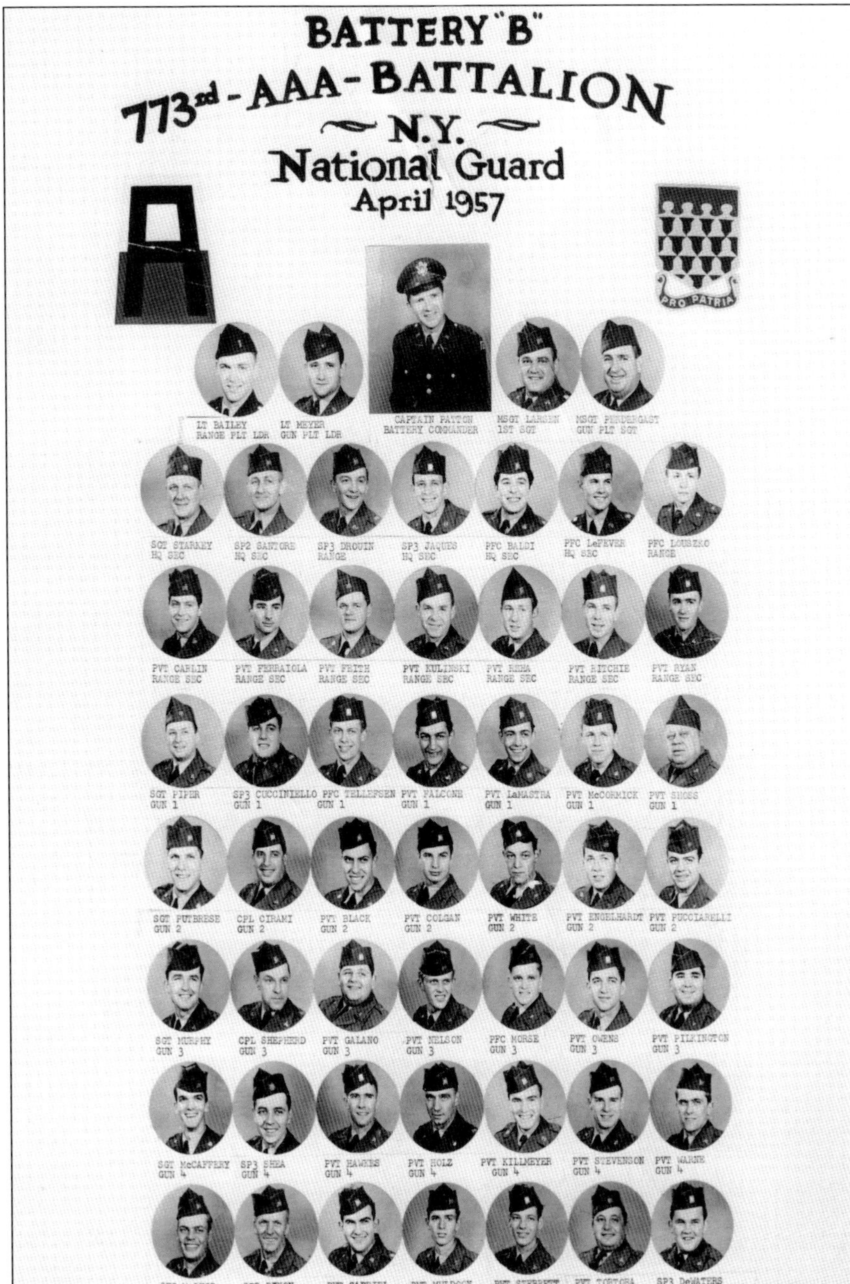

The armory on Manor Road near Martling Avenue was erected in 1926 on a site that had been used as early as 1912 to stable the horses for Troop F, a cavalry unit belonging to Squadron C Brooklyn of the New York State Guard. After World War I, Capt. William H. Morris, of Troop F, returned home determined to secure an armory for the troops. This image shows the men of Battery "B" 773rd AAA Battalion, New York National Guard. According to Gerard La Mastra (shown fifth from the left in the fourth row), all of these young men were from Staten Island. Since 1988, the Vietnam Veterans Memorial Park has been on the grounds of the armory. (Courtesy of Gerard La Mastra.)

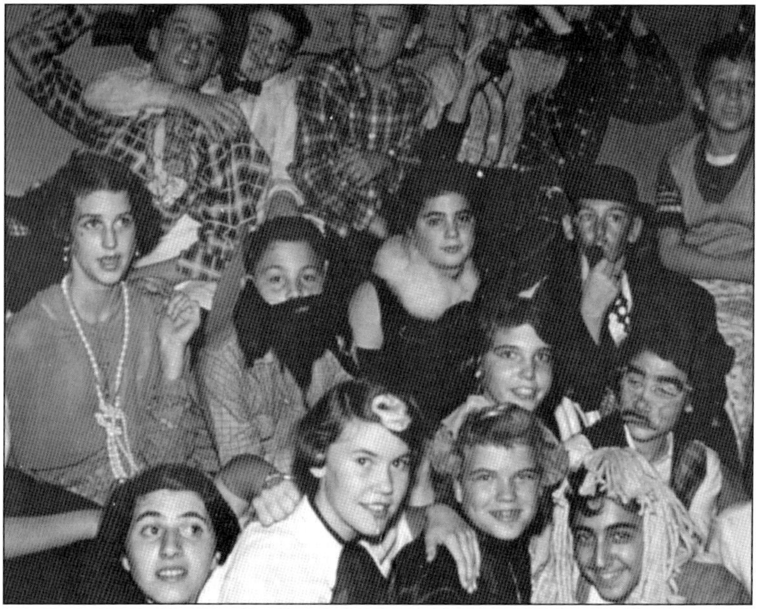

This photograph might bring back a lot of memories of growing up in West Brighton in the 1950s and 1960s. This is a Halloween party at Karin Kirchin's house on Davis Avenue with her classmates from PS 45. (Courtesy of Karin Kirchin Rooney).

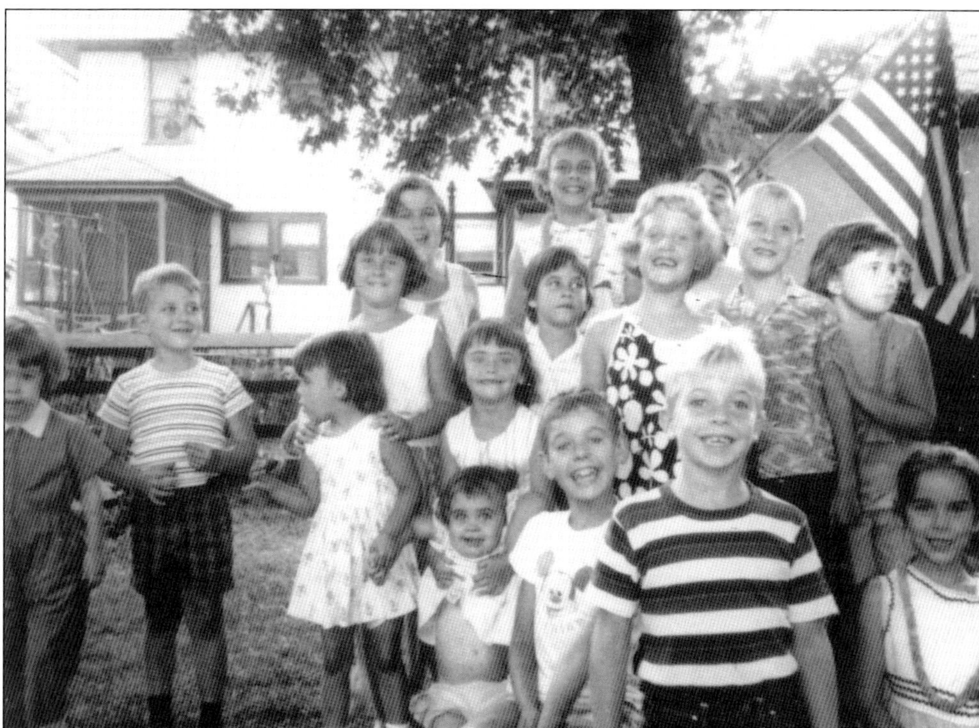

Years ago, a nice warm summer day meant plenty of kids playing on Pelton Avenue. Some of the family names in this group photograph from 1962 include Sprawa, Donovan, Finigan, Vanderbilt, and Dannemann. (Courtesy of the Vanderbilt family.)

The Honorable State Supreme Court justice Peter P. Cusick married Miriam Kearney in Sacred Heart Church in 1967. The West Brighton couple were married for 33 years. They have three sons—Peter, Michael and John. (Courtesy of the Cusick family.)

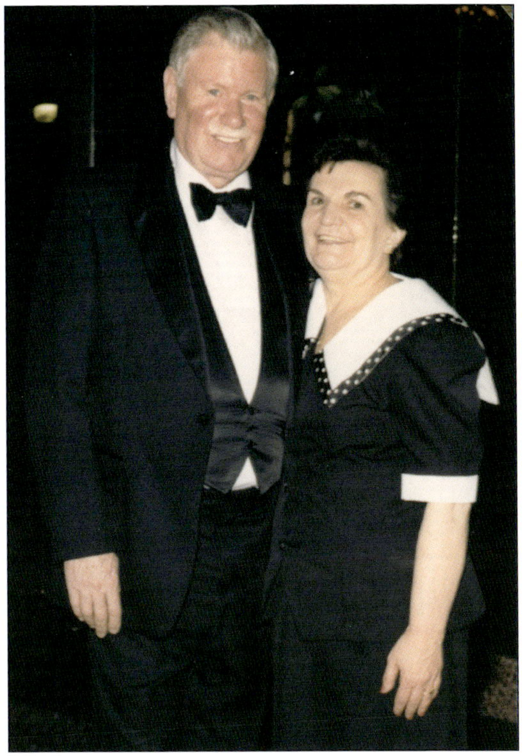

The Shea family of West Brighton is one of the largest clans on Staten Island. This photograph shows 15 of the 16 Shea children with their parents. With 11 girls and 5 boys under one roof, the kids had to share bedrooms, eat in shifts, care for younger siblings, and do 10 loads of laundry per day. Growing up in West Brighton, the Sheas had a large home full of people and love. (Courtesy of the Shea family.)

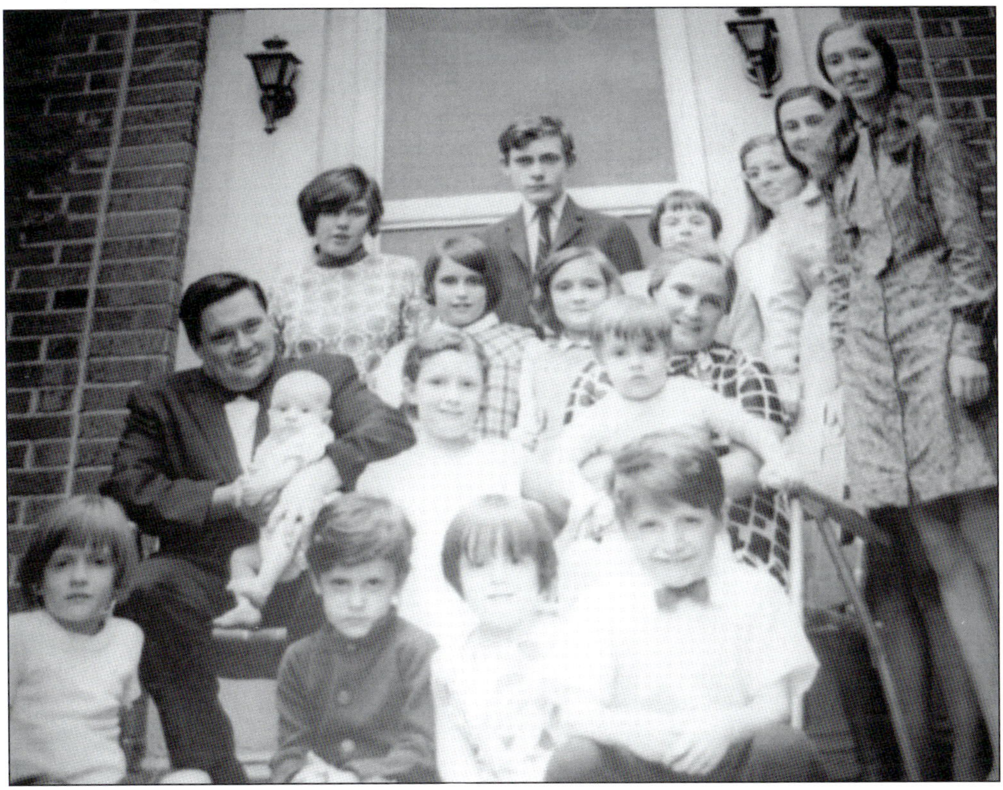

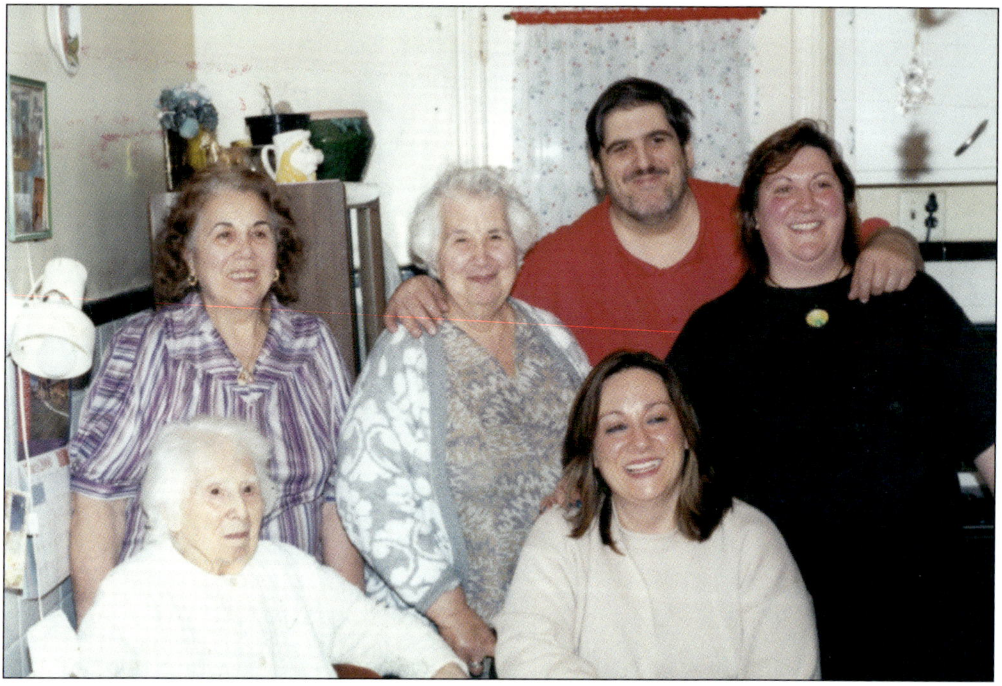

Fannie Cucuzza, matriarch of the Cucuzza family, founded the famous Staten Island business Boston Fish Market in 1918 with her husband, Vito. The Cucuzza family owned and operated Boston Fish Market for 91 years in West Brighton. Pictured below, Fannie's grandsons Vito Jr. (left) and Salvatore continued the family tradition until they closed the store in 2009. Pictured above are, from left to right, (first row) Fannie and Domenica Cucuzza Mousa; (second row) Domenica "Minnie" Cucuzza Benevento, Sarafina "Sadie" Cucuzza Avenoso, Paul Benevento, and Marilyn Cucuzza Ciaburri. (Both, courtesy of the Cucuzza family.)

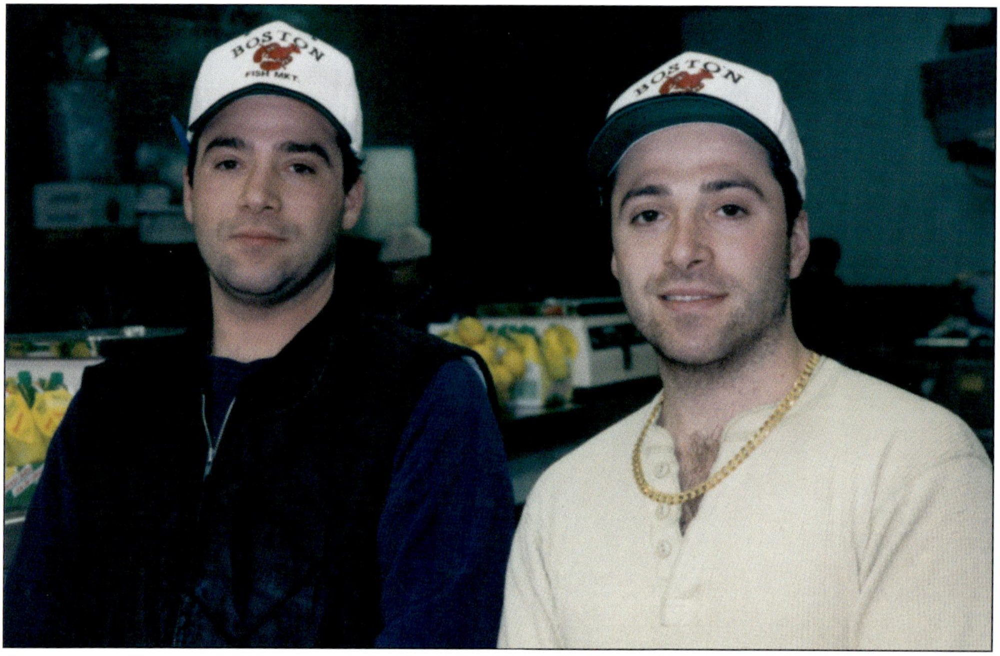

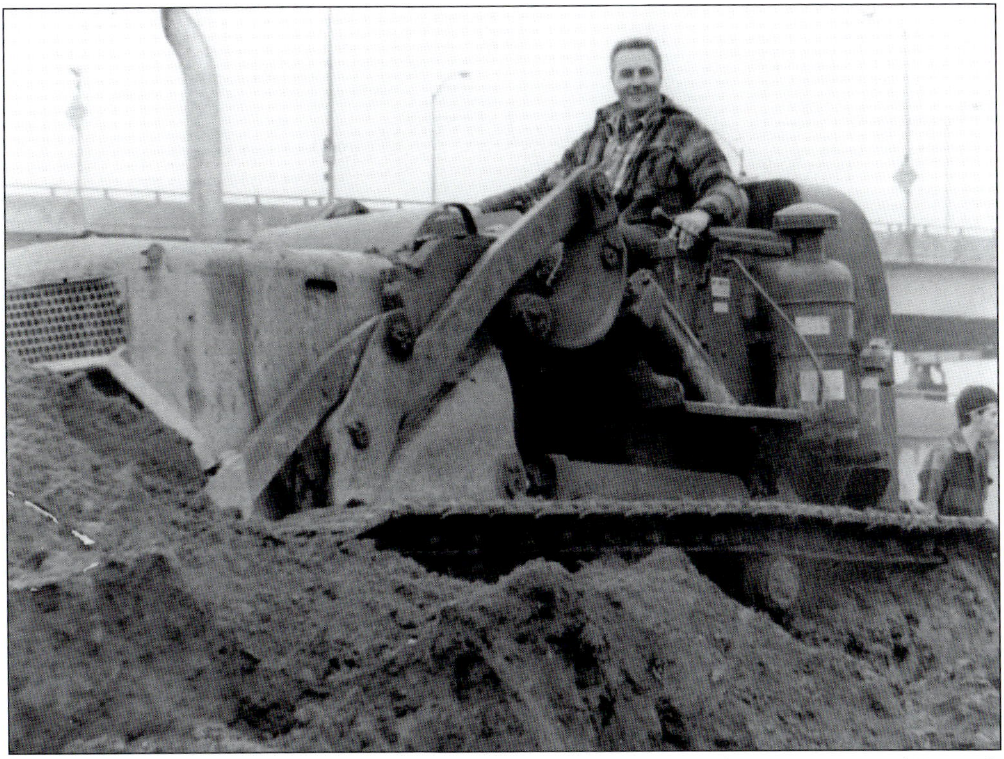

Ed O'Connor (above and below), the youngest of four children, was born to Peter and Hannah O'Connor in 1941. At age 12, Ed was struck with rheumatic fever, and his priest administered the last rites, but Ed went on to defy all odds against him. At age 16, he started his own business with his eldest brother, John, forming O'Connor Trucking (below). He went on to become the third generation of O'Connors in the construction industry. Ed was instrumental in the demolition and construction of numerous structures on Staten Island, including St. Michael's Boys Home, Demyan's Hofbrau, Miller Field airport hangars, Gateway Park, Staten Island Expressway, Fresh Kills Landfill, and the Verrazano Bridge. He also donated his time and equipment to anything involving children: Pouch Camp, Travis baseball and football fields, and St. Peter's football field. (Both, courtesy of the O'Connor family.)

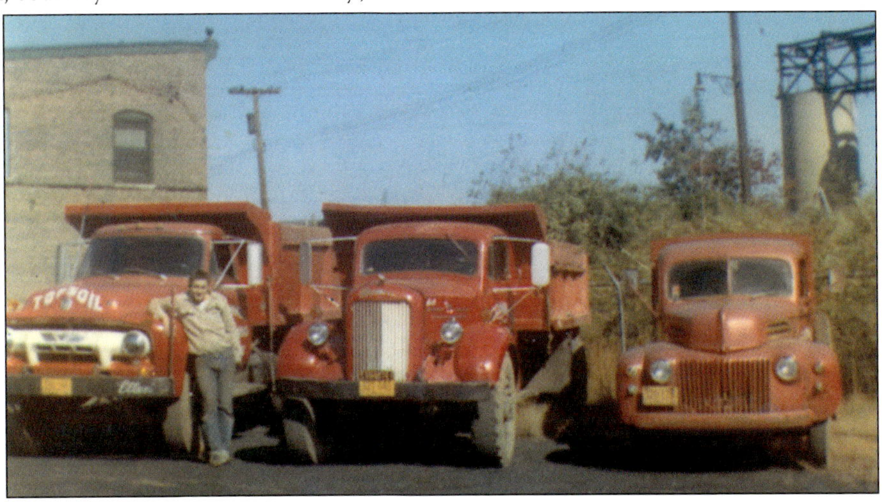

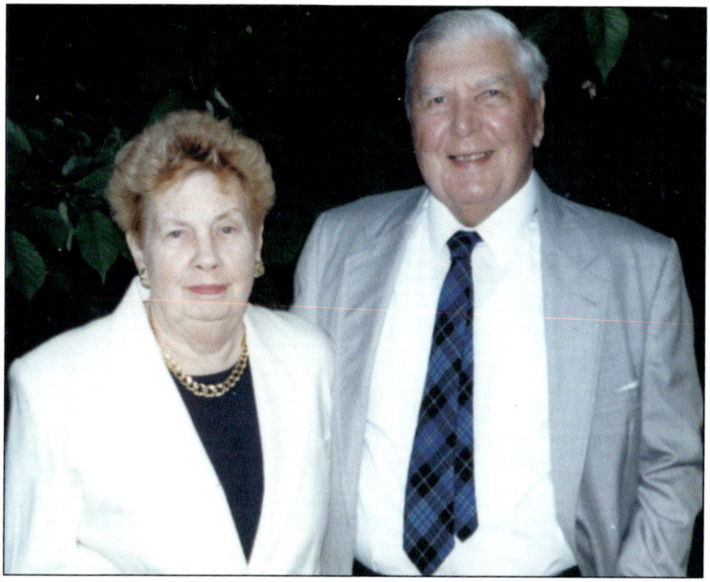

Nancy and Bill Beveridge were married for 62 years before Nancy passed away in 2012. They wed in St Mary's Episcopal Church on Castleton Avenue in West Brighton. They became very active at Christ Episcopal Church in New Brighton. Bill sang in the church choir for 84 years, and Nancy was active with the young people's group, the church directory, and running the coffee hour. (Courtesy of the Beveridge family.)

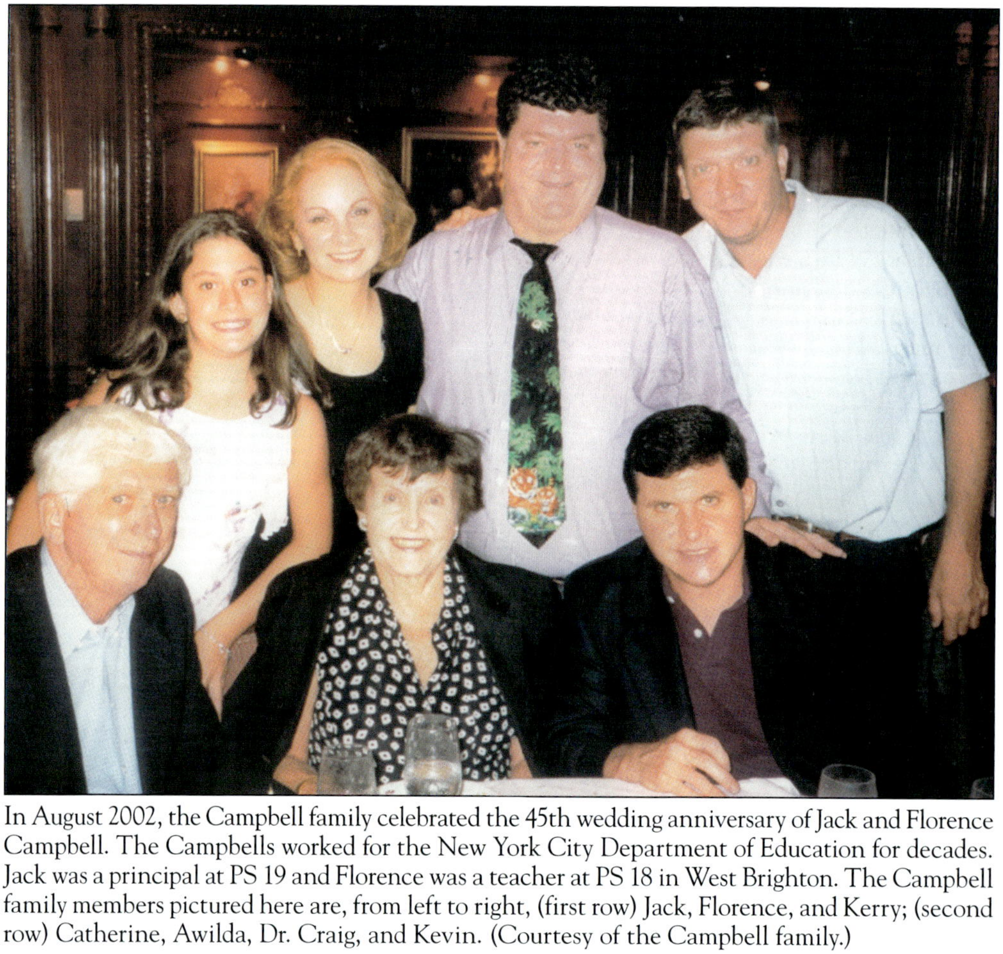

In August 2002, the Campbell family celebrated the 45th wedding anniversary of Jack and Florence Campbell. The Campbells worked for the New York City Department of Education for decades. Jack was a principal at PS 19 and Florence was a teacher at PS 18 in West Brighton. The Campbell family members pictured here are, from left to right, (first row) Jack, Florence, and Kerry; (second row) Catherine, Awilda, Dr. Craig, and Kevin. (Courtesy of the Campbell family.)

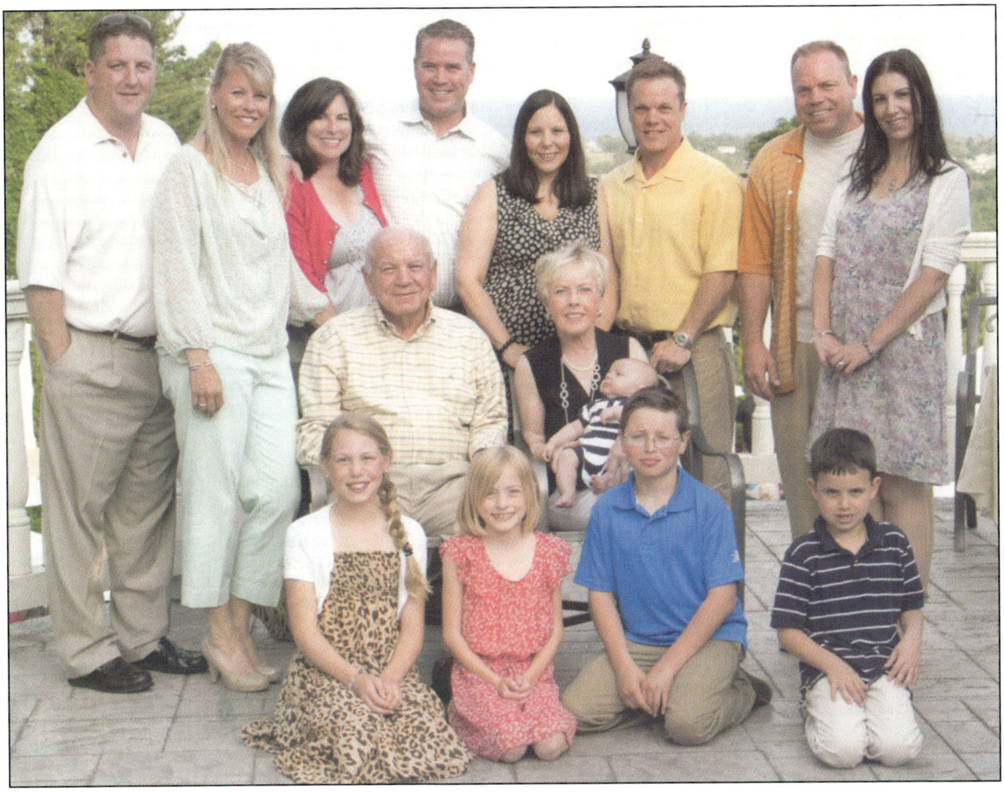

This 2013 gathering was held to celebrate the 50th wedding anniversary of former Staten Island borough president Ralph J. Lamberti and his wife, Susan. The Lambertis were married on June 22, 1963, and are surrounded here by their four children and their spouses, along with the five Lamberti grandchildren. (Courtesy of the Lamberti family.)

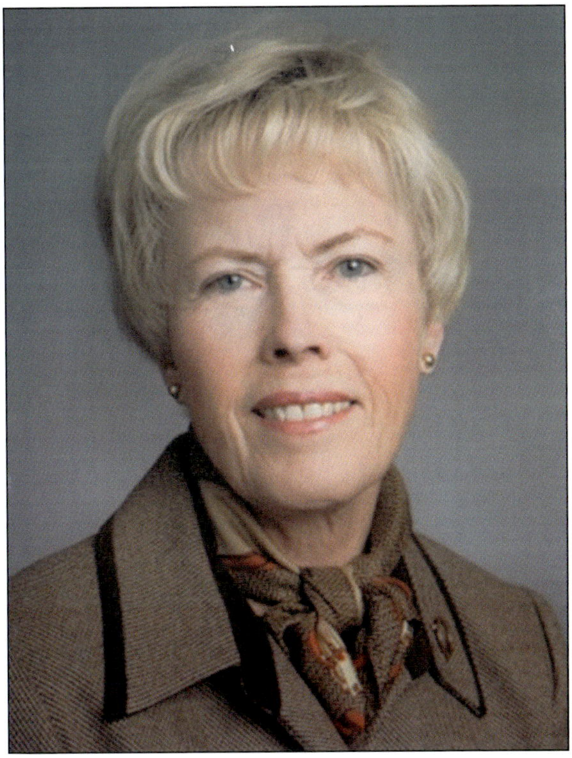

Susan Pederson Lamberti was Staten Island's first lady from 1986 to 1990. Lamberti was a special education teacher on Staten Island for 32 years and a Staten Island Woman of Achievement in 1986. (Courtesy of the Lamberti family.)

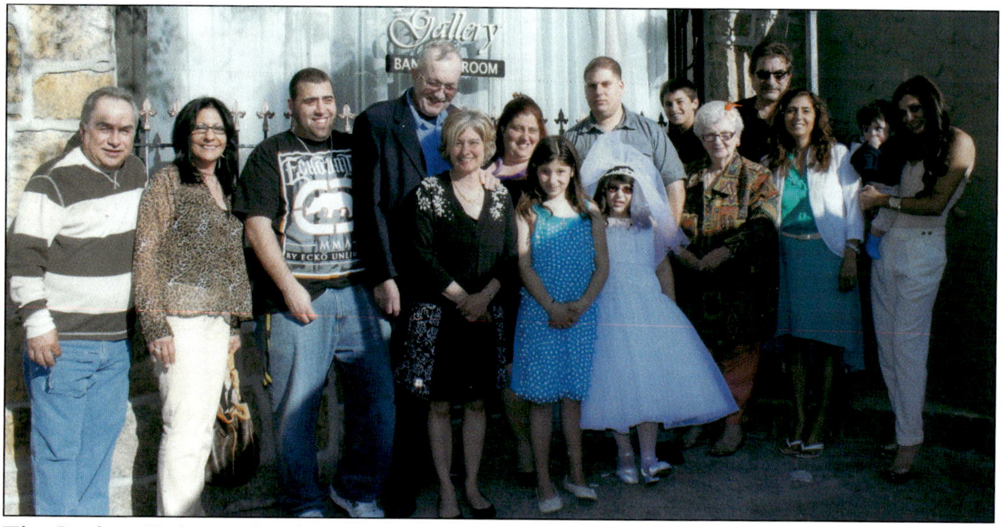

The Cardone-Eadicicco families pose together at a recent family gathering. Pictured are, from left to right, Joe Cardone Sr., Fran Varriano Cardone, Michael Eadicicco, Wayne Roucken, Victoria Maglio Roucken, Christina Eadicicco, Elizabeth Eadicicco, Joe Bauer, TerriAnn Eadicicco, Albert Maglio Cardone, Ann Maglio, Al Cardone, Ann Maglio Cardone, Salvatore Caminiti, and Talia Cardone. (Courtesy of the Cardone family.)

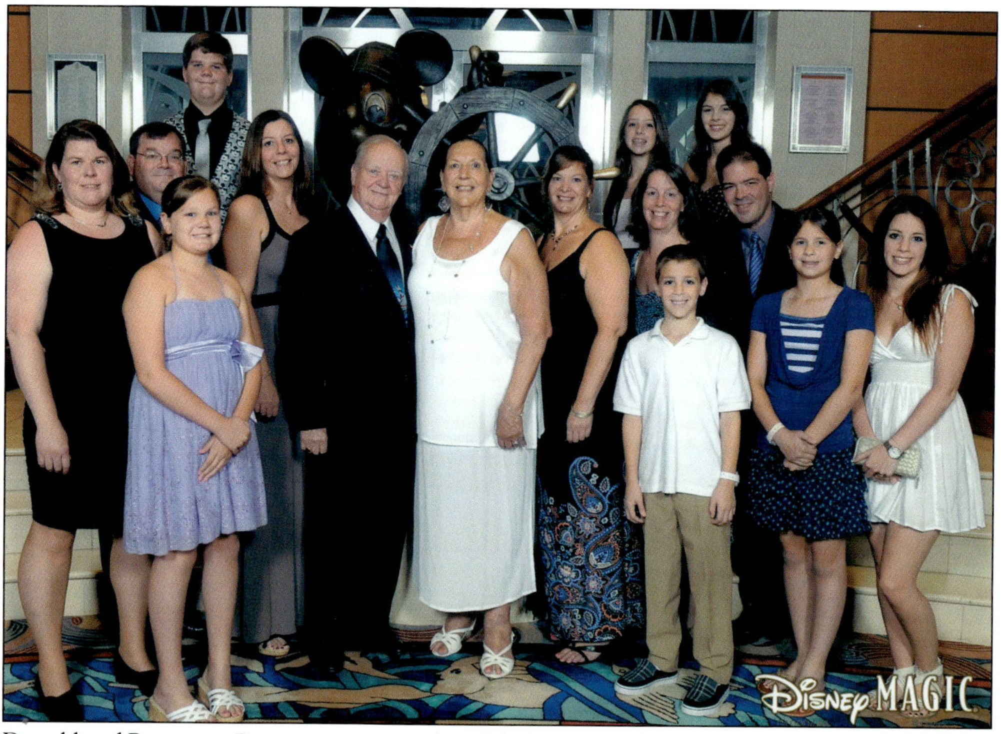

Donald and Rosemary Regan were married on July 28, 1962. The Regans renewed their marriage vows at a Mass celebrated in their home by Rev. Brian E. McWeeney. Donald and Rosemary are pictured at center and are surrounded by their four children and their spouses and the seven Regan grandchildren. They commemorated their 50th anniversary on a cruise to Florida and the Bahamas aboard the *Disney Magic*. (Courtesy of the Regan family.)

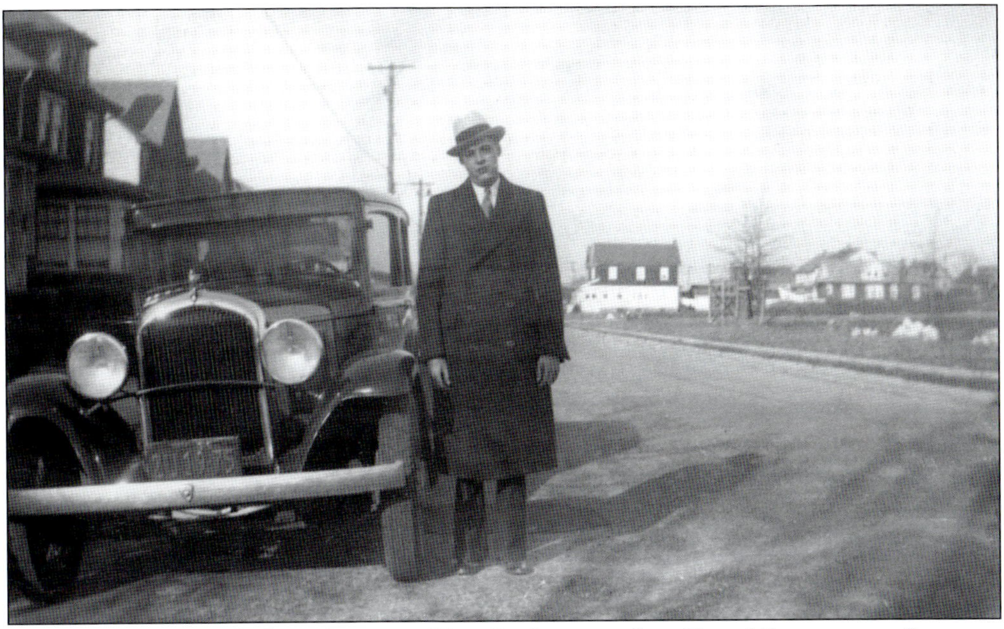

The above photograph shows longtime West Brighton resident Gerard Brunner standing on a very sparse Oakland Avenue many years ago. His granddaughter Debra Harkins is pictured below standing in the exact same spot in 2012. Brunner's daughter Cecelia recalled that "you could see clear over to PS 45 from our front steps before they built homes on Pelton and Davis Avenues." (Both, courtesy of the authors.)

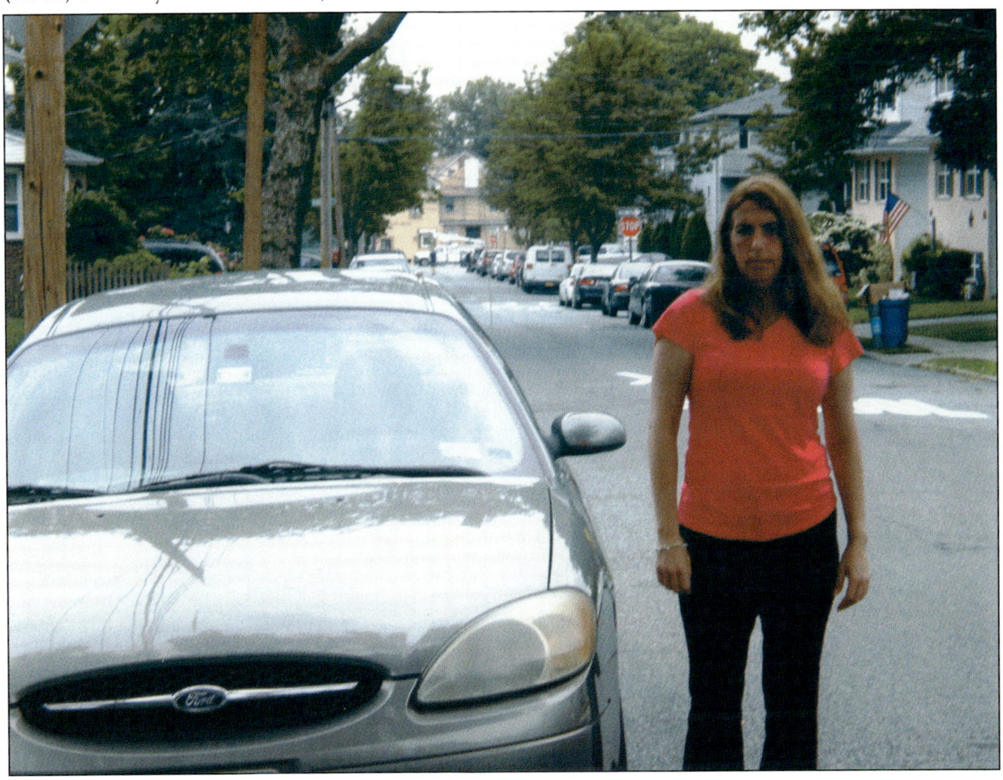

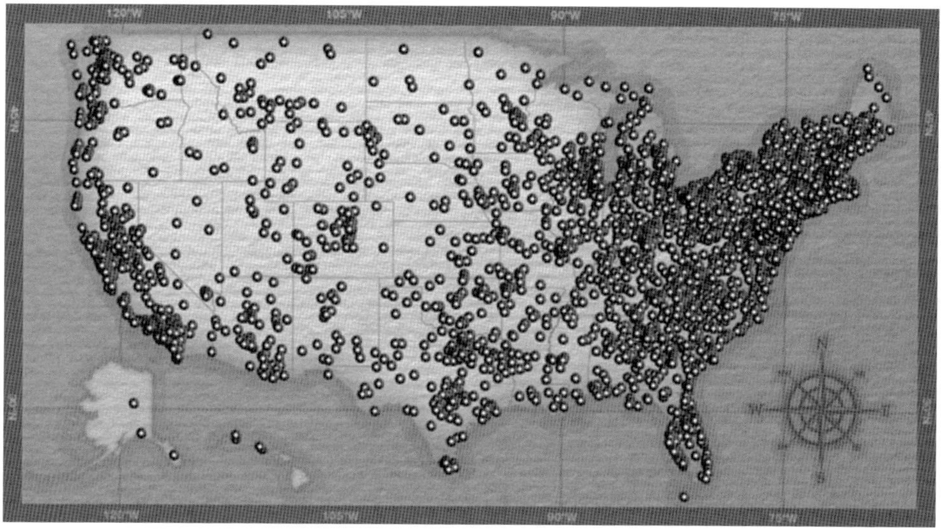

Consistent with our mission to preserve history on a local level, this book was printed in South Carolina on American-made paper and manufactured entirely in the United States. Products carrying the accredited Forest Stewardship Council (FSC) label are printed on 100 percent FSC-certified paper.

MADE IN THE USA